THE LIBERAL PARTY IN SOUTH-WEST BRITAIN

SINCE 1918

The Liberal Party

in

South-West Britain Since 1918

Political Decline, Dormancy and Rebirth

GARRY TREGIDGA

UNIVERSITY
of
EXETER
PRESS

First published in 2000 by
University of Exeter Press
Reed Hall, Streatham Drive
Exeter EX4 4QR
UK
www.ex.ac.uk/uep/

British Library Cataloguing in Publication Data
A catalogue record for this book is available
from the British Library.

ISBN 0 85989 679 X

Typeset in 11½pt Monotype Garamond
by XL Publishing Services, Tiverton

Printed in Great Britain by Short Run Press Ltd, Exeter

Contents

Figures and Maps

Figures

Maps

I would like to thank Helen Jones at the University of Exeter for designing the
maps. Also my thanks to Jack and Lillian Prowse at Barnstaple and Pauline
Quickfall, secretary at the Liskeard Liberal Democrat Office, for providing me with
the photographs for this book.

Tables

Foreword

by The Rt. Hon. Charles Kennedy MP
Leader of the Liberal Democrats

Much has been written over the years about the decline of the Liberal Party in the first half of the last century. Yet, very little has been written about areas where Liberals continued to be strong in the inter-war years. Even less about the relative revival of Liberalism and Liberal Democracy in the last fifty years, most memorably highlighted in the Liberal Democrat breakthrough in the 1997 General Election.

Nowhere was this resurgence more notable than in the south west of Britain where Liberal Democrats now dominate local government and in 1997 swept to parliamentary power in an almost unbroken run from Land's End to the borders of Wiltshire. The South West holds a special place in the hearts of many Liberal Democrats as a bastion of liberal revival and a sign of the party's new strength.

This book's focus on the significance of regionalism in political fortune is important. While political historiography has been moving in a regional direction recently, Garry Tregidga rightly asserts that the South West 'region', and for that matter any other, is not populated by homogeneous country dwellers with identical aspirations and political beliefs, but by a rather more diverse people. That is why he gives a rather more sophisticated analysis of the reasons for Liberal Democrat success in an area which encompasses the four counties of Cornwall, Devon, Somerset and Dorset.

Moreover, as a Highlander, I have some empathy with those

Cornishmen and women who see themselves, not as a part of south-west England, but as members of a 'Celtic fringe'. It is an interesting commentary on the nature of modern British politics that this great swathe of the United Kingdom stretching from Cornwall, through Wales, to the tip of Scotland does not have a single surviving Tory MP.

But perhaps that should be the subject of another book.

Introduction

The general election of 1997 will go down in history as the moment when New Labour finally ended eighteen years of Conservative rule. Only time will tell if Tony Blair can now achieve his second aim of laying the foundations for a new 'progressive' era to replace the supremacy that the Conservatives have usually enjoyed in British politics since 1918. In the South-West of Britain, however, the election was regarded as significant for yet another reason. The Liberal Democrats, generally acknowledged as the heirs to the old Liberal tradition of the peninsula, had finally made a breakthrough. Since the 1930s the regional party, while still a major force in a few isolated seats, had failed to return a large number of MPs to Westminster. Now only one seat, the three-way marginal of Falmouth & Camborne, disrupted an otherwise continuous bloc of Liberal Democrat territory that stretched from Land's End to the borders of Wiltshire. Not since 1923 had the Conservatives been reduced to a minority of seats, essentially Dorset and south Devon, in a region that they had once assumed was a loyal stronghold.

To understand this election in a historical context we need to start with the debate over the dramatic decline of the Liberal party after the First World War. In 1906 the party had returned nearly 400 MPs to the House of Commons. By 1924 its representation had fallen to forty, and by 1951 the Liberals appeared to be on the verge of total parliamentary extinction with a mere six seats. The view that the social foundations of Liberalism were being undermined by the emergence of Labour even before 1914 has proved very resilient, as seen by its advocacy by Matthew et al and Laybourn.[1] But this view has been seriously challenged. Wilson claimed that the Liberals were able to accommodate the

1

interests of the working class at this time, and that it was the political and social consequences of the First World War, especially the Asquith–Lloyd George split of 1916, which were really responsible. Such a view remains academically respectable, and in more recent years has been expounded in great detail by Tanner.[2] Cook, on the other hand, has made the distinction between the *decline* of the Liberal party and its *downfall*. In his view the party was still a serious contender for government as late as 1923, and it was not until the end of the following year that the Liberal decline had 'passed the point of no return'.[3]

But this core debate has tended to overshadow other issues relating to the history of British Liberalism in the twentieth century. After all, the demise of the Liberals as an alternative party of government does not really explain their unrelenting decline at every election after 1929. Was this simply inevitable given the fact that Britain's electoral system was a serious obstacle to a third force like the Liberals? Could the party have adopted an alternative strategy that might have limited the dramatic fall in its parliamentary representation during these years? Even in 1929 the Liberals had fifty-nine seats and nearly a quarter of the vote. In theory the party still had sufficient support to remain as a major force in British politics, since it was the main alternative to the Conservatives in half of the seats which they had won in that election (131 out of 260) and in a fifth of the constituencies captured by Labour (58 out of 288).[4] Attention should also focus on why the Liberals were able to survive their years in the political wilderness after the 1920s. Despite a consistent decline in representation until 1955, the party was able to maintain its existence as an independent force during the crucial period of the mid-twentieth century. The Liberals survived as a major electoral force in remote regions like rural Wales and the far South-West of Britain, and even in 1951 their 109 candidates could poll an average vote of 14.7 per cent. This provided the nucleus for a limited revival of the party from the late 1950s onwards. Yet the nature of that phenomenon also raises a number of important questions, which provide the essential background for understanding the recent history of third party politics. Why was it only a partial recovery? Was it simply an illusion based upon protest voting? What prevented the Liberals from creating a more secure electoral base during the years of Jo Grimond and Jeremy Thorpe?

This complicated process of decline, dormancy and rebirth can be seen especially well through a case study of the Liberal experience in south-west Britain. In the 1920s the four counties of Cornwall, Devon, Somerset and Dorset formed one of the few geographical regions in Britain where the party of Asquith and Lloyd George could still win a relatively large number of seats. The collapse of its regional powerbase here in 1931 also contributed to the national impotence of Liberalism throughout the mid-twentieth century. By the early 1950s, when the Liberals were fighting for their very existence, the South-West again played an important role, since it was the early revival in Cornwall and Devon which provided the morale and purpose that enabled the party to survive its darkest days. Victories at Torrington and North Devon in the latter part of the decade improved the credibility of the party, and effectively heralded the revival of Liberalism at the national level. By 1966 the three Liberals in the two western counties represented a quarter of the parliamentary party. In recent years the regional Liberal Democrats have built on these historic foundations to emerge under the leadership of Paddy Ashdown on equal terms with the Conservatives in Westminster elections, twelve seats each in 1997 and the remainder held by Labour, and as the dominant force in the area of local government.

The South-West, then, provides an ideal area in which to examine the changing fortunes of organized liberalism. Since the regional party obviously had to operate within a wider framework, this study will attempt to relate local developments to the situation at Westminster. It will consider whether the national leadership was able to harness the potential Liberal vote as effectively as it could have done, particularly in a region like the South-West where the party was still a significant political force. The 1920s had demonstrated that Liberalism was still a virile force across the four counties, and socio-economic factors appeared to give a long-term advantage to the party. Yet the Liberals were unable to establish a secure bloc of seats in the South-West after 1929. Was this failure purely inevitable given the fact that developments at the national level were not favourable to the Liberals for most of the period? Was there an alternative strategy that the party might have pursued? Thus, apart from explaining the particular reasons for the party's survival and rebirth in the South-West, the discussion will be expanded to consider the possibility that the Liberals would perhaps have had greater success with a strategy which was designed to maximize the electoral potential of certain regions.

While there have been a number of such regional political studies in the past, they have tended to focus more on the *rise* of Labour than on the *decline* of Liberalism.[5] This particular investigation will therefore move away from the conventional focus on urban Britain to the neglected world of rural and small-town politics. It will show how the political alignment of the South-West was created by a variety of factors, such as the survival of religious nonconformity, the relative weakness of the trade-union movement and the complex nature of political affiliation in a farming and service-dominated area. Above all, it will point to the wide regional variation at the heart of electoral change. Even in 1929 the Liberals could still poll at least 30 per cent in the vast majority of seats in regions like the Scottish Highlands, rural Wales and the East Midlands. By contrast, the party won less than 30 per cent in every division that it contested in Glasgow, Staffordshire and Sheffield. This regional diversity conflicts with the natural tendency to consider the Liberal decline as a straightforward national phenomenon. What accounts for this variation? Would the Liberals have been more successful after 1924 if they had concentrated on those seats which they still had a good chance of winning?

This case study, then, fills a current gap in the history of both Liberal and regional politics. Although it traces the wider story of the party in the South-West from 1918 to 1997, I have deliberately concentrated my chronological chapter structure on the middle decades of the century. Far from being a long, dreary and essentially uneventful epilogue to Liberal decline, the years from the late 1920s to the first stirrings of revival some thirty years later cover the central themes of decline, dormancy and rebirth. It was during this period that the destruction of organized Liberalism seemed inevitable following the party's fall from power. The reaction of both party activists and the wider electorate was to lead to the processes of both decline *and* survival, while the limited nature of recovery in the 1950s, it will be argued, was influenced by earlier events at the local and state level. The final chapter, which combines the role of a conventional conclusion with a fresh insight into later events, brings this story to an appropriate finale with a look at the memorable breakthrough of 1997.

1

Politics in the Provinces

Introduction

The long-term decline of the Liberal party after 1918, whether at the national or regional level, should not be seen in isolation from similar developments taking place throughout Western Europe. During the first quarter of the twentieth century the rise of Socialism was seriously undermining older political allegiances across the Continent, and it was organized Liberalism, the popular ideology of the previous century, which tended to be the principal loser in this new phase of realignment. Yet the uneven nature of historical development *within* a state could significantly influence the extent and timing of this process. Variations, both in terms of cultural and economic development, ensured that the provinces did not conveniently fall into line with political developments taking place in the national arena. This could lead to a complex pattern of alignment, with some regions embracing class politics at an early stage and traditional cleavages surviving in other areas. It is this vital factor of regional diversity that provides the context for understanding the changing fortunes of the Liberal party in South-West Britain.

Alignment and Diversity

Until the late 1960s the conventional view of British politics was that political change took place on an essentially national basis. Regional variations were insignificant given the basically homogenous nature of the electorate, and the seemingly inexorable rise of the Labour party in the House of Commons after the First World War, from sixty seats in 1918 to 288 by 1929, tends to confirm this view. Since the old Liberal agenda no longer appealed to modern voters, particularly Free Church issues like temperance and Anglican disestablishment, political realignment seemed inevitable. Yet the rise of Socialism was in reality a regional phenomenon. As Kinnear points out, Labour victories in the crucial election of 1922, when the party moved from being 'an ineffective minor group in Parliament to that of a vigorous and determined Opposition', were based on 'a few well-defined areas'.[1] But this creates a new problem in understanding the relationship between regional diversity and electoral behaviour. While a common link for the Socialist victories in 1922 was that they occurred in urban and industrial areas, it was also a diverse list in the sense that it ranged from gains in London to remote centres like Glasgow and industrial Yorkshire. A diverse pattern also emerges with those areas that still looked to Liberalism in 1929. The Celtic fringe of Cornwall, North Wales and the Scottish Highlands provided the bulk of Liberal representatives elected in that year, but the party remained a credible force in areas like Wiltshire and East Anglia on the borders of the prosperous Home Counties. A simplification of this process, which just concentrates on the centre–periphery cleavage in isolation, does not really explain the full nature of political change at the regional level.

It is important to draw on the work of political scientists looking at other comparable societies and their regional politics to put the experience of both Britain and the South-West into some kind of perspective. A good example can be seen in Rokkan's views on the formation and consolidation of core political cleavages. He concluded that voters at the regional level throughout Western Europe were subject to conflicting influences by the 1920s that could vary in significance from election to election. In the first place were the main issues being debated at the centre. The rise of Socialism, the New Left, led to a class-based agenda at the centre based on the 'owner–worker' cleavage. This encouraged a polarization of opinion based on class and/or ideology (Socialism versus anti-Socialism), and such ideas began to dominate political debate throughout the state. However, traditional issues could still have a significant impact, especially in regions remote from central government. In the Nordic countryside the predominance of small farms, the relative strength of religious nonconformity and an essentially 'egalitarian class structure' preserved a traditional culture which provided a more secure base for the Liberals and other Old Left parties.[2] This meant that voting decisions were an interactive process between two basic concepts: class-based ideas from the centre and the old values and community issues of the region.

Rokkan simplified these regional factors into three basic cleavages: (1) centre–periphery; (2) state–church and (3) rural–urban. The centre–periphery conflict was an early form of cleavage in which the provinces defended their culture against control from the centre. An obvious source of discontent was where an ethnic minority, such as the Basque community in Spain, was in conflict with the dominant nation-building culture. Yet a milder form of territorial politics could be found in Norway where the peasants in the provinces were disgruntled with the metropolis because the bureaucracy and the urban bourgeoisie were attempting to impose their ideas on the countryside. The geographical remoteness of the peripheries could well lead to economic problems and a feeling that the regional culture and general economic prosperity of the community was being undermined by the actions or indifference of central government. This would invariably give rise to some form of regionalism or nationalism. Some remote provinces, however, could be integrated into the state system if the owner–worker cleavage was strong. An example of this process can be seen in the extreme periphery of the northern region of Norway. The hierarchical nature of society in this area encouraged the early breakthrough of class politics, which was demonstrated in 1903 when the first Socialist representatives to enter the Norwegian Parliament were elected by the fishermen of the northern communes.[3] A comparison can be made with the extreme North-East of England. Despite a sense of provincial identity and a geographical remoteness from central government, the Labour party became the dominant force in the urban and industrial areas during the 1920s, while the outlying rural areas, with the exception of the marginal seat of Berwick-upon-Tweed, remained loyal to the Conservatives.

This suggests that the Old Left was likely to fare better after the First World War in those areas where the centre–periphery cleavage was combined with other factors. It is worth noting that the three traditional cleavages outlined above could be connected, thereby providing an even more secure foundation for the survival of older movements. For example, political differences over religion tended to be related to the centre–periphery divide. In Roman Catholic countries the state–church cleavage was based on a conflict between secular parties and the church over issues like control of the education system. However, it took on a different form in Protestant countries where religious nonconformists expressed their opposition to the 'latitudinarianism of the national Mother Church' by either forming evangelical parties or working within an existing anti-establishment party. In the provinces, particularly those areas which were most remote from the state capital, the opposition of the Free Churches to 'urban secularism' and the 'evils of modern life' naturally appealed to the local inhabitants. Religious nonconformity was often integrated into the culture of a 'subject' province, as in Wales, and became a key factor in what Rokkan termed the 'politics of cultural defense'.[4] These traditional forms of alignment were often connected to the land issue. Rural peripheries were likely to feel neglected by the dominant urban/industrial interest, while agrarian parties have rarely emerged in Roman Catholic countries because Christian Democratic groups have been able to 'cross-cut' the rural–urban cleavage.

Exploring the South-West

In theory this meant that the British Old Left was also in a strong position to survive the onslaught of class politics in those regions where the Liberal party was still sustained by a combination of Protestant nonconformity, rural discontent and regionalism. Yet to apply Rokkan's work to the history of regional Liberalism it is essential to focus on a specific region in Britain. The four south-western counties of Cornwall, Devon, Somerset and Dorset form a suitable model for such purposes since all three of the traditional cleavages were present. In the first place climatic and geographical factors had produced a landscape of small farms that specialized in stock rearing, dairying and grass-land farming. This was particularly the case in rural districts in the west of the region where the isolated uplands of Dartmoor and Bodmin Moor encouraged a pastoral form of agriculture. In some of the eastern parts, such as the areas around Dorchester and Exeter, arable farming was more suitable, and the power of the 'Squire and his Lady' gave an advantage to the Conservatives. Yet the neighbouring county of Somerset was one of the principal dairy regions of England, with the farms of the Somerset levels tending to be quite small in size with an average acreage of 30 acres.[5] Another general feature of the South-West was the relative absence of major urban settlements. Plymouth (population in 1921: 210,036) was the only large borough, and borough constituencies only accounted for five of the region's twenty-seven divisions (Bath, Exeter and the Plymouth seats of Drake, Devonport and Sutton) after 1918. Even in the eastern counties, which were close to the urban centres of Bristol and Bournemouth, it was still essentially a very rural area. North Dorset, for example, was the third-largest English division in terms of size and contained 'more than 120 villages, with six small towns', while Wells contained a 'number of smaller towns and many villages and hamlets [but] no large mass vote'.[6]

It was only to be expected that the economic agenda of this rural and small town society would differ from the national scene. The Old Left issue of free trade was an obvious example. While Britain's economic problems, combined with the perceived threat from Socialism, were encouraging many voters to transfer their allegiance from Liberal to Conservative by the early 1930s, the traditional belief in free trade as the core economic issue survived longer in the South-West when compared to other regions. Key groups across the peninsula, such as agricultural labourers, female voters and old age pensioners, believed that protectionism would lead to an increase in the cost of living. Many local industries during the 1920s were also likely to be affected adversely by tariffs. Dairy farmers depended on cheap supplies of farm implements and feeding stuffs, while the clay and fishing industries feared that they would lose their foreign markets.[7] Admittedly, there were local industries that favoured some form of protection. The glove industry, which employed several thousand workers on the borders of Dorset and Somerset, welcomed the introduction of Safeguarding in the 1920s in order to keep out a 'flood of foreign gloves', while the Heathcoat Amory family in east Devon had defected to the Conservatives by 1931 on the grounds that tariffs were essential for the prosperity of their lace business.[8] Despite these exceptions, free trade was still relevant to many voters in the region. This was particularly the case in Cornwall where the Liberals completely monopolized the county's parliamentary representation on those occasions when free trade was an issue. Leif Jones, Liberal MP for Camborne (1923–4 and 1929–31), pointed out in October 1930 that this loyalty to the old cause of free trade was based on the view that the prosperity of virtually all of Cornwall's staple industries would be undermined by tariffs:

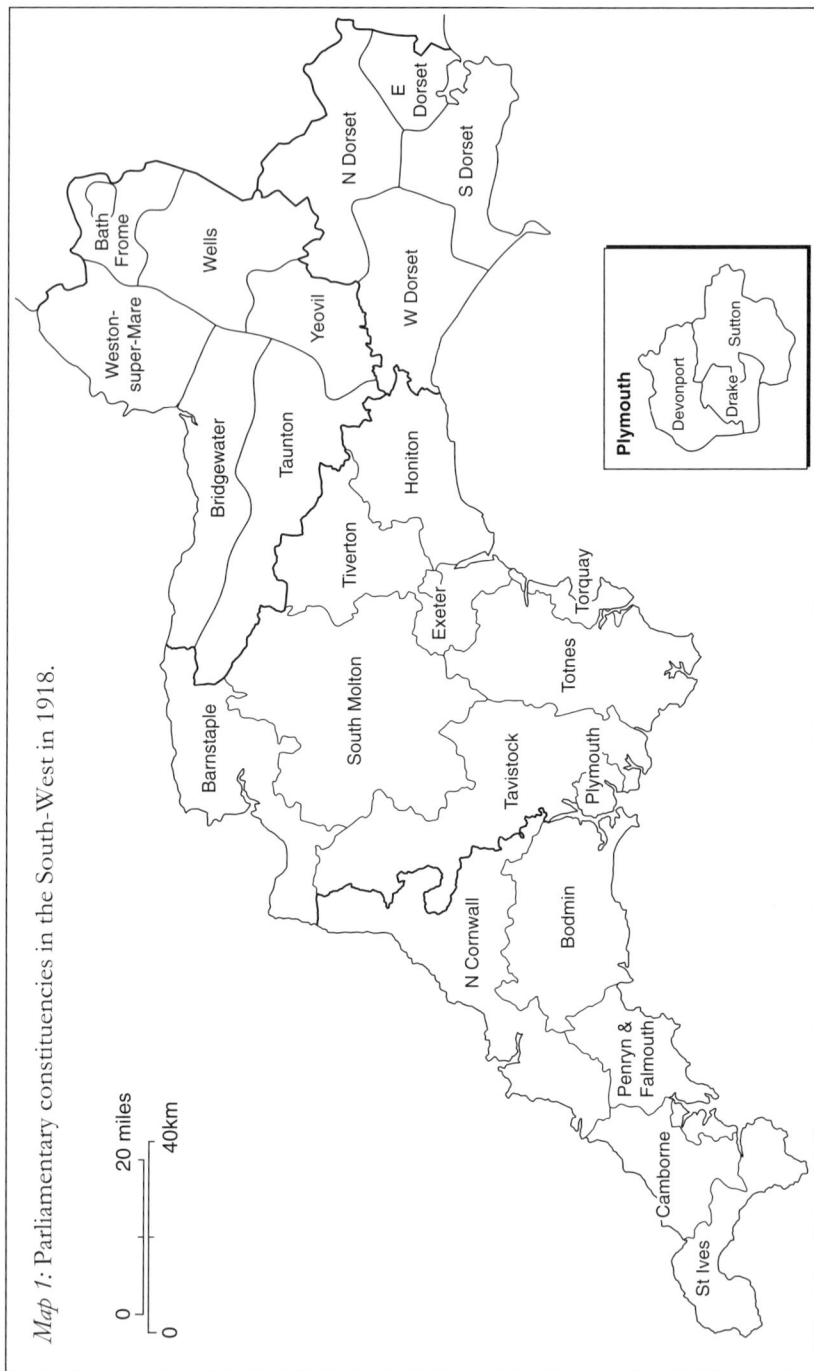

Map 1: Parliamentary constituencies in the South-West in 1918.

Any Protectionist system set up in this country was going to hit Cornwall. It was not possible to afford Protection to tin and china clay, which were export trades. Cornish agriculture, which depended very largely upon cheap feeding stuffs and fertilisers, was going to be penalised under any system of Protection set up.[9]

The final point about the threat to agricultural prosperity was typical of the way in which the Liberals attempted to rouse the traditional supporters of free trade. Jones emphasized the local benefits of cheap agricultural imports. He argued that the region should 'take advantage of the present situation, buy all the feeding stuffs we can, and feed all the stock our farms will carry on the cheap corn our neighbours are good enough to send to us'.[10] A general acceptance of such sentiments by small farmers in the South-West ensured that the Liberals were in a stronger position to win votes here than in arable areas. Furthermore, developments after the First World War pointed to the continuing existence of the rural–urban divide, with many farmers throughout the four counties still speaking of the 'urban menace' that interfered with the prosperity and general way of life of the countryside.[11] There was always the possibility that the Conservatives, as a national party of government, could alienate the farming vote in seeking to balance the interests of rural and urban Britain. Subsequent chapters will demonstrate that Conservative defeats at parliamentary by-elections like Bridgwater in 1938 and Torrington in 1958 were based on that party's unpopularity with the farming community when in government.

Given Labour's weakness in most rural areas in Britain, it was inevitable that the Socialists would find it difficult to stage a break-through. The party did not even put forward any parliamentary candidates in the region until 1918, and even in 1929, when Labour first became the largest group in the House of Commons, it was only able to win two seats in the region. Labour appeared to be making definite progress throughout the South-West in 1945 when they captured six seats and became the main opposition to the Conservatives, but by the 1950s their representation had fallen to just one seat (Camborne). In that sense the region was similar to South and West Norway where Socialist parties had only minimal success in their efforts to 'entrench themselves in the countryside outside the isolated industrial enclaves'.[12]

The majority of businesses employed only a small workforce, while a system of agriculture based on family farms obviously required fewer labourers. Indeed, it was only railwaymen, quarrymen, dockers and lorry drivers who tended to join a trade union in the 1920s, which limited the potential Labour vote. Even in the mid-1960s it was still common, certainly in the rural West, for workers on farms or in small industrial concerns to vote in the same way as their employer.[13]

What was perhaps even more surprising was the failure to sustain the impact of Socialism in those seats where conditions were supposedly more conducive. Even the coal-mining division of Frome went to Labour on just three occasions (1923, 1929 and 1945), while only in 1945 did all three of the Plymouth seats return Socialist candidates. In Cornwall, where Radicalism had been strongly entrenched in industrial seats like St Austell and Camborne before the First World War, the Socialists failed to elect a single MP throughout the inter-war period. This will be discussed in greater detail at a later stage, but a closer study of the experience of the St Austell area suggests a possible explanation. A.L. Rowse, the historian and Labour candidate for the area in the 1930s, claimed that in the first two decades of the twentieth century the rise of class politics was delayed by the 'egalitarian' spirit that prevailed in local communities. There was a tendency for workers to retain their independence by remaining outside the trade-union movement by having a 'second string to their bow, a small holding, a part-time job, a small shop'. He concluded that 'there was never any ill feeling, let alone class-hostility, between the workers and the owners and 'captains' of the works; they were all still close together … for that; they came from the same people, they attended the same chapels, they shared the same tastes—football and brass-bands—they were all Liberals together'.[14] Although the 1913 clay strike obviously revealed another side to the class issue, it could be said that in a region where industry was restricted to small zones, such as St Austell and Frome, the rise of class politics was likely to be more gradual.

In order to really understand the impact of Socialism in the region we need to consider another social group: the *petite bourgeoisie*. Research in the past, as terms like *petite bourgeoisie* and the *piccola borghesia* clearly indicate, has been focused on continental Europe. Until the 1980s the core trend in the 'historiography of this stratum', as Morris puts it, was to find a long-term explanation for the emergence of European Fascism, particularly in Germany where the discontent of the lower middle class was seen as the central factor in the rise of Hitler.[15] Whilst recent studies on this subject have extended the debate to cover the wider political activities of small entrepreneurs, such as the relationship between shopkeepers and the state in inter-war Belgium and Sweden, the real interest still seems to lie with the continental experience. This is a debate, however, which can be applied to Britain and the South-West in particular. A crucial issue after the First World War was how to reconcile the social and economic interests of the small man within the new corporatist state. In Britain, as in other countries like Italy and Sweden, the tendency was for small entrepreneurs to regard the Socialists, with their commitment to nationalization and links with the co-operative movement, as the main proponent of collectivism.[16] But bourgeois parties in alliance with big business could also pursue state intervention and economic rationalization, which was effectively undermining the position of small economic concerns. Small traders in Britain, just like the farmers, were prepared to withdraw their allegiance from Conservative governments, at least on a temporary basis, if they felt that their interests were being neglected.

The Liberals, as the only other non-Socialist party, recognized that they could fill this vacuum. As James Bateman, the party's candidate for the Somerset seat of Yeovil remarked in 1945, there were 'three main roads before the nation today'. The Conservative 'road led to big business [and] the small man had little hope of reaching the end of it'. Since the Socialist road would lead to the 'overpowering monopoly of the state', only Liberalism would result in 'true economic freedom' which would ensure the survival of the 'smaller business and manufacturer'.[17] During the Second World War the party had appointed an Independent Trader Inquiry at the national level which recommended an anti-monopoly code to protect the small entrepreneur from unfair competition. A pressure group, entitled the Independent Trades Alliance, was even set up by the Liberals at this time. In July 1945 the Liberal report was unanimously approved at a conference of traders in Somerset. Edward Gallop, a local Liberal activist and chairman of the Western Area of the ITA, declared that 'thanks were due to any Party bold enough and good enough to bring out such a Report'. He added that the small traders had to become 'politically minded' in order that Parliament would be 'obliged to listen to their voice'.[18]

But what exactly do we mean by the term *petite bourgeoisie?* The usual emphasis is just on a specific group covering shopkeepers, artisans and service providers like innkeepers and taxi drivers. Bechofer and Elliot concluded that the small entrepreneur differed from other members of the wider bourgeoisie in that he relied on his own labour. Even when he employed some workers outside his own immediate family, this was 'an extension of, rather than a substitute for [his] own labour'.[19] When we come to a remote geographical region like the South-West one could argue that the term should be extended to include small farmers, fishermen and even Rowse's clay workers: an essentially rural *petite bourgeoisie.* If one adds those groups on fixed incomes, such as old age pensioners, then a clear majority of electors in many rural and residential seats did not fit neatly into the collectivist two-party system that had emerged by the Second World War.[20]

Despite the potential for Liberalism, it was the Conservatives who were the dominant party in South-Western politics from 1924 onwards. Britain's electoral system was a serious obstacle to a third force, and the business community, 'big and small alike', tended to identify with the Conservatives through their basic fear of Socialism.[21] This attitude can be seen in regard to the events of the early 1930s when many Liberals rejected the free trade cause and defected to the National government. Part of the explanation for this process may well have been due to a growing belief that some form of protection was essential to safeguard British industry at a time of economic depression. Nevertheless, many voters, including small farmers and traders who still preferred a free trade system to keep down the cost of living, might well have been attracted to the National parties on the grounds that the new coalition was the only bulwark against Labour. A good example was Henry Hobhouse, MP for East Somerset from 1885 to 1906. He had previously been a staunch free trader; he had actually moved from the Liberal Unionists to the Liberals over the free trade issue in 1906, but his greater fear of Socialism led him to compromise over the tariff issue in 1931. Although still opposed to the 'extreme doctrines of Protection', Hobhouse believed that free trade was not a 'gospel for which we ought to go to the stake. It [was] only a means to an end, the end being the commercial and industrial prosperity of our country.'[22] In that sense it was the Conservative party, not Labour, which emerged as the real beneficiary of the impact of Socialism in the South-West.

This did not mean, however, that the local Liberals had no future. Mayer claimed that the *petite bourgeoisie* was united only in 'moments of extreme crisis', giving rise to an 'erratic and intermittently frenzied politicisation' as the group defended its interests against external economic forces. This process was evident in the brief popularity of parties that specifically appealed to the small man, such as the proto-Fascist Rex party in Belgium in 1936 and the Poujadist movement in France during the 1950s.[23] A similar process can be detected in Britain, particularly the South-West, where the Liberals enjoyed temporary success in 1929, 1964–6 and 1974 only to lose ground in the subsequent election when the anti-Socialist vote reunited in order to remove the Labour party from office. By-elections offered an even greater opportunity for protest voting and, as Chapter 7 will suggest, the Liberal advance at Torquay and Torrington in the late 1950s was based principally on the discontent of the *petite bourgeoisie*. Further research needs to be carried out into the political activities of this group in Britain after the First World War, but the evidence from the South-West certainly points to its crucial role in regional politics. Indeed, the discontented *petite bourgeoisie* acted as the mainstay of the Old Left after 1918. It was their flexibility as a group in moving to and from Liberalism that accounted for political change in an increasingly 'fixed' two-party system. As Maurice Petherick, the prospective Conservative candidate for Penryn & Falmouth, put it in 1930, it was essential to convince this floating group that the anti-Socialist issue had to take precedence over other cleavages:

> We Conservatives must realise that unless we can recapture the Liberals who voted for us in 1924 our chance of office is remote. We have got to realise in the West-country that while for many years to come we might fight out the old-fashioned battle of Tory versus Radical, it is only a local battle, and remote from the great national issue of Socialism.[24]

When we come to the religious cleavage it is difficult to establish a regional generalization. The national Census of Religious Worship in 1851 revealed that there was considerable variation in the strength of the Free Churches. In Cornwall, which was more akin to North Wales than the shire counties of England, the nonconformists accounted for

71.8 per cent of all those attending a place of worship, but this figure fell to 43.1 in Devon and was lower still in Somerset (38.4) and Dorset (37.8). There were no further official censuses of worship after 1851, but Coleman has concluded that the distribution of nonconformity in the South-West would have been quite similar in the 1930s.[25] This view is supported by Kinnear's estimate of nonconformist membership for 1922. His statistics actually underestimate Free Church strength in the far west since attendance at nonconformist chapels was not restricted to members, and this was particularly the case with Methodist congregations in Cornwall. In addition, Kinnear did not include the Bible Christians, part of the United Methodist Church after 1907, who were rather small at the state level but a prominent denomination in east Cornwall and west Devon. Nevertheless, the survey suggests that Free Church members accounted for at least 10 per cent of the electorate in North Devon and every constituency in Cornwall. In the rest of the region the nonconformists represented less than a tenth of electors in all but two seats (North Dorset and Yeovil).[26]

Religious nonconformity provided a secure niche for Liberalism in the western divisions. Probert commented that the chapel was still the 'social centre of the community' in remote areas, and this ensured that a large section of the population identified with Methodism after 1918. During the first decade after the war the Wesleyans and the United Methodists, the principal nonconformist groups in the West, had even experienced a modest revival.[27] Many rural Methodists, like their counterparts in Scandinavia, were committed to a traditional agenda, while the strength of family loyalties in rural communities encouraged the younger generation to share the same values. Martin concluded that the 'hard core' of nonconformists in west Devon were even 'resistant to cultural change' in the 1960s.[28] In addition, Methodism had always been a major socio-political force in the West. The leadership of the 1913 clay strike came from the nonconformist chapels. Sunday sermons were concerned with wages and labour conditions during the rest of the week, and Methodist ministers would encourage the clay workers with readings from the book of Exodus.[29] The nonconformist societies, in particular the Bible Christians who were a major force in the farming communities of the Cornwall–Devon borderland, also provided the opposition to the squirearchy and the clergy. According to Martin, this reflected the fact that the Bible Christians were the principal opponents of the payment of tithes by those farmers who had no connection with the Church of England:

> Behind the frontage of faith there were economic urges. The farmers hated tithe and the power of gentry and clergy. Religion ... opened the floodgates of emotion. This was a farmer's religion, a rural Methodism; and it reflected the peculiarities of its area of birth.[30]

Whilst there is a growing need for a major study of local Methodism that examines the wider framework of class and politics, we can at least establish that the rise of socialism and the owner–worker cleavage had little relevance for the rural communities of Cornwall and the Devon border zone. In Bible Christian chapels it was common for a 'labourer' to take the service while his 'master' was in the congregation.[31] Furthermore, whilst Wesleyan Methodism at the state level appealed primarily to the middle class, it embraced all classes in Cornwall. In those regions where Primitive Methodism was strong, such as Durham, the Labour party usually achieved and sustained an early predominance after the First World War, but this denomination was much weaker in the far west. It was only in the Camborne division, even then with just 489 members in 1922, that the Primitive Methodists attracted much support.[32] In addition, the local Liberal leaders, many of whom came from the farming community, were usually Methodist lay preachers, and in general they remained loyal to Liberalism. Rural Methodists tended to follow the lead of the lay preachers, their local heroes, and they also continued to vote Liberal.[33] As with the Rokkan model, links could be established between the rural and religious cleavages in this part of the region. Even after the Second World War many local nonconformists still associated Liberalism with Christianity, while the old suspicion of the Anglican/ Conservative landlord was reinforced by a growing concern that the small farmer was being neglected by both Labour and the Conservatives.[34]

Defining the South-West

This example of diversity *within* the South-West raises the wider problem of assessing the extent of the region. The vagueness of such labels as the 'West of England' and the 'West Country' reflects the failure of both academics and the wider community to establish a consensus in regard to regional boundaries. The four counties are certainly considered as a specific region in Smart's fairly recent study of political alignment in the inter-war period.[35] Pelling, however, divided the four counties into three separate areas in his *Social Geography of British Elections, 1885–1910.* Basing his regions on a model devised by C.B. Fawcett in 1919 he treated the two western counties as a distinct region, while Somerset and Dorset were divided and combined with neighbouring counties to form the regions of Wessex and the Severn.[36] Yet Manning-Sanders, writing in 1949, assumed that the region of the 'West of England' covered Cornwall, Devon and Somerset, while Hollis in 1958 believed that the central Wiltshire seat of Devizes was a typical 'West Country' constituency.[37] The Liberal party itself divided the four counties for organizational purposes. Somerset and Dorset were included with Bristol, Wiltshire and Gloucestershire in the Western Counties Liberal Federation, while the counties of Cornwall and Devon formed another federation.

A valid argument could also be advanced for saying that Cornwall should be treated as a distinct region in its own right. Payton's pioneering study on this subject written in 1992, entitled *The Making of Modern Cornwall,* was placed firmly in the broader centre–periphery framework developed by Rokkan and more recent scholars. Adapting and developing Tarrow's idea of various 'phases of peripherality', he concluded that 'in each historical period the experience of Cornwall has been highly individual when compared to that of the English "centre", or indeed other areas of Britain'.[38] Historical and geographical distinctiveness certainly ensured that the socio-economic factors that assisted the Old Left in Norway (religious nonconformity, family farms and a peripheral economy) were more evident in the county than anywhere else in the 'South-West'. Cornwall was also the only part of the peninsula where a cleavage between the dominant nation-building culture and a subject region could have conceivably occurred along ethnic lines. Indeed, the history of modern Cornish nationalism can be traced back to the end of the nineteenth century. Following the Liberal split of 1886 over the question of home rule for Ireland, Gladstone and his supporters decided to make the issue appear more relevant to mainland Britain by advocating a federal system of government: 'Home Rule All Round'. Although Cowethas Kelto-Kernuak (the Celtic-

Cornish Society) which was formed in 1901 operated on a non-political basis, the Cornish Liberals used the cultural themes raised by this organization for political purposes. Thus, the cause of Irish home rule was defended on pan-Celtic grounds, while some Liberal activists echoed their counterparts in Wales by calling for the disestablishment of the Anglican Church in Cornwall. Significantly, Lloyd George's suggestion in 1905 of combining Devon and Cornwall in a single region was rejected on the grounds that the Cornish people were a 'separate race'.[39] When Winston Churchill proposed the creation of regional legislatures for England in 1912, Alfred Browning Lyne, the editor of the *Cornish Guardian* and a prominent local Liberal, called for domestic self-government:

> There is another Home Rule movement on the horizon. Self government for Cornwall will be the next move ... The Metropolis is coming to mean everything, and all the provinces approximate towards the fashion of the centre ... We think this is much to be deplored, and we do not see why Cornwall should not join in the 'Regionalist' movement which is striving in various parts of Western Europe to revive local patriotism.[40]

Yet the outbreak of the First World War removed those conditions which had allowed these ideas to flourish. The focus in British politics gradually shifted away after 1914 towards social and economic subjects, and it was not until the 1960s that devolution again became a major issue at Westminster. The loss of this external stimulus was crucial. Cornwall, in contrast to the other Celtic nations, lacked a recent tradition of political nationalism, while the debate over Cornish self-government had not developed sufficiently to make a lasting impact on party politics. Nonetheless, the experience of the inter-war period was to ensure that the potential for regionalist discontent was to remain. The Liberals claimed that their party, unlike the new Labour–Conservative alignment at Westminster, could 'understand Cornish folk and be in sympathy with their traditions and outlook on life'.[41] Lyne, by then the Chairman of Bodmin Liberal Association, developed this anti-metropolitan theme when he wrote in 1923 that Isaac Foot, with his ability to relate to the radical and nonconformist interests of the community, was the natural champion of Cornwall. He added that the region was a 'long way from

London and unless the powers that be are made to realise that Cornwall does really exist and is entitled to some of the money that goes up from Cornwall … we shall not get what is our fair proportion of public expenditure'.[42] This left the Liberals well placed to take advantage of the rise of anti-metropolitanism in Cornwall after the Second World War.

Paradoxically, this difficulty in defining the borders of the region actually justifies the case for seeing south-west Britain as a suitable area for studying Liberalism. Although some similarities were inevitable in such a basically rural area, the real interest perhaps lies in analysing the social and political differences which existed from Bristol to Land's End. The idea of change across a particular area was hinted at by Urwin who developed the centre–periphery model by pointing to the additional existence of 'inner' and 'outer' zones. Thus, while London and the Home Counties form an 'Inner Centre', there was also an 'Outer Centre' based on regions like Wessex and East Anglia, with even an 'Inner Periphery' (Cornwall, Wales and northern England) and an 'Outer Periphery' (Scotland and Ireland).[43] Applying this model to the decline of the Liberals after the First World War, it can be argued that the decisive moment for the party finally came in 1929 when it failed to recapture control of the 'Outer Centre'. Somerset, Dorset and east Devon form the western districts of Wessex, the key region that moved away from Liberalism after 1923. After that date the party had only limited parliamentary success, briefly winning East Dorset in 1929 and North Dorset in 1945, and it was not until Paddy Ashdown's historic victory at Yeovil in 1983 that the party obtained a secure presence in the eastern counties. Only recently with the electoral breakthrough of the Liberal Democrats in 1997 was the third party once again in a position to challenge the supremacy of the Conservatives in Wessex, winning eight constituencies in Devon and Somerset and an additional seven seats, including Newbury and Winchester, in the other counties.[44]

In many ways the county of Devon actually forms the borderland between this 'Outer Centre' region and the 'Inner Periphery' of Cornwall. The residential nature of towns and villages on the south and east Devon coast certainly gave an advantage to the Conservatives. The climate and geography of this area was milder than north Devon, and the coastal resorts of Paignton, Budleigh Salterton and Exmouth were the fastest-growing areas in the county. The Conservatives were therefore being 'constantly reinforced', as Pelling put it, by new middle-class supporters, and the Liberals were to find it increasingly difficult to win seats like Torquay and Totnes after 1918. Pelling concluded that the influence of the Church of England was also 'stronger' in this part of Devon. The Free Churches were usually weaker in the rural parishes, and their only major stronghold in the area was the fishing community of Brixham (Torquay). Moreover, the nonconformists were divided into a variety of groups, in particular the Congregationalists, Baptists and Wesleyans, and this meant that there was no principal denomination to consolidate the Liberal–Free Church nexus, unlike in Cornwall and western Devon.[45] It was therefore understandable that Barnstaple in the north of the county was the only seat to return a Liberal in the 1930s. This remote area also witnessed the first real signs of rebirth in the 1950s with Jeremy Thorpe obtaining a good second place at North Devon in 1955 and narrowly winning the seat in the subsequent election.

This leads us once again to consider the experience of the Cornish periphery. One could easily classify the whole of the county as the real heartland of Liberalism in the South-West. After all, in 1929 it was the only area where the Liberals staged a complete recovery, with victories in all five seats. This landslide result was nearly repeated again in 1997 when four seats went to the Liberal Democrats and the sole exception, Falmouth & Camborne, fell to Labour. As Andrew George, the new Liberal Democrat MP for St Ives, pointed out, 'the Celtic nations of Scotland, Wales and Cornwall were a Tory-free zone'.[46] Yet the seventy years between these elections also witnessed variations within Cornwall. By 1951 the Labour party had forced the Liberals into third place in the western seats of Truro, Falmouth & Camborne and St Ives. Although conditions in west and mid-Cornwall were not so favourable for Labour as in some other regions of Britain, the party was able to establish a base for itself in some industrial communities. When the Liberal revival started a few years later it was really focused on the eastern constituencies of Bodmin and North Cornwall. With similar developments taking place in North Devon, Torrington and Tavistock, this created a rural heartland for the Liberals centred on the River Tamar. The effect was to create a rural periphery in the east, where the Liberals could win seats at Westminster on an anti-metropolitan platform, and a more complex pattern west of Bodmin, consisting of relatively prosperous areas like Truro and St Austell and the peripheral industrial/rural zones of Camborne/Redruth and the far west.[47] Only with the victory of David

Penhaligon at Truro in October 1974 did the Liberals start to move back into the western parts of the Duchy.

Conclusion

Ideas developed in a European context provide an interesting approach for studying the survival and eventual rebirth of South-West Liberalism after the First World War. By looking at the process of inter-war realignment purely in terms of the rise of Socialism it is tempting to assume that the decline of the Liberal party was inevitable. However, the real arena for electoral change lay in the regions. Traditional cleavages, combined with the long-term discontent of the *petite bourgeoisie*, ensured the party's survival as a credible force in some regions during the crucial decades of the mid-twentieth century. By focusing on the South-West this process can be explored in greater detail, particularly since the four counties covered both central and peripheral zones. Indeed, it is this comparative framework within one particular area that holds the key to enhancing our wider understanding of political change.

2

Keeping the Faith: 1918–1929

Introduction

While historians might debate the actual timing of the start of the decline of the Liberal party, it was undoubtedly the decade after the First World War which witnessed its demise as a party of government. Despite a respectable showing in 1923, when the Liberals on 157 seats were still able to compete on fairly equal terms with their opponents, represen-tation in the House of Commons dropped to just forty in 1924 and only rose to fifty-nine in 1929. This period, dubbed the 'Age of Alignment' by Cook, paved the way for a new two-party system, Labour versus Conservative, that survived intact until the Liberal revivals of the 1960s and 1970s.[1] Yet in the rural South-West the Liberals were to retain their historic role as the radical alternative to the Conservatives. Although the regional party certainly struggled to meet the new challenge posed by Labour in the early part of the period, good election results in 1923 and 1929 demonstrated that Liberalism was still a powerful force across the four counties. This chapter traces the main political developments at Westminster and in the region during the immediate post-war period before focusing on the significance of the 1929 election, which paradoxically pointed both to the survival of Liberalism and to its failure to retain a permanent ascendancy in the region.

Meeting the Socialist Challenge

The electoral breakthrough of the Labour party during the first quarter of the twentieth century has been well documented. This is even the case at the regional level with a growing number of studies on the party's industrial or urban strongholds, places such as Yorkshire, Nottingham and Clydeside, where the rise of Socialism seemed almost inevitable.[2] With hindsight the South-West appears to be a political backwater at this time. Labour remained firmly in third place until 1945, and after the Second World War the party still had to struggle to win seats at Westminster. Nevertheless, the disastrous performance of the Liberals in 1918 was so serious that a unique opportunity was briefly created for the early advance of Socialism. Whilst the Conservatives and their Lloyd George Liberal allies dominated the parliamentary representation of the four counties, with twenty-four out of twenty-seven seats, a surprisingly good performance by Labour meant that those Liberals who still followed Asquith could not even console themselves with the thought that they were still the obvious alternative to the government.

The threat from Labour was most noticeable in Cornwall. Although the party lacked a pre-war parliamentary tradition in the Duchy, its two candidates at Camborne and St Ives both achieved good results in 1918 with 48.0 and 38.4 per cent of the vote respectively. This was particularly the case in Camborne where it was commonly accepted that if the prospective Conservative candidate had stood, Labour would probably have won the seat. What is even more surprising is the fact that west Cornwall was briefly at the forefront in the rise of Socialism, at least when it is compared to some other parts of Britain more usually considered as Socialist strongholds. Both Sheffield and Stepney had emerged as key Labour areas by the late 1920s, but in the first post-war election a relatively low share of the vote, roughly only a fifth to a third, was normal. Labour's share of the vote was actually greater in Camborne and St Ives than it was in future strongholds like Bermondsey, Doncaster, Aberavon and Motherwell, while the result in Camborne was even fractionally better than in Keir Hardie's old seat of Merthyr Tydfil.[3]

This success reflected the local expansion of the trade-union movement. In 1914 the Workers Union only had 400 members in the county, but by the end of the war membership had apparently risen to over 15,000 and union activists were already calling on Labour to contest every seat in Cornwall since 'they had no concern for either Liberal or Tory'.[4] This was quite evident in Camborne where Francis Acland, the sitting Liberal MP, was seriously considering the idea of withdrawing before the election in favour of a Labour candidate. The Workers Union had established a 'strong and effective membership' as wartime conditions enabled the movement to attract support amongst tin miners and munitions workers, while political activists were able to build on a radical tradition established by C.A.V. Conybeare's election victory in 1885 when the seat was, as Deacon put it, 'at the leading edge of British politics'.[5] Even in 1917 Acland was informing his wife that the power of the Labour movement in Cornwall was at least equal to counties more usually regarded as Labour strongholds:

> We only got 30 at the meeting in Redruth yesterday out of 200 [invitations] sent out. I think the Labour party have sent word round to the working men that they're not to come, and they feel proud of staying away. At nine meetings I've had under 300 people & I doubt if one could pick out nine villages in Yorks or Lancs where I should have had such a poor attendance.[6]

The rise of the Labour movement in Cornwall was echoed in other parts of the South-West in 1918. At Frome the Socialists pushed the sitting Liberal MP into a poor third place and were only a few hundred votes behind the Conservatives. Even more surprising was the fact that Labour came second in all but one of the three-cornered contests in the region, while the party benefited from straight fights with the Conservatives in Bridgwater and Taunton, seats which were to go Liberal only five years later. It was symbolic of the weakness of the old Radical cause that the Liberals only fared reasonably well in a limited number of rural seats like Barnstaple and North Dorset which were not contested by the Socialists. Even in rural Tiverton, the one seat where Labour came third, the Liberal share of the vote was nearly 30 per cent behind the Conservatives. Labour's average share of the regional vote was 29.4 per cent, which compared favourably with the Liberals on 34.7 per cent. This figure was not to be equalled again until after the Second World War, and Labour candidates in seats like Bridgwater, which was contested for the first time ever with very little organization, were greatly encouraged by these 'remarkable results'. Since the Liberals were totally demoralized by their defeats throughout the four counties, with only Acland at Camborne being regarded as a true Asquithian, it almost seemed that realignment was inevitable. The Conservatives were quick to recognize this point, talking of the 'end of the Liberal Party' and the 'true Bolshevist spirit' that was now being introduced into regional politics by Labour. Only the Lloyd George coalition, it was claimed, could preserve stability since the 'old party names were now quite meaningless', a view that appeared to be confirmed by the decision of Acland's two remaining Asquithian colleagues, George Lambert (South Molton) and J.T.T. Rees (Barnstaple), to take the Coalition Liberal whip after the election.[7]

Figure 2.1: 'The Farmers' Friend': George Lambert, MP for South Molton (1891–1945), and his family.

Figure 2.2: Isaac Foot, MP for Bodmin (1922–24 and 1929–35), campaigning at Tideford in 1922.

Within less than four years, however, the tide was turning in favour of the Liberals. Isaac Foot's landslide victory over the Conservatives in the Bodmin by-election in March 1922 pointed the way to recovery, with his evangelical style of campaigning restoring the party as the true heir to the old Radical tradition. Liberal activists in neighbouring divisions were suddenly talking of a 'great revival', and in the general election of that year the party captured three seats from the Conservatives (Tavistock, North Dorset and Taunton). Contemporary observers, such as Sir Robert Sanders, Conservative MP for Bridgwater, generally expressed their surprise at this 'curious wave of Liberalism'. Part of the explanation rested with a general disenchantment with the Lloyd George coalition, but it was significant that the Liberal gains in 1922 were all in essentially agricultural seats. The farmers were increasingly disenchanted with the Conservatives because of a decline in farm prices, while agricultural workers voted Liberal in protest at lower wages. Throughout the election campaign the regional Liberals believed that this rural protest vote would hold the key to their revival in the West.[8] While the fall of Lloyd George a few weeks before the election gave the

Conservatives an opportunity to distance themselves from the record of the previous administration, this did not benefit the party in counties like Somerset and Dorset. The party was certainly not helped by the fact that the Minister for Agriculture during the coalition years, Sir Arthur Griffith-Boscawen, was the Conservative MP for Taunton. His unpopularity amongst the farming community led to his defeat at the hands of Hope Simpson, the Liberal candidate and a local farmer, while the neighbouring seats of Bridgwater and Tiverton only just resisted the swing to the Asquithians. Only three seats, St Ives, Barnstaple and East Dorset, went against the trend by moving to the Conservatives. Significantly, these victories were at the expense of sitting Lloyd George Liberals who presumably attracted the blame for falling prices and wages.[9]

The precarious state of the rural economy also ensured that Labour was now relegated to the sidelines in the region. Howard suggests that unions representing rural labourers 'suffered more than most' from the onset of depression in 1921. Falling membership, due to rural poverty and indifference from the national Labour movement, ensured that local union branches were in 'no position to lead a Labour assault on the countryside', and in rural areas like East Anglia the party actually lost electoral support throughout the 1920s. In much of the South-West there was the added problem that the trade-union movement had just started to target agricultural labourers after the war. Without a secure social and organizational framework it was not until 1929 that Labour finally put forward candidates in the remote rural seats like North Cornwall, South Molton and North Dorset. But the immediate effect of rural depression was reflected in a decline in the regional Labour vote. At Westminster the 1922 election was the crucial event which confirmed that the Liberals, still divided between the followers of Asquith and Lloyd George, were now the third force in British politics. Yet Kinnear makes the point that, while the Labour party was consolidating its grip on many industrial and urban areas, 'in 77 seats it actually lost ground in comparison with 1918, and in 63 more, Labour did not contest seats it had fought' in that earlier election. The party's overall share of the vote in the South-West only dropped from 15.3 to 14.3 per cent, but this modest fall disguised the fact that the party was performing far worse in 1922 in those divisions which were also contested by the Liberals. In 1918 Labour candidates polled an average vote of 28.7 per cent, compared to just 21.3 per cent for the independent Liberals, in the seven seats contested by both parties. Four years later these positions were reversed with the Liberal vote rising to 34.5 per cent and the average percentage for Labour nominees dropping to 18.2.[10] A good example occurred at Tiverton where the decision of Acland to fight his home constituency in 1922, following his resignation as MP for Camborne, galvanized local party workers into activity. Both discontented farmers and labourers backed his challenge, and this resulted in an impressive swing to the Liberals, who were only seventy-four votes behind the Conservatives, while the Labour candidate lost his deposit. In June 1923 Acland won Tiverton with a narrow majority in a by-election, a result that he repeated at the subsequent general election.

These setbacks revealed that what the Labour party really lacked in the South-West at this time was an urban centre or industrial sub-region which could provide a focus for socialist propaganda. Apart from providing a more stable environment which could have sustained the party's advance during the early and crucial years of development, an industrial/urban base would have produced a critical mass of union activists and party workers, such as university students, who could have developed the local organization in adjacent rural areas where conditions were less favourable. A model for such a process can be seen in Wales where the Labour party first established a core area in the southern mining seats during the years immediately before and after the First World War. Having obtained credibility and electoral strength it was natural to expand into the more remote parts of the principality where

Table 2.1: Election results for the Tiverton constituency, 1918–1923 (percentages).

	1918	1922	1923 (by.)	1923
Conservative	57.2	46.9	48.1	50.0
Liberal	28.7	46.5	49.9	50.0
Labour	14.1	6.6	2.0*	—
Turnout:	64.8	80.1	88.1	87.4

* F. Brown, the official Labour nominee at Tiverton in 1922, stood as an Independent Labour candidate in the June 1923 by-election.

Liberalism, sustained by the political dominance of Lloyd George, remained strong. Although this proved to be a slow process, by the early 1950s Labour was finally replacing the Liberals as the premier party in rural North Wales.

West Cornwall was the obvious powerhouse for the expansion of Socialism. The respectable showing of the party in the first post-war election had confirmed this sub-region's reputation as the premier radical area in the South-West, and by 1920 there was even speculation that Labour would be unopposed by the other parties in Camborne. But just two years later there was a dramatic decline in Labour fortunes. The party did not even contest St Ives in the 1922 election, while in Camborne the Socialists polled just over a fifth of the vote in a three-cornered contest. Local observers questioned the party's ability to recover from such a 'staggering blow', and this proved to be an accurate prediction since the Labour vote barely increased above the 20–25 per cent level until 1945.[11] The underlying reason for this decline was undoubtedly the collapse of the Cornish tin industry after the war. Although the party's rise was possibly assisted by the anger generated by the first wave of mine closures, the prospect of long-term unemployment after 1920 was disastrous. The terrible social consequences of unemployment and poverty totally undermined the confidence of the movement. Emigration had 'considerably weakened' the party in the area as key activists left in search of employment, while many working-class voters apparently supported the Lloyd George Liberal candidate, Algernon Moreing, in the desperate hope that he could restore the industry's 'old prosperity' because of his financial interests in mining. Labour could thereafter make little progress in a climate of apathy and despair, and by the 1930s the constituency organization had virtually ceased to exist.[12] Without a core base in the industrial heartland of the Duchy, it was understandable that the rural divisions of Bodmin and North Cornwall were not even contested on a regular basis until after the Second World War. Only the mid-Cornwall division of Penryn & Falmouth started to move towards Labour, partly because the relative prosperity of the china clay industry in the St Austell area provided more conducive conditions for the party, but even then it was not until 1945 that the seat elected a Labour MP.

In Cornwall as a whole, however, the failure of the early Socialist challenge meant a return to, as Payton put it, the 'Politics of Paralysis'.

De-industrialization, which had followed the original collapse of the mining industry in the late nineteenth century, had prevented the development of secure social foundations for the New Left. The brief success of Labour in 1918 was probably due to Perry's idea of a social and economic 'remission in the Great Paralysis' during the years leading up to the First World War, when large productivity increases had occurred for important sectors of the local economy like mining and agriculture.[13] Thereafter, radical politics was to remain focused on the sacred and traditional agenda of the Liberal–Methodist nexus, while poverty and unemployment in the peripheral–industrial West resulted in apathy rather than widespread support for socialism. Non-Conservatives in the county returned to figures that symbolized the Old Left tradition, particularly Leif Jones, Liberal MP for Camborne (1923–4 and 1929–31) and Foot. Jones was well known to Cornish voters as president of the United Kingdom Alliance, a leading temperance organization, and son of a famous poet-preacher from Wales. Yet it was Foot who emerged as the real symbol of the Liberal revival. His ability to identify with radical and local interests ensured that he was able to capture Bodmin on three consecutive occasions, while his reputation proved to be a real asset for the party throughout the far west. A report on the 1922 by-election by the *Observer,* which used such words as 'crusade', 'fiery cross' and 'ancient faith in Liberalism', clearly pointed to the fusion of religion and local culture at the heart of Liberal politics:

> The scenes on Saturday afternoon at the declaration of the poll beggared description ... the enthusiasm of nonconformist farmers, of earnest young preachers, of dark-eyed women and fiery Celtic youth had something religious about it. No such fervour could be seen outside Wales.[14]

Plymouth, as the largest urban centre in the region, had the potential to provide another gateway for the Socialists to move into the rural hinterland of both Cornwall and Devon. During the early 1920s the Labour party was steadily consolidating its position in the Drake and Sutton constituencies, and in 1929 the city elected its first Labour MP when James Moses captured Drake. Yet Labour was unable to make a breakthrough in Devonport. Despite some initial success after the war, the party was forced into third place throughout the 1920s. Many

Figure 2.3: Isaac Foot (centre), with Mr Heath, election agent, on the right, March 1922.

Figure 2.4: Isaac Foot showing a supporter the party colours, March 1922.

working-class voters feared that a 'Labour man' would not defend the dockyard interest, and the Socialist candidate in 1922 described Devonport as 'probably the most reactionary part of the country'.[15] Leslie Hore-Belisha, who represented the division from 1923 to 1945, was able to benefit from this situation. He developed a maverick form of Liberalism, conservative on defence and imperial issues but radical on social reform, which suited the unique conditions of the area. His reputation as an effective champion of key groups like the dockyard workers and small traders was further sustained by an active organization at the local level. While this period saw a decline in municipal Liberalism in urban Britain, including much of Plymouth, the Liberals survived as the main party in the Devonport wards of the city by concentrating on such issues as better housing for working-class families. By 1929 the local association had 2,000 members, while parliamentary and municipal campaigns were conducted on a professional basis.[16] Only with Hore-Belisha's defection to the Liberal Nationals in 1931, which resulted in the creation of a single centre-right force across the city and the final disappearance of an effective and independent Liberal challenge, was there an opportunity for Labour. After the Second World War Labour captured all of the three Plymouth divisions, and by the early 1950s the party was finally emerging as a serious force in adjacent rural seats like Bodmin and Tavistock. But this process came too late since by 1955 there were already signs of a revival of rural Liberalism.

Only Bristol, just outside the four counties, provided a secure base for Socialism. Even in 1922 the Labour party seemed to be on the verge of a major breakthrough in Bristol East, and by the end of the decade the party held four out of the five parliamentary divisions in the city. This progress was repeated, albeit at a slower rate, in adjacent constituencies. The most notable example in Somerset was Frome where Frank Gould, who was elected as Labour MP in 1923 and again in 1929, could rely on the support of the bulk of the constituency's 14,000 coal miners. The relative strength of Primitive Methodism in the mining villages around Radstock provided another advantage.[17] Larger towns and a mixed economic base in much of the county, including glove making, cloth mills and slate quarries, were to ensure that by the late 1920s Labour could expect to poll about a fifth of the vote in Bridgwater, Yeovil and Taunton. The party's candidate for Bridgwater, J.M. Boltz, symbolized this process. Boltz, a former Liberal and a local trade union official, was able to raise the party's vote from 7.3 in 1924 to a respectable 19.4 per cent in 1929 by targeting agricultural labourers and building up support amongst industrial workers in the towns.[18] Even in Somerset, however, the road to Socialism was far from inevitable. Yeovil was another classic case of a seat where the Labour vote had actually fallen after the immediate post-war period. Despite Labour's coming second in the first post-war election, a new Liberal candidate, C.W. Cohen, had pushed the Labour party into third place by 1923.

It was Yeovil and not Frome that represented the wider regional picture. By 1923 the Liberal resurgence seemed unstoppable as Stanley Baldwin's decision to call an early election on the central issue of protectionism provided a traditional rallying cry for party activists and led to a reunion of the Asquith and Lloyd George factions, with the notable exception of the Camborne division. In the far west the subsequent Liberal victory marked a return to the golden days of 1906, with the party capturing all of the five Cornish seats and, perhaps even more surprisingly, winning seven out of the eleven divisions in Devon. Yet this advance was not restricted to the western counties. The proud boast of the Conservative MPs for Somerset following their landslide victory in 1918 was 'We are Seven'. A reversal in their fortunes started in 1922 when they had lost Taunton to the Liberals and this was confirmed in the following year when the party was defeated in every constituency in the county with the exception of Yeovil. Only Dorset, where the Liberals were successful in just the Northern division, survived as a Conservative stronghold.[19]

This sweeping success left Liberalism as the dominant force from Land's End to Bristol. Social and political developments, at least so far as the South-West was concerned, had clearly moved the political advantage back to the Old Left. Rural depression had undermined the Conservatives and blunted the impact of Labour, while a return to poverty and unemployment in the working-class communities of West Cornwall resulted in the loss of a potential stronghold for the New Left. The Conservatives had believed that they could win back the rural vote in the region by offering a subsidy to the farmers on the eve of the election. Yet, as the *Western Morning News* pointed out, this did not stop the Liberals' defeat at Bridgwater of Sanders, who had replaced Griffith-Boscawen as Minister for Agriculture. The parliamentary committee of

Table 2.2: Election results in the South-West, 1918–1923.

	1918		1922		1923	
	Seats	% Vote	Seats	% Vote	Seats	% Vote
Conservative	21	54.1	20	48.6	8	47.6
Coalition Liberal	3	4.4	2	4.1	—	—
Liberal	3	25.9	5	32.3	18	40.4
Labour	—	15.3	—	14.3	1	12.0
Other	—	0.3	—	0.8	—	—

the Devon Farmers' Union appeared to favour Conservative candidates in just Totnes and the mainly urban division of Torquay. Elsewhere, the farmers were given a 'free hand' in regard to Conservative and Liberal candidates since the industry was divided over the likely benefits of the subsidy. Besides, the Liberals could generally count on the support of rural labourers, who were probably the key group behind the party's landslide in the western counties. Already discontented over the problem of low wages, the land workers and their wives feared that tariffs would significantly increase the cost of living.[20] With Labour candidates withdrawing in many seats, an issue which will be discussed in greater detail later, the full force of anti-Conservative sentiment provided the catalyst for a remarkable revival of the Liberals just five years after an election which seemed to mark their demise.

Turning of the Tide

The question after the 1923 election, however, was whether the Liberals could succeed in turning the South-West into a permanent regional stronghold. At the state level the reunified party had increased its parliamentary representation from 116 to 159 seats, but it was Labour, with 191 MPs, which was able to form a minority government under Ramsay MacDonald. With the Liberals effectively keeping Labour in office, the potential for an anti-Socialist reaction amongst the electorate seemed obvious. This left the Liberal MPs in the South-West in a particularly vulnerable position since the Achilles' heel of their advance in 1923 was that the majority of them were returned with relatively slender majorities over the Conservatives. As Table 2.1 suggests, it was actually remarkable that the Liberals had been so successful in 1923. Despite winning two-thirds of the region's representation at Westminster, the Liberal share of the vote was over 7 per cent less than the figure secured by the Conservatives. Part of this discrepancy can be explained on the grounds that the Liberals contested fewer seats than their Conservative opponents. Nevertheless, the average Liberal vote per seat was fractionally lower as well. Whilst the Conservatives retained their eight divisions with comfortable majorities, with the exception of Drake and Honiton, the new political masters of the region were vulnerable to even a small swing of opinion

Surprisingly, the precariousness of their position did not seem to bother the local Liberals who broadly welcomed the formation of the Macdonald administration. Many of the newly elected MPs felt that they owed a debt to Labour, pointing out that the reduction in the number of that party's candidates in 1923 and even examples of actual co-operation in seats like Camborne and Bridgwater had 'played an important part in securing a magnificent victory in the West of England'.[21] There was also a more cynical view of the situation at Westminster. It was reported that the general feeling 'down west' seemed to be that 'we should have a Labour government which would live dangerously and die quickly making way for a Liberal administration'.[22] Yet events soon proved that this approach was hardly realistic. Moderate Liberal opinion was generally opposed to 'experiments, whether in the direction of a change in the fiscal system or in the direction of Socialism'.[23] This desire for stability had assisted the party's recovery in 1923, but by effectively keeping a Socialist administration in office this factor now undermined its position. Indeed, the threat to Liberal dominance in the South-West was already present at the beginning of 1924 as the Conservatives began to distance themselves from protection. The emphasis was now on 'progress under the Union Jack, and not ruin under the Red Flag'.[24] This foreshadowed the circumstances that the Liberals were to find themselves in during the election campaign of the autumn of that year.

In order to avoid an electoral disaster it was essential for the Liberals to contest the next election on more favourable grounds. One option was to give constant support to Macdonald. The Liberals would probably have benefited from this line, as Labour would have been under a greater obligation to introduce proportional representation, especially if this had been pressed during the formative weeks of the new administration. When electoral reform was finally debated in May relations between Labour and the Liberals had been embittered by the defeat of the Rent Bill, and minority or coalition government, the likely outcome of proportional representation, had been discredited. But the basic reason for this delay lay with the Liberals themselves who had no clear position on the issue of electoral reform. At a meeting of the parliamentary party at the end of January 1924 the party could not agree on whether to press for proportional representation or the alternative vote, and it was decided instead to appoint a committee to examine the subject.[25] This suggests that the Liberals were simply in no position to exploit the parliamentary situation to their own advantage. They had fought the election as a party of government, a strategy which had nearly succeeded considering that their share of the vote was only slightly less than that secured by Labour, but the practical reality of working with larger parties in the House of Commons revealed the weakness of the Liberal position and their inability to adjust to a new role as the third party.

When the election finally came in October 1924 there was little attempt to define a distinctive image. The basic message of the Liberal candidates was that, given the lack of progress of both the Conservatives and Labour since 1922, the time was now right for a Liberal administration.[26] However, with the Conservatives having relegated tariffs to the background and the Liberals, except for individuals like Lloyd George, failing to develop an inspiring programme for office, the political landscape had been transformed. The one local exception was Alec Glassey, the new Liberal candidate for East Dorset, who, despite the disastrous showing at the state and regional level, actually succeeded in raising the party's share of the vote in his constituency in a three-cornered contest. In contrast to the vast majority of Liberal candidates he fought a vigorous and positive campaign, concentrating on social issues and incorporating Lloyd George's plan to develop the coal and power industries in his election address. This paved the way for his success in 1929 when he won the seat from the Conservatives.[27] But the general pattern was one of confusion. The instability of the past year was one of the dominant issues in the election, and, as the idea of a Liberal government did not appear credible, this encouraged wavering

Liberals to vote for another party. In such circumstances the party's aim throughout 1924 of acting as a moderating influence on the government was clearly not a viable option. Forced to decide between being pro-Labour or anti-Socialist, the Liberals were indecisive and lost votes across the political spectrum.

The position of the local Liberals was especially difficult given the changing nature of the agricultural issue. By the time of the 1924 election there was a growing perception that the Labour administration, just like its post-war predecessors, was failing to address the needs of rural Britain. Some Liberals, particularly John Emlyn-Jones, MP for North Dorset since 1922, tried to exploit this situation by pointing to the refusal of the Macdonald government, assisted by the Conservative opposition, to incorporate a provision for a minimum wage for agricultural labourers in the Minimum Wages Bill. Maxwell Thornton, the MP for Tavistock, echoed these sentiments when he declared that only a Liberal government could provide 'security for the farmer and a good wage for the worker'.[28] Yet the agricultural community already had a vociferous champion in the form of Stanley Baldwin. Well aware of the need to play on rural grievances he declared at Taunton during the election campaign that 'Townspeople do not really understand us countryfolk'. The lack of purpose of the Liberal parliamentary party during 1924 ensured that the role of rural guardian had been lost to the Conservatives. Baldwin warned agricultural voters that another Labour administration would lead to bureaucratic interference from Whitehall, while the Liberals would be indifferent to the plight of the farming community. Above all, his comments at Taunton clearly point to the hidden significance of the rural–urban cleavage in British politics:

> There has grown up in the towns during the last generation or more large vested interests in the handling and distribution of foreign foodstuffs who will fight to the death against any improvement of rural conditions that will lessen their prospects of trade. We have also to reckon with the ignorance that exists in urban districts about country life, and that in itself is a serious thing. This country is almost split up into two nations now—the urban and the rural.[29]

With many farmers also seriously concerned by the wider threat posed by Labour, which had effectively been kept in office by the Liberals, rural discontent was now fused with anti-Socialism to provide a vote-winning platform for the rejuvenated Conservatives. The 1924 election resulted in a dramatic turnaround in the fortunes of rural Liberalism. Popular MPs who had assiduously cultivated the farming vote, such as Simpson and Thornton, were swept away by the Baldwin landslide. Even Lambert, MP for South Molton since 1891 and affectionately known as the 'Farmers' Friend', lost his seat because of the defection of the bulk of the local agricultural vote.[30] Indeed, in the South-West as a whole only the urban seat of Devonport, defended by Hore-Belisha on a local needs platform, remained with the Liberals. Moreover, an increase in the number of Labour candidates, from twelve to eighteen, combined with an official announcement from Transport House that its supporters should abstain in those seats which were not contested, lost the Liberals vital votes amongst the agricultural labourers. A propaganda campaign in the rural areas during the summer months led to the adoption of new Labour candidates, which ensured that the Liberals had to fight on two fronts to retain their ascendancy in the farming areas.[31]

Finally, the religious cleavage was effectively sidelined by the nature of the election campaign. Foot, for example, lamented that anti-Socialism had taken precedence over the old issue of local option, pointing out that virtually 'all the members of the House who were closely associated with the cause of temperance had gone down in the fight'. This reflected a wider problem as moderate adherents of Liberalism were now forced into making a decision as to whether to support the traditional agenda of the Old Left or vote against the Socialist threat. Political observers in the region attributed the party's defeat to the 'Russian business' which had given 'Nonconformist Liberals a shock [and had] led them to break away from their allegiance to Liberalism'. These voters came from a 'very thrifty class' who feared that their 'hard-earned savings would be jeopardised if a Socialist Government came into power'. Many of these floating voters were tenant farmers or 'small householders', the local *petite bourgeoisie*, who had traditionally voted Liberal.[32] Their desertion of the Liberal faith appeared to mark the end of the pre-war system and the final triumph of class politics.

Back to the Old Faith?

In the immediate aftermath of the Conservative landslide there certainly appeared to be little prospect of a Liberal recovery. Asquith's defeat in the election led to his elevation to the House of Lords, a move that left the depleted parliamentary force in the Commons under the effective control of Lloyd George. The divisions which had had bedevilled the Liberals since 1916 now intensified. While to some extent this was due to the personal antagonism that existed between Lloyd George and his Asquithian opponents, differences at this time also reflected an ideological split. Lloyd George's desire to remould Liberalism as a modern and progressive force alienated some supporters, such as Sir Alfred Mond, but were welcomed by former Asquithians like Acland and Hore-Belisha. In the South-West the suggestion of a form of land nationalization, contained in the *Land and the Nation* proposals in 1925, led to the resignation from the party of former MPs like Thornton and Sir Courtney Mansel (Penryn & Falmouth). Although this controversial idea was eventually deleted from the final document, Acland was forced to resign as prospective candidate for Tiverton because of his close association with the proposals. His wife, Lady Eleanor, summed up the state of the party in May 1926 when she wrote that 'I'm afraid there is no Liberal Party, in the real sense of the word—no organised body of people who haven't quite made up our minds what we think'.[33]

Table 2.3: Election results in the South-West in 1924 and 1929.

Election	Party	MPs	Candidates	% Vote	Average % Vote
1924	Conservative	26	27	52.7	53.1
	Liberal	1	23	33.3	38.5
	Labour	—	18	14.0	20.9
1929	Conservative	16	27	43.2	43.1
	Liberal	8	26	35.5	37.1
	Labour	2	27	19.4	19.0
	Other	1	2	1.9	27.9

Yet despite these internal problems, the subsequent election of 1929 was to result in a definite improvement in the electoral position of local Liberalism. The Conservatives lost ten of their twenty-six seats across the South West, and it was the Liberal party, retaining Devonport and winning an extra seven seats, that was the principal beneficiary of this swing. Cornwall saw the most sweeping change on this occasion with all five seats moving from Conservative to Liberal. Foot and Jones regained the seats which they had lost at the previous election, while three former cabinet ministers who had moved to the area in search of potentially safe seats, Walter Runciman, Sir Donald Maclean and Sir John Tudor Walters, won St Ives, North Cornwall and Penryn & Falmouth respectively. Elsewhere, only East Dorset and South Molton, which was captured by Lambert, fell to the Liberal advance. It should be pointed out, however, that the party had come quite close to regaining first place in the South-West. An extra swing in 1929 of less than 1.8 per cent from the Conservatives would have made the Liberals the single largest party with thirteen seats.

This election marked the culmination of a period of revival following the final struggle between Asquith and Lloyd George. Asquith's death in 1928, combined with growing support for the new leadership, effectively marginalized Runciman and the more vociferous Asquithians in the so-called Liberal Council, while generous financial assistance from Lloyd George's political fund enabled the party to put forward sufficient candidates to form a government. Moreover, a series of by-election successes at places like Bosworth in May 1927 and Holland-with-Boston in March 1929 suggested that 'at long last a real recovery was at hand'.[34] This mood of optimism was very evident in the South-West. In March 1928 the Liberals gained St Ives from the Conservatives, while seven months later they failed to win the Tavistock by-election by just 173 votes. Western Counties Liberal Federation reported in September 1928 that there was 'increasing activity of Liberalism throughout every Division which, if retained will once more place the Western Counties in the front rank of Liberal representation in the House of Commons'.[35] Similarly, at a meeting of the Devon & Cornwall Federation in January 1929 it was announced that fourteen of the sixteen constituencies were 'well equipped with excellent candidates' and that a 'considerable amount of work had been accomplished'. Torquay Women's Liberal Association had won the Wintringham Cup for the largest increase in

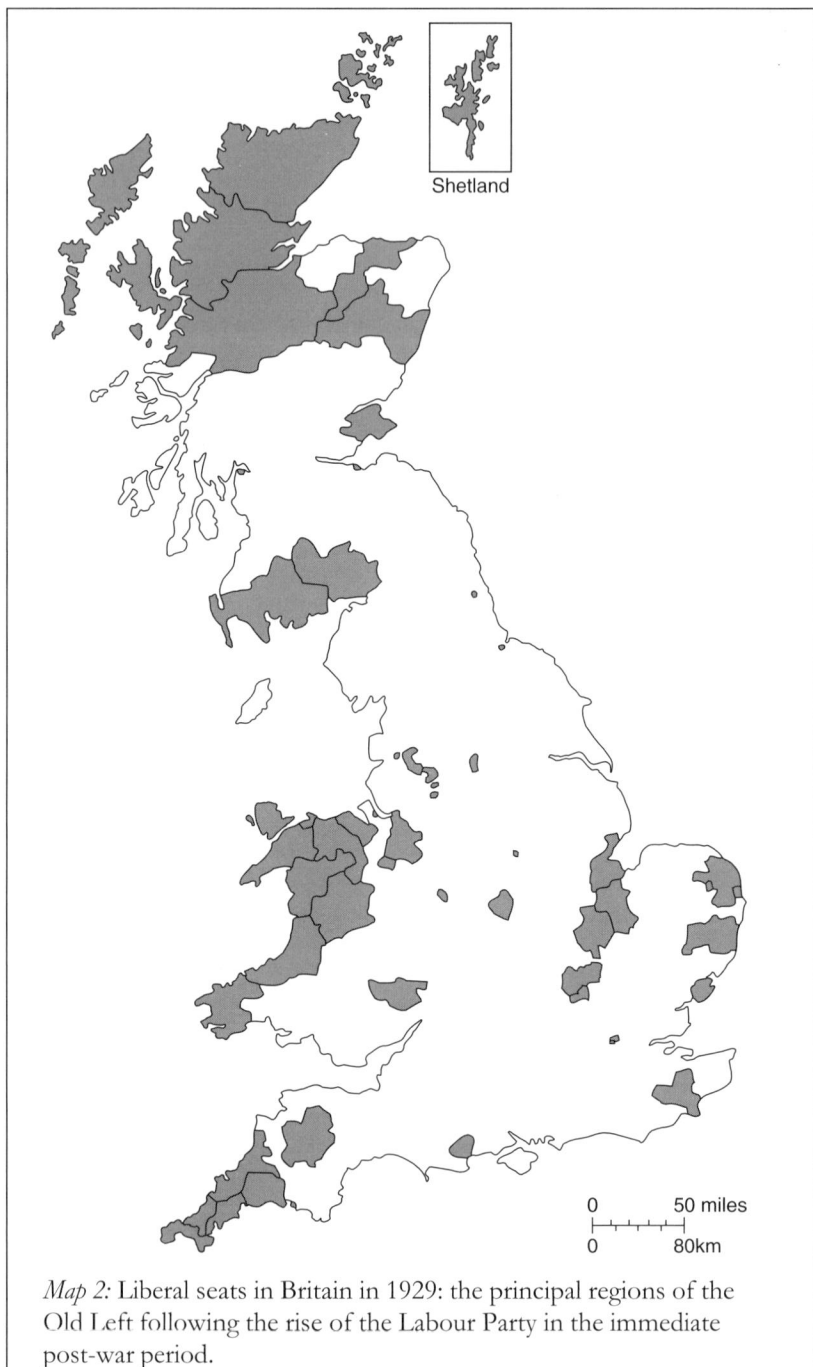

Map 2: Liberal seats in Britain in 1929: the principal regions of the Old Left following the rise of the Labour Party in the immediate post-war period.

female members in Britain, while the North Cornwall Liberals had the country's highest number of pledged supporters.[36]

This growing momentum in the region was strengthened by a belief that the Liberals would at least become the second-largest party in the House of Commons. The *Western Morning News* reported that the Liberals considered 100 seats as their 'absolute minimum, while the more optimistic members of the party ... regard 150 or even 200 as being nearer the mark'. Some activists even talked of a repeat of 1906, while Maclean claimed that it was 'well within probabilities that the Liberals would be called upon [to] form a Government'.[37] This enabled the party, which with hindsight was able for the last time to present an alternative cabinet of former ministers, to campaign as a party of government. Posters, entitled 'The Liberal Party with its able leaders', appeared in newspapers, and they displayed pictures of Lloyd George, Walter Runciman, Sir Herbert Samuel, Viscount Grey, Marquis of Reading, Sir John Simon and Earl Beauchamp. It was emphasized that these individuals were all cabinet ministers in the pre-war Liberal governments, and that under their guidance the country would be able to return to prosperity. It was no wonder that the defeated Conservative candidate for Penryn & Falmouth claimed that the Cornish Liberals were so successful in 1929 because they had been able to convince the electorate that there was 'a great Liberal revival in progress which was to resuscitate a middle party'.[38]

A distinctive image was obviously an essential factor in any Liberal revival. Lloyd George's financial resources and energetic leadership had led to detailed investigations into subjects like land reform and unemployment. The most famous of these reports, *Britain's Industrial Future* (1928), was produced by a committee of economists and politicians, including John Maynard Keynes. It recommended government planning in order to create employment, and in 1929 Lloyd George's pledge to conquer unemployment formed the basis of the party's national campaign. The conventional view of historians is that the party needed such a 'forward looking programme' in order to remain a relevant force. For example, Wilson claimed that it was better for the Liberals to follow Lloyd George 'along radical paths than to attach themselves to the ... stale doctrine of the Liberal Council'.[39] The party obviously could not afford to ignore changes in British politics and society. Even in the conservative South-West the Liberals had been

Figure 2.5: David Lloyd George at Barnstaple on his land reform tour of the South-West in 1926.

criticized in 1924 on the grounds that 'no young man joins the Liberal Party, and a party that is not recruiting from the youth of the country is bound to pass away'.[40] Younger candidates, such as Richard Acland (Torquay) and Dingle Foot (Tiverton), tended to be enthusiastic supporters of Lloyd George's policy review, and their presence in the Liberal ranks was a symbol that the party had a future. By putting forward innovative solutions for topical issues like unemployment the Liberals could present a modern and positive image to the electorate. Hore-Belisha believed that the party's new policies provided Liberalism with a distinctive identity that compared favourably with the negative approach of their opponents:

> I am fed up with this attitude of 'safety first'. That is not the spirit of adventure of this Elizabethan city [of Plymouth], and it is time we got an honest-to-goodness fellow like Lloyd George who … is full of courage, vitality and enterprise and ready to tackle [unemployment].[41]

But the alternative approach of the Liberal Council should not be ignored. They argued that candidates should appeal to the basic instincts of party supporters by emphasizing traditional policies, such as free trade and economy, which had proved so successful in 1906 and 1923. This was especially the case in the remote parts of the South-West where the Gladstone agenda, as Dawson recognized, was still 'deeply ingrained'. Maclean even asked Herbert Gladstone to visit North Cornwall because the local inhabitants regarded the name 'Gladstone' with 'deep reverence'.[42] The danger of a modernist approach in such circumstances was that it could alienate some of the party's most committed adherents, but still fail to attract a large number of new supporters. A traditional agenda would at least have enabled the Liberals to appeal to their core supporters in conservative areas, which was essential at a time when the party was already in long-term decline.

Walter Runciman was a leading exponent of this policy. In 1927 he had put forward his own proposals in *Liberalism As I See It*. The main theme of his book was that the Liberals would never 'win the confidence of the country until they deserve that confidence by a consistent reassertion of the principles associated with Gladstone'. In his opinion the 'force of a Liberal candidate's appeal [was] lost through trying to outbid Tory or Labour sentiments', and the party should instead concentrate on traditional issues like free trade, self-help and economy. Runciman also believed that local option, or even prohibition, should be one of the main priorities of the party. He claimed that intemperance was 'one of the worst curses of Great Britain, industrially, morally and financially'. The country could not afford to waste £300,000,000 per annum on alcohol, and therefore temperance should become a prominent objective of the party.[43] Such views naturally conflicted with the new proposals for dealing with unemployment. Although Runciman accepted the need for limited public work schemes, he was 'against trying to work on borrowed money [because] to do so compels you to pay the penalty at some time or other'.[44] His analysis of the unemployment problem was influenced by his personal involvement with the shipping industry. Runciman emphasized that the rise in unemployment in Britain was due to the decline of the great staple industries like coal, iron and shipbuilding. The 'only permanent cure' for unemployment was the 'extension and restoration of trade at home and abroad', and in order to obtain economic recovery he advocated a reduction in debts and taxes. Instead of moving in an interventionist direction, he believed that government should create the right conditions for a free market economy to flourish:

> Every step in the right direction depends upon national solvency, which in its turn depends on active and abundant industry and commerce, which again is only possible under conditions of free trade with restraints withdrawn and interference reduced to a minimum.[45]

The 1929 election confirmed that traditional Liberalism still appealed to the basic political instincts of many Liberal supporters. Jones and Maclean expressed their public support for the party's employment programme, but they preferred to give more space in their election addresses to traditional issues. Hilda Runciman, the wife of Walter and candidate for Tavistock, did not even mention the new policy, while Lambert emphasized that the 'Liberalism he learned was that of Mr Gladstone'.[46] Even in Dorset, where the four Liberal candidates had 'unbridled faith in Mr Lloyd George's unemployment cure', party activists seemed more interested in the 'raiding of the Road Fund by Mr Churchill' and the 'race for armaments'. Questions at political meetings throughout the four counties tended to be concerned with free trade, pensions and the government's Rating and Valuation Act. Indeed, the latter measure was seen as the 'issue which the Liberals regard as likely to bring voters to their side'.[47] The new changes especially affected small businessmen who had tended to support the Liberals in the past, but had voted Conservative on anti-Socialist grounds in 1924. A Liberal activist in West Dorset was even able to link the Act with the party's traditional hostility to the drink trade:

> Then, there was the matter of Rating Reform. It was claimed that this offered relief to industry. It possibly did so to the brewers, but not to persons like himself. He was an employer of between 70 and 80 persons, and he was being taxed an additional £300 a year in order that relief might be given to the brewers.[48]

The regional importance of religious issues in 1929 had the effect of restoring the Liberal–Nonconformist bond. In the first place the

Liberals were able to exploit the attempted revision of the Prayer Book in the previous year. Although this was ostensibly a matter for the Church of England, the nonconformists were alarmed at the spread of Roman Catholic practices. Algernon Moreing, now the Conservative MP for Camborne, was criticized for voting in favour of the 'Romish book', while questions at election meetings in North Devon were 'mostly centred on the Prayer-Book'.[49] Temperance reform seemed even more popular amongst its adherents in the 1920s because of the prohibition experiment in the United States. One of its attractions was that it was a distinctive cause that appealed to all wings of the party. George Chappell, the candidate for West Dorset, was a keen advocate of both local option and the proposals contained in the *Yellow Book*. His Conservative opponent was opposed to temperance legislation, while the Labour candidate suggested a Royal Commission. Chappell, however, could give his total support to Local Option and Sunday closing of 'liquor bars'.[50] Temperance figured even more prominently in the Liberal campaign in Cornwall. Jones intended to introduce a Cornish Local Option Bill in the House of Commons if he was elected, and this meant that it was essential for the Liberals to do well in Cornwall in order to show that there was popular approval for such a policy. Whilst local temperance groups held public meetings on the subject, the Fellowship of Freedom and Reform, which opposed local option, held counter-demonstrations throughout the county. Camborne Conservative Association concluded that religion was the main local reason for Moreing's defeat:

(1) The Temperance issue affecting the Women's vote. The Division was canvassed extensively by Liberals on this question.
(2) The vote of the candidate for Prayer Book disturbing the strong Non-Conformist feeling in the Division.[51]

A potential threat to free trade was another factor in the Liberal revival. Key groups in the region, from many local industries, such as dairy farming, mining and fishing, were likely to be adversely affected by tariffs, while key sections of the regional electorate like agricultural labourers, women and old age pensioners believed that protectionism would lead to an increase in the cost of living. During the late 1920s many Conservatives had favoured an extension of protection, including the 'safeguarding' of the iron and steel industries, and Runciman had claimed in 1928 that free trade would therefore become the 'dominant question of the election'.[52] Yet as Ball remarked, Baldwin wanted the Conservatives to present a moderate image, and in the event the party campaigned on its legislative record and the threat from Socialism. Nevertheless, the question of safeguarding was still a prominent issue in 1929. Lord Grey, the president of the Liberal Council, even declared that it was the main issue of the election, while parliamentary candidates like Runciman claimed that the Conservatives had 'added more new taxes to the tariff list than any of their predecessors of the last 50 years'.[53] Dire warnings that a Conservative victory would lead to an extension of tariffs for iron and steel were reinforced by the maverick statements of 'die-hard' Conservatives like Sir Basil Peto, MP for Barnstaple (1924–35). The Conservatives subsequently concluded that the 'misrepresentation' of safeguarding was one of the principal reasons for their loss of support.[54]

Although Liberal voters were enthusiastic about traditional issues, they were less certain in regard to the party's new policies. For example, voters in Totnes appeared to have doubts about the pledge to reduce unemployment to normal levels within a year, while in Wells the wife of the Liberal candidate was asked 'whether it was true the Liberal Party was going to take the dole away [and] put all the unemployed on road-making'.[55] The party's opponents naturally exploited this uncertainty. Sir William Joynson-Hicks, the Home Secretary, claimed in a speech at Blandford that the Liberals would be giving 'a pick and shovel to … clerks and shop assistants, who would not be able to carry out such strenuous work for more than a few days'.[56] In addition, both Labour and the Conservatives argued that in view of Lloyd George's failure to keep his election promises in 1918 he was not to be trusted. The Liberal leader was presented as the 'wizard [who] had a past' and a man who 'would betray if he had the opportunity again'.[57]

It could also be argued that the party's new policies were of little assistance in winning protest votes. In May 1929 the *Western Morning News* commented that the Conservatives 'have had nearly five years of office, and … they have disappointed, as all Governments do, some of the hopes on which they were elected'.[58] Many of these 'disappointed' voters were probably former Liberals, but the government had also alienated floating voters and even loyal Conservatives. Ball has remarked that during the late 1920s many Conservatives had 'lapsed further and further into apathy'. In their view the government had failed to give sufficient attention to issues like agriculture and finance, while they also 'resented' the decision to enfranchise women under 30.[59] The Liberals were still the alternative to the Conservatives in the region, and were the obvious home for protest voters. Yet a campaign that was based on new and controversial policies was likely to alienate some of these voters. Indeed, a study of the farming issue suggests that the Liberals had only qualified success in attracting this source of support. Once again there was growing concern over central government's perceived failure to assist agriculture. Although farmers were now exempt from having to pay rates on agricultural land because of the Rating and Valuation Act, they were still not satisfied with Baldwin's record. Ball and Kinnear concluded that the discontent of the farmers benefited the Liberals, particularly in Cornwall and the East Midlands.[60] While small farmers had tended to support the Liberals, many of the larger farmers who defected must have been purely protest voters. Yet Dawson claims that the Liberals were still on the defensive over the issue of land nationalization, while the *Western Morning News,* which adopted a neutral editorial policy in 1929, concluded that the Liberal proposals for land reform had 'not awakened the sympathy of country voters'.[61] The fear of being placed under 'bureaucratic control' could well have deterred some cautious farmers from voting Liberal, and this may have been a factor in the party's defeat in some marginals.

Admittedly, the party's pledge to reduce unemployment may have attracted support in some seats. Walters claimed that the party's victory in Penryn & Falmouth had been 'secured by the exposition during the past two years of a constructive Liberal policy, which found a fitting complement in the scheme for dealing with unemployment'. The Taunton Unemployed Association decided to support the Liberals on the grounds that their 'scheme was the only practical one for providing work for the unemployed', while voters seemed interested in the proposals in Devonport and East Dorset.[62] But it is perhaps significant that these seats were not predominately rural. During the election campaign it was said that the 'effect of Mr Lloyd George's unemployment policy may be different in large industrial areas, where there is more unemployment; but here [in the South-West] it has not been received with great enthusiasm'.[63] Unemployment in the region was concentrated in urban and industrial areas like Devonport and Penryn & Falmouth, and in rural districts it tended to be low.[64] The Liberal employment scheme was therefore irrelevant to the personal needs of rural voters. Yet even this explanation is not totally satisfactory. The success of the Labour party in the industrial regions of Britain confirmed that radical policies alone could not prevent the rise of class politics. Jones, however, captured the depressed mining division of Camborne on an essentially traditionalist platform, and the local Conservatives did not even mention unemployment as one of the reasons for the Liberal victory.[65]

The real explanation was that these results reflected the demise of the Liberals as a *national* party. The emergence of a new class-based political system meant that the Liberals could only win those seats where local factors had prevented or delayed the rise of Labour. This tended to be in rural areas where traditional issues still had considerable appeal, but some charismatic Liberals, such as Hore-Belisha and Glassey, were able to convince voters in individual urban seats of the practical benefits of the party's employment policy. What the Liberals really needed in 1929 was a national strategy which focused on their strength in the countryside. An alternative programme might have enabled the Liberals to win those urban seats where Labour was weak, while at the same time the party would probably have had greater success in attracting vital votes in marginal rural divisions.

Socialist Incursion

In 1929 the Labour party contested every seat in the four counties for the first time. A specific study of this vital aspect of the election is an appropriate way in which to link the various themes of the entire decade after the war. To start with, the 'incursion of Labour' seems to be one of the main reasons why the Liberals failed to repeat their 1923 landslide since only three of the sixteen Conservatives returned in 1929 polled more than half of the vote. Although the Liberals may not have captured all of these seats, the absence of Labour candidates would have probably enabled the party to have won most of them. Furthermore, the general absence of Labour candidates in 1923, following their failure to sustain their initial success, had enabled the hostility of Liberals and Conservatives to continue virtually uninterrupted. The subsequent election, however, had shown how the Conservatives could exploit anti-socialism at the local level. While the Liberals were able to limit the full force of this fear in 1929, this issue presumably led a number of voters to stay with the Conservatives.

The conventional view of historians is that the presence of Labour candidates in rural seats was responsible for the failure of the Liberals to stage a major breakthrough in 1929. Kinnear, basing his conclusions on the experience of Wiltshire, found that Labour usually obtained 'just enough votes to deny victory to the Liberals'. For example, in 1923 the Liberals had won all four of the rural divisions in that county, but they failed to win a single seat in 1929 because of the presence of Labour candidates. 'Similar developments took place in many agricultural districts. Labour, though not strong enough to win, was strong enough to cause a Liberal defeat.'[66] Cook claims that the 1923 and 1924 elections had 'removed the Liberals from their industrial bases'. By 1929 an increase in support for Labour, combined with their greater number of candidates, prevented the Liberals from recovering the rural seats they had lost in 1924.[67] However, this view has been challenged by Smart in a case study of the four counties of the South-West. He emphasized that 'any realignment of voting behaviour … actually transforms the social bases of the party system itself'. The ultimate failure of the Liberals to repeat their 1923 triumph was not due to a swing from Liberal to Labour, since the latter party was so weak in rural areas, but rather to the success of the Conservatives in attracting anti-Socialist votes. The fact that three of Labour's best results, Penryn & Falmouth (28.9 per cent), Camborne (25.3) and St Ives (17.1 per cent), occurred in seats which were won by the Liberals, appears to confirm his view that Labour was not a major obstacle to Liberalism. He concluded that it is 'difficult to find signs in any [seat] of Labour interventions so dividing the "radical " vote as to present the seat to the Conservatives'.[68]

Smart is certainly correct in challenging the assumption that electoral change was a simple matter of 'radical' voters transferring their support from Liberal to Labour. It was quite possible that a number of voters would either have abstained or even voted Conservative in the absence of a Labour candidate. Peto believed that it was 'perfectly impossible for anyone to say how many who voted for Labour, a new party in that part of the world, would have otherwise voted Liberal or Conservative'.[69] Alfred Browning Lyne, chairman of Bodmin Liberal Association, recognized the existence of a section of the working-class electorate which would not vote Liberal, possibly because of the party's support for temperance, and which, in the absence of a Labour candidate in the past, had formerly voted Conservative.[70] Nevertheless, all three parties generally accepted that *most* of Labour's support came from former Liberals. Labour admitted that the 'swing of the pendulum' towards Socialism had 'obtained its impulse' from the Liberals, who had been concerned by the threat throughout the campaign, while the Conservatives also believed that Labour intervention was a 'sure sign' that they would retain their regional supremacy. Even Lyne recognized that Labour had mainly attracted votes from the Liberals. He concluded that what 'upset all the Liberal calculations in the West of England was the incursion of Labour. Such incursion presented the Conservatives with anything from 50 to 100 seats'.[71]

By examining the 1923 election we can see the significance of Labour intervention. In that year Labour had only put forward twelve candidates across the four counties, and in seven seats the Liberals were either not standing (Exeter, West Dorset, Sutton and Frome) or were in no position to win the seat (East Dorset, Drake and South Dorset). The division in the opposition vote in Yeovil meant that it was the only seat in Somerset to elect a Conservative, and in St Ives the Liberal candidate had the smallest majority in Cornwall. In Barnstaple the Labour vote was less than 5 per cent, while Hore-Belisha succeeded in reducing that party's share of the vote in Devonport. Wells is another good example of the way in which the strength of the Socialist vote could influence the outcome of an election. Whilst in 1923 Labour support had collapsed in favour of the Liberals, in 1929 the Conservatives were able to retain the seat with a narrow majority.

The vital fact about the Liberal landslide in the South-West in 1923 was that so many of the party's victories were by narrow margins (see Table 2.2). Indeed, the party had won Tiverton and Torquay by only 3 and 372 votes respectively. Fourteen out of the eighteen Liberal victories had been achieved in straight fights with the Conservatives, and if the party was to repeat its 1923 landslide the non-Conservative vote had to be united. This was particularly a problem outside of Cornwall. Although the average percentage majority of the Cornish Liberal MPs was 13.7 per cent in 1923, it was only 3.1 per cent in Devon and 4.0 per cent in Somerset and Dorset. It was only to be expected that the greater number of Labour candidates in 1929 prevented the Liberals from

Table 2.4: The percentage vote of the three parties in Wells, 1922–1929.

Election	Conservative	Liberal	Labour
1922	47.7	33.4	18.9
1923	44.2	48.2	7.6
1924	52.6	36.1	11.3
1929	43.6	41.4	15.0

making a major advance throughout the region. The only seat which the party was able to win in Devon was South Molton, which usually had the lowest Conservative vote in the county, while in Somerset and Dorset it failed to capture any of the seats which it had lost five years earlier. Smart's claim that Labour 'achieved some of its best regional results in seats regained by the Liberals' does not take into account the fact that these three seats were in Cornwall. Cornish Liberalism was able to resist the 'incursion of Labour' because of the traditional weakness of the Conservatives. The electorate of 1929 was vastly different from that of 1885, but the basic difference in the Conservative vote between Cornwall and the rest of the South-West was still present (see Table 2.5). In 1929 the Liberals could win Penryn & Falmouth and Camborne with a vote of less than 40 per cent because the Conservative vote was less than 35 per cent. But in Conservative seats like Totnes and Bath the party's vote had never fallen below 45 per cent, and even a small Labour vote would prevent a Liberal victory.

There was another sense in which Labour was an obstacle to a full

Table 2.5: A comparison of the Conservative share of the vote in the four counties.

Election	Cornwall	Devon	Somerset	Dorset
1885	40.8	47.4	48.5	46.4
1906	39.6	47.4	45.2	49.4
1923	41.9	49.3	47.9	51.7
1929	38.4	43.0	45.3	46.2

Liberal recovery. Smart claims that the anti-Socialist vote was already 'consolidating itself', and he concluded that in 1929 the Conservatives were able to 'retain much of the support obtained in the "special" circumstances of 1924'.[72] Anti-Socialism was definitely a key asset for the Conservatives. In 1926 the chairman of the party's Bodmin association urged members to 'enrol in their ranks all who were opposed to Socialism'. The association's annual dinner that year was addressed by a 'life-long Liberal' who had now joined the Conservatives on the grounds that the 'only bulwark against Socialism was a progressive Unionist party'.[73] Conservative candidates reiterated this message in 1929. Wallace Wright (Tavistock) believed that the issue was simply 'Socialism versus anti-Socialism', while Charles Williams at Torquay said that the 'coming election would be with the Conservatives on one side and the Socialist Party on the other'.[74] The most that the Liberals could achieve was to hold the balance of power, which, according to Sir Robert Sanders, would create uncertainty:

> He had not yet once heard of [a Liberal candidate] giving a straight answer to the question 'Are you going to support Labour, or are you going to support the Conservatives?' ... he really could not understand how anyone could vote for a candidate who refused to give a straight answer to that question.[75]

Fear of another Labour government was undoubtedly a problem for the Liberals. In West Dorset the party's decision to contest the seat divided their supporters. E.J. Wotton Buckpitt, an 'old-time Liberal', sent a letter of support to Major Colfox, the Conservative candidate, in which he expressed his opinion that the adoption of a Liberal was a 'grave mistake, seeing that there was already a Socialist ... in the field'. Colfox claimed that Liberal 'intervention could only have the effect of splitting the anti-Socialist vote [and] he felt justified in believing that many rank-and-file' Liberals would continue to support him. This issue forced the local Liberals onto the defensive, and the chairman of the local association had to advise 'any Liberals who might be wavering to waver no longer ... because they had as good a chance as any party of winning West Dorset'.[76] Even the mere presence of a Labour candidate could help the Conservatives. Lady Eleanor Acland claimed that one reason why her son Richard had failed to win Torquay was the 'presence of a third candidate who never had a chance of winning, but [who] frightened some of the more timid voters' into supporting Williams.[77]

But it is important to recognize that the Socialist bogey was limited by the circumstances of 1929. Labour attempted to present a moderate image during the election campaign, which might well have benefited the Liberals. In addition, by campaigning as a party of government the regional Liberals were able to appear as a more credible force, while their local concentration on traditional issues was likely to appeal to those Liberals that had defected at the last election. The Baldwin government's poor record in international and financial affairs also alienated support, and it was symbolic that a large group of 'Anti-Socialist' voters that had signed the nomination papers of the Conservative candidate for Bodmin in 1924 now returned to Foot. Above all, anti-Socialism was not sufficient to prevent a serious loss of Conservative support in those seats where the old ideological alignment was most deeply ingrained. While it is impossible to make a true comparison between 1924 and 1929 because of the increase in the size of the electorate, it is interesting that the Conservative percentage vote fell by 10.3 to 13.3 per cent in the former Liberal strongholds of Camborne, North Cornwall and St Ives. Conservative claims that they were the 'bulwark against Socialism' were more effective in seats to the east of the main Liberal strongholds where their share of the vote in Tiverton, Honiton, Weston-super-Mare and Torquay only fell by 2.7 to 5.5 per cent. The problem for the Liberals really lay in the long term. While fear of Socialism may have limited the scale of the recovery, the actual experience of keeping the second Labour administration in office was to lead to a more secure alignment on Socialist versus anti-Socialist lines.

Conclusion

In the 1920s, liberalism in the rural South-West was still sustained by the forces that had motivated the party before the war: a deep reverence for the cause of Gladstone, the moral fervour of religious non-conformity and a belief that the Liberals were still a potential party of government. The strength of these traditional cleavages undermined the early challenge of Labour and ensured that Liberalism remained a major force even at the end of the Age of Alignment. Yet 1929 also effectively marked the end of the old era. The greater number of Labour candidates, combined to a lesser extent with fear of the 'Socialist menace', effectively limited the scale of the Liberal revival. Furthermore, this critical election, like 1923, did not point the way to success in the future. Runciman was proved correct in his assessment that the party needed to appeal to the basic instincts of traditional supporters, but the events of the following two years would threaten its very existence.

3

Into the Wilderness: 1929–1935

Introduction

After 1929 the long-term decline of the Liberal party resumed with intensity. Set against the background of the fall of the second Labour government and the creation of a National coalition under Ramsey MacDonald, this period culminated in the general election of 1935 when the Liberals found themselves struggling to survive as a separate party in the House of Commons. The first part of this chapter traces the bewildering sequence of political events which took place at this time, placing regional developments in the South-West within a broader framework and showing how the Liberal party's position at Westminster and in the localities was being steadily undermined. But there was another side to the party's performance at this time. Since attention usually focuses on the various factors that threatened to destroy the party, it is so easy to forget that the Liberals actually survived. This was certainly the case in the South-West where the party, sustained by the conservative nature of rural society, remained a vibrant force in many constituencies. However, the absence of a coherent strategy which could reflect the changing fortunes of the party meant that a further reduction in the party's parliamentary representation, both at the national level and in the South-West, seemed inevitable by 1935.

'Their party has gone to pieces'

The 1929 election had confirmed that the Liberals were no longer seen as an alternative government. Although the party was still a major force in terms of its national share of the vote, its bloc of just fifty-eight MPs in the House of Commons was disappointing to many activists. Even the electoral position of Liberalism in the South-West was far from secure. Six of the eight Liberal MPs possessed majorities of less than 5 per cent, and this meant that they were vulnerable to only a small swing of votes. Four days after the election George Lambert, MP for South Molton, remarked that the future of the 'old party hardly bears thinking about', while Walter Runciman, MP for St Ives, felt 'nearly hopeless'.[1] Lloyd George's refusal to provide any financial assistance after June 1930 created further uncertainty. Ramsay Muir, the chairman of the National Liberal Federation, claimed that the Liberals would lose all credibility at the next election as an alternative party of government since they had only sufficient funds to contest 200 seats. The problems that this caused for the party were evident at the local level. For example, in April 1931 the Western Counties Liberal Federation announced a dramatic reduction of expenditure from £3,082 to £1,330 per annum. This reduction in income meant that the party's organization in some constituencies, such as Frome and Plymouth Sutton, had become moribund by the time of the 1931 election.[2]

Lloyd George's opponents exploited this situation. During the election campaign they had kept a relatively low profile, but over the following two years there were frequent attacks on the leadership. Leading critics, such as Lord Grey and Sir Charles Mallet, called on the party to 'dissociate itself from the political fortunes of Mr Lloyd George'.[3] Personal differences were combined with criticism of the interventionist ideology of modern Liberalism as the seriousness of Britain's financial and economic situation led to calls for a return to a strict policy of retrenchment. By March 1931 the Liberal *West Briton* newspaper was claiming that many in the party were 'not in love with the proposals which emanate from some of their leaders for borrowing and spending huge sums of money'. The 'best way' to help the unemployed was to 'lessen the present punishing burdens on industry'.[4] Such statements were often linked to a nostalgic yearning for the glory years of the nineteenth century. In April 1931 the chairman of the Somerset Liberal Conference declared that 'what they wanted today was another Mr Gladstone', while a few months earlier Lambert had publicly called for a return to a Gladstonian platform:

If they had Mr Gladstone to lead them today there would not be 58

Liberal members of the House of Commons, there would be a great many more. Mr Gladstone's principle was man-making, not reliance on the State for everything. Self-help instead of State help. They had got to get back to Mr. Gladstone's principles of finance.[5]

Yet the traditionalists were mistaken in their belief that a Gladstonian agenda was a solution to the party's difficulties during this period. To start with, the severity of the economic situation led many Liberals to question the wisdom of their formerly sacred icon of free trade. By 1931 there were reports from Somerset to Cornwall of a 'most decided falling off in enthusiasm among Liberals for the purely negative attitude of the Free Trade argument', and a growing belief that 'something must be done to redress the balance of trade'.[6] The first Liberal MP in the region to publicly question the free trade doctrine was a Gladstonian. By November 1930 Lambert was arguing that the limit of direct taxation had been reached, and that a 10 per cent duty on import manufacturers had to come.[7] This development was of long-term significance. In the past free trade had been the main issue which had separated moderate Liberals from the Conservatives. Now that there was a belief that 'something must be done' to remedy the economic situation, there was little to stop them from leaving the party. Moreover, at the previous election the Liberals had benefited from the belief that Baldwin's 1924–29 administration had a poor record in regard to financial affairs. By 1931 the Conservatives were also concentrating on the need for public economy and, as Thorpe remarked, a 'point of unity' was now being made with Liberal supporters.[8] The speeches of Conservative candidates in the South-West were specifically designed to establish the party as the real and independent heir of the Gladstonian tradition.[9] The Liberals, in contrast, lacked a credible position from which to exploit the old cause of retrenchment. By keeping a Socialist administration in office they were unable to emerge as the clear champions of economy, and this created further tensions. In August 1931 Sir Charles Hobhouse, a former Liberal minister and president of the Western Counties Liberal Federation, warned his party that he would 'look elsewhere' if it did not move even further in the direction of retrenchment:

> If the Liberal Party will take up the cause of public and private economy … I am prepared to serve them as in the past. If they will

not make economy their principal project in their electoral campaign ... then I myself must ... find other co-operators where I can.[10]

Many of the traditionalists in the parliamentary party, however, actually believed that they had more in common with leading members of the Labour government like Snowden. The Old Left heritage shared by old-style radicals in the Liberal and Labour parties ensured that there was common ground on issues like retrenchment, free trade, temperance and foreign policy. Leif Jones, MP for Camborne, declared that 'Mr Snowden gives me a restful feeling as compared with his predecessor [Churchill]', while Hilda Runciman felt that the party could afford to be patient with Labour because it was 'curious how Liberal they seem to become when they are in office. Their Socialism seems to fall away from them. This, indeed, is inevitable.'[11] The Cornish MPs played a key role in these events since they formed the nucleus of the opposition to Lloyd George's policy. In March 1930 the *Western Morning News* commented that the 'Runciman–Maclean group', which included Jones and, to a lesser extent, Isaac Foot, were in a 'key position, and on them may very well depend the fate of the Government and the date of the election'. There was even speculation that Runciman and his supporters in Cornwall were preparing to set up an independent Liberal party in the House of Commons that would be sustained at the local level by electoral pacts with Labour.[12]

Lloyd George's next move, however, transformed the nature of the divisions within the party. In March 1930 he announced that the parliamentary party would abstain in any further votes relating to the Coal Bill, on the grounds that they did not want to 'embarrass' the government while the Naval Conference was still sitting. This decision signalled the beginning of a new approach, with the Liberals holding regular consultations with government ministers and providing guaranteed support for agreed policies like unemployment and agriculture. In exchange for this support the MacDonald administration included the alternative vote in an Electoral Reform Bill that was put before the House of Commons early in 1931.[13] An agreement with the Labour government certainly had potential benefits for the Liberals. Dingle Foot believed that the 'Protectionist campaign in the country [was] definitely losing impetus' by the summer of 1931, and it was therefore in the interests of the party to keep Labour in office until this offensive had 'done its worst'. If the government could survive until 1932 it would enable the Liberal 'rank and file' to prepare for the 'fight of their lives'.[14] In addition, electoral reform would help the party to survive as a significant force in British politics. Although the Liberals would have preferred the introduction of proportional representation, they thought that the alternative vote would benefit the party in areas like the South-West where the intervention of Labour candidates had enabled many Conservatives to retain their seats on a minority vote in 1929. John Day, Liberal candidate for Tavistock, argued that if the alternative vote was introduced in time for the next election it would ensure that the far west of the region in particular would become a permanent Radical stronghold:

> Every seat in Cornwall would become an absolutely safe Liberal one, and the same might be said for at least three of the Devon constituencies—Barnstaple, Tavistock and South Molton. In fact, if the alternative vote was carried, the Tory candidates in those seats might as well throw up the sponge at once.[15]

But this policy depended upon the survival of the government. Although it was quite possible that the Liberals would have benefited from the alternative vote if the Conservative revival had lost momentum, the delaying powers of the House of Lords meant that electoral reform would not have been passed until 1933 and it appeared that the government's days were already numbered in 1931. MacDonald had alienated key groups like the trade unions and the Independent Labour Party, while observers claimed that the government itself was 'full of the consent to die'. Its position was further weakened during the summer of 1931 by the escalating financial crisis that followed the collapse of the Kredit Anstalt in Vienna and the publication of the report of the May Committee with its prediction of a £120 million budget deficit. Growing divisions within the Liberal party further undermined MacDonald's position. Lloyd George's decision to co-operate with Labour was regarded as a 'great triumph' for his opponents in the Runciman–Maclean group, while it alienated those Liberals who were determined to maintain an independent identity for the party.[16] The new nucleus of discontent was a small group of MPs under the leadership of

Sir John Simon, which was prepared to co-operate with the Conservatives in order to remove the government. In March 1931 the authority of the party leadership was seriously weakened when only thirty-three Liberal MPs supported a vague motion in favour of co-operating with 'this or any Government' which put Liberal policy into effect.[17] These developments were reflected in the South-West. By November 1930 Lambert, who had previously announced his intention of voting against all increases of expenditure, had emerged as a leading member of the Simonite group, while a few months later the Western Counties Federation passed a motion which called on the party to maintain its 'complete and real independence'.[18]

More surprisingly, Leslie Hore-Belisha, MP for Devonport and a leading modernist within the party, moved to the Simonite group. His hostility towards Labour was influenced by the government's decision to reduce the size of the Royal Navy at the time of the Naval Conference. While the vast majority of Liberals supported the government on this issue, including Runciman who declared that he wanted to 'see the battleship abolished once and for all', Hore-Belisha had consolidated his position in Devonport by championing the interests of the Royal Navy and the local dockyards.[19] This event confirmed his general view that the party was making a serious mistake in allowing the Conservatives to have a monopoly in opposing the government. It made more sense for the Liberals to preserve their independence, and to exploit the government's failure to deal with problems like unemployment. This attitude was clearly expressed at the party's Buxton conference in May 1931 when he declared that during the

> first few months of this Parliament …we prided ourselves on our independence. … On that day when we withdrew our opposition to the Coal Bill the heart was taken out of the Liberal Party. We ceased to have the respect of the constituencies. The public became at a loss where to place the Liberal Party.[20]

The strategic position of the party was further complicated on 27 July when Sir Herbert Samuel had to take over the leadership of the party after Lloyd George was taken seriously ill. Samuel's inheritance was effectively a poisoned chalice. With the party totally divided over its attitude towards the government it was now struggling for its very existence. On 23 August, however, the second Labour administration finally drew to a close. The cabinet, which was unable to agree on a proposal to reduce unemployment benefit, was forced to resign, and on the following day MacDonald took office as Prime Minister of a new National government consisting of four Labour ministers, four Conservatives and two Liberals. A meeting of Liberal MPs, peers and candidates gave their support to the decision to join the new government, while the move was widely approved at the constituency level. After all, party activists actually regarded the new administration as the 'nearest approach to a Liberal government' since the war.[21] This was especially the case in Cornwall where three of the county's MPs became ministers. Maclean became President of the Board of Education, while Walters took over as Paymaster General and Foot accepted the post of Secretary of Mines.

However, the new administration proved to be only a temporary solution to the party's problems. Once the government had agreed on measures to balance the budget there was growing pressure from the Conservatives for an early election. The Samuelite wing of the party was naturally appalled at the prospect of a protectionist landslide, and the general feeling of activists at the local level was that 'this unnecessary election' was simply a 'Tory ramp'.[22] But on 5 October the cabinet agreed that the parties which formed the National government would appeal to the country for a 'doctor's mandate' to introduce any measures which would create economic prosperity and a favourable balance of trade. Samuel's authority as party leader was further undermined by defections at opposite ends of the party. Lloyd George refused to support his decision to participate in the election as National candidates, and he was one of seven independent Liberals, mainly relatives like his daughter Megan Lloyd George, who stood in opposition to the government. In addition, 24 Liberals led by Simon and Hore-Belisha announced their decision to fight as Liberal National candidates in full alliance with the Conservatives. With the loss of many of its prominent figures the party's position appeared even more precarious.

This disintegration within the parliamentary party was reflected at the regional level. Runciman, formerly a die-hard champion of the cause of free trade, now apparently underwent a rapid conversion to protectionism in order to stand in the election as a Liberal National. In September 1931 he suggested the prohibition of luxury imports, but at the end of the month he withdrew his signature from a Simonite memorandum on the grounds that he did not realize that it involved the acceptance of tariffs. A few days later, however, he was stressing the need for 'wartime measures for dealing with wartime problems', and his new view was that the government should take any steps necessary, including tariffs, to deal with the economic situation.[23] Yet it is worth noting that he remained opposed to tariffs on imported food, which meant that in 1931 he was technically contravening the 'doctor's mandate'. The final defector to the Liberal National camp was Glassey. His decision to sign the Simonite memorandum at the end of September seems surprising in view of his earlier loyalty to the party leadership. It is interesting that his wife continued to address Samuelite meetings in other parts of the region during October, while Glassey himself returned to the Liberals after the election and became treasurer of the Western Counties Federation.[24] This suggests that his decision to join the Simonites was really based on the fact that his 277 vote majority in East Dorset was obviously vulnerable to even a small swing of votes. As a Liberal National Glassey could expect the Conservatives to withdraw their candidate, but in the event he was to be just another victim of the Conservative revival.

In these circumstances it was no wonder that the Liberal campaign in 1931 was conducted in total confusion. Many Liberals still believed that it was their duty to oppose the Conservatives and protectionism. This led to a series of bitter contests in places like Wells and North Cornwall between the old parties, while in South Dorset the constituency association backed the Socialist candidate. Other activists, however, backed Conservative candidates in order to stop the 'spread of Socialism and Bolshevism'.[25] Significantly, these individuals took the view that the danger of Socialism had to take precedence over the old fear of protectionism. A leading Liberal in North Dorset claimed that if the party carried free trade to its 'extreme limits' it would merely 'play into the hands' of Labour. He argued that contests between 'National' candidates were 'against the best interests of the country', and on this occasion it was far better for the anti-Socialist parties to unite against the common enemy. Although he still preferred the idea of a Liberal government, 'such an event [was] outside the range of practical politics ... We must have either Mr MacDonald's National Government, with the strong probability of their imposing tariffs under certain conditions *or* a Socialist Government ... whose policy spells ruin for us all.'[26]

This anti-Socialist attitude ensured that the Conservatives and their Liberal National allies swept to a landslide victory. The Liberals retained only North Cornwall and Bodmin, where Foot was returned unopposed, while ten of the successful National candidates were elected with substantial majorities of over 30 per cent. Although the Socialists also lost ground, with Frome and Drake captured by the Conservatives, the Liberals were the real losers. In previous elections the South-West had been one of the few regions where the party was in a strong enough position to win a large number of seats on a relatively small swing of votes. However, in 1931 the Liberals only came close to victory in Barnstaple (Conservative majority of 4.4 per cent) and Penryn & Falmouth (5.9 per cent). The election also revealed the long-term significance of the formation of the Liberal Nationals. A crucial factor in the success of individuals like Hore-Belisha, Lambert and Runciman had been their success in building up a strong personal vote. Their defection was compensated to some extent by freak gains from Labour in other parts of Britain, such as Dewsbury and Leicester West, but these temporary victories proved no substitute for the loss of a considerable number of the party's few surviving strongholds. In the South-West this meant that it would be even more difficult for the party to establish itself as a powerful regional force. In that sense 1931 marked an important stage in the collapse of its parliamentary base.

The paralysis of Liberalism intensified after the election. Although party activists at the local level were calling for an early move into opposition almost immediately after the election, the party leadership

Table 3.1: Election results in the South-West in 1929 and 1931.

	Seats		Percentage Vote		Average % Vote	
	1929	1931	1929	1931	1929	1931
Conservative	16	22	43.2	55.6	43.1	60.1
Liberal National	—	3	—	7.9	—	66.9
Liberal	8	2	35.5	20.0	37.1	37.6
Labour	2	—	19.4	15.6	19.0	21.5
Other	1	—	1.9	0.9	27.9	24.5

was reluctant to resign from the government at a time of instability. Incredibly even an ardent free trader like Sir Donald Maclean had no desire to leave the cabinet over tariffs. He agreed that the 'convictions of a lifetime are not cast off overnight', but it was essential to preserve the national character of the government in view of the other 'vital matters on which we all agreed'. The situation was still not stable enough for a return to party politics, and Maclean believed that this justified the continuation of the National government. He accepted that there 'were some good Liberals who want my colleagues and myself in the Government to come out if it as a protest against Protection ... I have a good deal of understanding with that "come out of it" slogan [but] I think the cry comes from the emotions rather than from the reason'.[27]

But political developments created a momentum that eventually forced the party into opposition. By March 1932 three tariff measures (Abnormal Importations Bill, Horticultural Products Bill and the Import Duties Bill) had been enacted. An 'agreement to differ' over the introduction of tariffs in January 1932 enabled the Samuelite ministers to stay in the government, but the party's annual conference at Clacton in 1932 confirmed the opposition of both backbenchers and party activists.[28] The North Cornwall by-election in July 1932, which was called following the death of Maclean in the previous month, led to further friction, with the Conservative and Liberal parties in a state of 'open war' over the issue of free trade. Following the protectionist agreement at Ottawa in the September of that year, the Liberal ministers decided to resign from the government and move to the backbenches. However, many activists wanted a complete separation. Isaac Foot and Sir Francis Acland, the new Liberal MP for North Cornwall, were increasingly critical of the party's stance, while in February 1933 the Devon and Cornwall Federation passed a resolution calling on the party to 'cross the floor'. When the party eventually moved into opposition on 13 November, it was widely welcomed throughout the four counties of the region on the grounds that it would 'save Liberalism from disintegration'.[29]

The Liberal party's new role in opposition proved to be no solution to its problems. Parliamentary by-elections indicated that there was little popular support for Samuel's decision to leave the government backbenches. It is interesting that in the last two by-elections held before the Liberals went into opposition (Altrincham and Skipton) they achieved a more credible result than in by-elections held after that date. After moving into opposition on 13 November the Liberals rarely achieved a good by-election result (see Table 3.2). Samuel's late decision to move into opposition meant that the party was increasingly seen as an irrelevance. No longer able to contribute to government decisions, or share in its apparent successes, the Liberals also failed to establish themselves as a credible alternative. The Weston-super-Mare by-election in June 1934 was a good example. There was considerable apathy on the part of many voters, which proved to be a serious problem for the Liberals since they needed a 'definite turnover of opinion' in order to win the seat. Even some activists disagreed with the decision to contest the seat. Although it was reported that a number of the party's traditional supporters, particularly the nonconformists, were returning

Table 3.2: The by-elections that the Liberals contested from June 1933 up until the 1935 general election compared to the 1929 general election.

Constituency	Date	Conservative* %	Labour %	Liberal %	Other %
Altrincham	14 Jun 1933	+ 0.5	+ 0.4	–0.9	—
Skipton	7 Nov 1933	+ 3.5	+ 2.3	–7.5	+1.7
Rusholme	21 Nov 1933	+ 8.0	+15.8	–23.8	—
Harborough	28 Nov 1933	+ 9.1	+ 0.2	–9.3	—
Cambridge	8 Feb 1934	+ 8.0	+10.3	–18.3	—
Lowestoft	15 Feb 1934	+ 8.2	+13.2	–21.4	—
Basingstoke	19 Apr 1934	+ 3.3	+ 1.3	– 4.6	—
Merthyr	5 Jun 1934	–17.6	– 7.8	+ 6.1	+19.3
Weston-super-Mare	26 Jun 1934	+10.4	+ 5.5	–15.9	—
Rushcliffe	26 Jun 1934	+ 7.1	+ 3.0	–10.1	—
Lambeth, North	23 Oct 1934	+ 0.6	+14.1	–16.3	+ 1.6
Wavertree	6 Feb 1935	– 8.8	+ 3.2	–18.3	+23.9
Edinburgh, West	2 May 1935	+ 21.3	– 4.7	–16.6	—

* The Conservatives did not contest Merthyr in 1934, while National Labour represented the government at Lambeth in 1934. An Independent Conservative also contested Wavertree in 1935.

by the end of the campaign, the eventual result was a serious setback with both Labour and the Conservatives consolidating their grip on the constituency.[30]

By-election defeats created a negative environment which led to further decline. As Ramsay Muir remarked in October 1934, the Liberals were 'beaten in advance by the public's idea that we are done for, and this affects our own people'.[31] Even in comparative Liberal strongholds like Cornwall there was a general acceptance that the party was now fighting for its very survival. In 1935 the *West Briton* declared that Liberalism had to be kept 'alive as a definite force. ... The representation of Liberalism in every election in Cornwall is welcome whatever the result of the polling may be.'[32] Closely connected with the party's lack of credibility was a belief that the new alignment in British politics meant that organized Liberalism was now irrelevant. Lord Lothian, the prominent Liberal peer, concluded that the party was in an 'almost hopeless position' with both Labour and the Conservatives 'essentially liberal minded'.[33] Those Liberal voters who deserted to the Conservatives had concluded that the party ticket had 'almost dropped out', while the comments that the other parties used to describe the Liberals, such as 'a thing of the past' and a 'dwindling few political Rip Van Winkles', reinforced this view.[34] The malaise had even extended to party members as can be seen in the appeal by Sir Ronald Wilberforce Allen, the prospective Liberal candidate for Penryn & Falmouth and a former MP for Leicester South, for a more dynamic approach:

> Let us not apologise for our existence as Liberals. There is a tendency to feel ... ashamed to call ourselves Liberals, that we are not up to the times, but to be proud of our ... existence and not go on talking as if we are remnants of a historic but virtually defunct party.[35]

The continuing decline of the party in local government was another symptom of the paralysis of Liberalism. Cook has commented that the 'most consistent feature of municipal Liberalism in the 1930s was the absolute lack of an attempt to provide a Liberal challenge'.[36] By 1935 the party was only a major force in a small number of borough councils in the North of England, while there was a gradual but sustained decline every year in the number of seats that it contested. The weakness of the party in local government encouraged Liberal councillors to participate in anti-Socialist pacts with the Conservatives. As Stevenson remarks, it was usually only a 'short step from local pacts ... to the disappearance of independent Liberal candidates from the scene altogether'. The party's image was further tarnished by local government defeats, such as the failure to hold a single seat in the London municipal elections of 1934, which enabled its opponents to claim that it marked the 'end of the party'.[37]

To some extent the party fared better in municipal politics in the South-West than in Britain as a whole. In November 1935 the Liberals were still the second-largest party on the borough councils of Bath, Exeter and Poole, while Table 3.3 suggests that until 1933 the party actually enjoyed more consistent success than its opponents. Yet the party's position in local government was much weaker than it appeared. Relatively few council seats, with the exception of the Plymouth wards, were contested in the region during this period, and this meant that many Liberal councillors were returned unopposed. The Liberals, in particular, adopted a low-profile approach to municipal elections. In the previous decade the party was still prepared to challenge the other parties, especially in Plymouth and Poole. During the early 1930s, however, the party rarely contested wards held by its opponents. The main concern of the Liberals was to retain their existing seats, and isolated victories at Plymouth (1932) and Bath (1934) were obtained in straight fights. In 1932 the Plymouth Liberals even formed an anti-Socialist alliance with the Conservatives.[38] Moreover, Labour's active involvement in local elections assisted in the rise of class politics. Municipal candidates tended to come from the local business community and, since the vast majority of borough councils in the region were quite small, elections were invariably fought on non-party grounds. Labour candidates therefore represented the main opposition to the local 'establishment' in the smaller towns in the region. The general absence of an independent Liberal challenge reinforced the claims of Labour candidates that the 'real issue' in local politics was between the 'progressive programme of the Labour Party and those who represented vested ... interests'.[39] The significance of this development in local government was that it consolidated the owner–worker cleavage at the expense of traditional issues.

A wider problem was the general perception that the very nature of

Table 3.3: Net changes in representation on borough councils in the region.[40]

	Conservative	Labour	Liberal	Other
1928	−1	−2	+3	—
1929	−7	+10	—	−3
1930	+5	−6	+1	—
1931	+1	−5	−	+4
1932	+4	−8	+2	+2
1933	−6	+11	−1	−4
1934	—	+ 3	—	−3
1935	—	−1	—	+1

politics had apparently changed since the previous decade. It was not that the Liberals lacked policies, since in 1934 they had published 'wide and detailed' programmes, *Address to the Nation* and *The Liberal Way,* which covered such subjects as peace, industry, agriculture and the constitution.[41] However, many traditional supporters associated Liberalism with *causes* like free trade, retrenchment and religious nonconformity rather than *policies*. Baines has concluded that the National government had 'adopted the traditional Liberal slogans of retrenchment and fiscal probity, while throwing Liberalism off balance through its abandonment of the Gold Standard and free trade'. Even on the free trade issue the Samuelites lacked a distinctive policy. The Liberals were forced to admit that the return to free trade would 'have to be by stages', and by the spring of 1935 the official policies of all three Liberal groups were 'no longer so clear cut, nor so different'.[42] In such circumstances the Samuelite Liberals were unable to reconstruct their old electoral base, especially at the national level.

Supporters of traditional causes were, in addition, unlikely to be attracted by a greater emphasis on a modernist programme. At the local level there were indications that the Liberals were distancing themselves from the Gladstonian principles which had exerted such a strong hold in previous years. For example, the secretary of the Devon Union of Women Liberals called for family allowances, a minimum wage and the elimination of unnecessary competition. There also had to be social justice for the workers and 'fair play' for consumers within an organized plan for the British economy. She concluded that it could 'no longer be said that Liberalism is purely individualistic'.[43] Allen described the party's beliefs as an attitude of mind to national and international problems, and that because of this it 'grew and changed'. The nature of politics had so changed in the last thirty years that the important issues had become 'bread and butter politics, affecting employment, unemployment [and] wages'. He believed that the party should address these problems by relating Liberalism to the present and future since the Gladstonian agenda, 'for which he had great respect, was now Conservatism and he was sure that if Gladstone was living today he would still be a Liberal because he would have advanced with the changed conditions'.[44]

In the long term the party had to accept modern conditions, but in order to preserve its existing share of the vote the manner in which change took place was crucial. The dilemma for the party was essentially the same as in the late 1920s: how to retain traditional stalwarts and yet, at the same time, appeal to younger voters. This would have been a difficult task at any time, but the paralysis of Liberalism after 1929 meant that the party lacked the will and imagination to even attempt to deal with this difficulty. For example, some Liberals believed that the party should formulate a radical manifesto for women voters. In January 1935 it was proposed that the party should support equal status for married women and the removal of the marriage bar for teachers, and there was even a suggestion that 'all the Women's societies might be … moulded into an effective political force in alliance' with Liberalism. The response was extremely cautious, however, because of a fear of losing further electoral support. Economic depression made it 'unwise to press the point concerning the marriage bar', while a programme might 'entail many electoral disadvantages'. In the event the vague Liberal manifesto of 1935 made virtually no mention of specific issues for women.[45] The cautious attitude of leading Liberals on this issue demonstrates why no real attempt was made to devise a distinctive programme that could motivate party supporters. In 1929 the emphasis on Gladstonian principles in the South-West had provided a popular and distinctive image which appealed to many voters, but Liberalism in the thirties, as Wilson remarked, lacked 'crude assertion [and] violent appeals to the emotions'.[46] The emphasis on balance and caution was supposed to unite libertarians and collectivists, but this negative response was no solution to the party's dilemma, as young Liberals 'drifted into the Socialist camp' while many older stalwarts looked to the National government.[47]

It was only to be expected, then, that the party would fare badly in the 1935 general election. In terms of actual votes the Liberals only just remained in second place in the South-West, while their share of the vote in every three-cornered contest was less than in 1929. Although Richard Acland, the eldest son of Sir Francis, narrowly won Barnstaple by 464 votes, the party's parliamentary representation did not increase because Foot lost Bodmin to the Conservatives. Sir Francis Acland, who retained North Cornwall with a narrow majority of 836, was the only other Samuelite Liberal to be elected. Far worse results were recorded for the residential seats of East Dorset, Torquay and Weston-super-Mare where there was a quite significant decline in support. It was the Conservatives and their Liberal National allies, winning 25 out of the 27 seats in the region, who were the principal beneficiaries of this process. Labour, in contrast, lacked sufficient support in the rural South-West to emerge as an adequate successor to the Old Left. Although the Socialists appeared to be gaining ground across the four counties, they actually polled less in some divisions (Tavistock, Bodmin, Totnes, North Dorset, Frome, Drake and Sutton) in 1935 than in 1929. Far from heralding an opportunity for rural Socialism, the election appeared to confirm a decisive shift from Radicalism to Conservatism.

Factors for Survival

Yet perhaps the most surprising aspect of the 1935 election was that it also pointed to the likely survival of the old Radical tradition. At the national level the dramatic fall since 1929 in the party's vote (23.6 to 6.4 per cent) and parliamentary representation (59 to 21) has tended to encourage a generalization of the state of the party. Stannage, for example, concluded that in comparable seats the Liberals lost approximately one-third of their 1929 voting strength.[48] Yet in some three-cornered contests, such as Worcester, East Birkenhead and Wolverhampton East, the Liberal vote had actually risen. This was reflected in the South-West where the change in the party's percentage vote varied from a fall of 19.1 in Weston-super-Mare to a rise of 14.1

Figure 3.1: Liberal candidate Richard Acland (MP for Barnstaple 1935–45), campaigning in the North Devon countryside in 1935.

Figure 3.2: Richard and Anne Acland following the declaration of the Liberal victory at Barnstaple in 1935.

per cent in West Dorset (see Table 3.4). In a third of regional contests the Liberals fared disastrously with their share of the vote falling by more than 10 per cent, but in three-cornered contests at Tavistock and Totnes it was remarkable that the party's support was only slightly down. Even in 1935 the Liberals remained the main challengers to the National government in the majority of seats in the region, while their average percentage vote in the region was over 30 per cent. This was especially the case in rural constituencies. In the nine most agricultural seats that the Liberals contested they could still poll 40.8 per cent of the vote in 1935 while Labour took a mere 7.7 per cent.

Table 3.4: The percentage change in Liberal support on a constituency basis, 1929–1935.

Weston-super-Mare	−19.1	Camborne	−10.0	Bodmin	−3.9
East Dorset	−18.4	Penryn & Falmouth	−8.7	Tavistock	−3.6
Torquay	−16.1	Bath	−6.4	Totnes	−1.2
Wells	−15.3	North Dorset	−5.9	* North Cornwall	+ 1.6
South Dorset	−13.4	Yeovil	−5.7	* Barnstaple	+ 6.7
Bridgwater	−10.4	Frome	−4.4	* West Dorset	+14.1

* No Labour candidate in 1935.

These results reflect the fact that organized Liberalism must be considered as a local rather than a national force by the 1930s. The personal appeal of individual candidates could influence the outcome of an election in urban and rural divisions, while in some of the more remote parts of Britain socio-economic factors were more conducive to the survival of the Old Left. The rural nature of the South-West meant that the region was still rather insulated from the full impact of the political changes taking place at the Westminster level. Contemporary observers emphasized that it was the villages and hamlets of the countryside which provided the core of the Liberal vote, and this was demonstrated at the North Cornwall by-election in 1932 when Acland's nomination papers represented 'half the voting strength' in some of the

remoter settlements in the constituency.[49] Political rivalry between the
Liberals and Conservatives had developed over generations, and voters
were often reluctant to switch to the new political alignment that had
emerged in London. The *Western Morning News* concluded that the
continuing 'acceptance of the Liberal faith' in the area was due to a
'remarkable loyalty to family tradition'. This factor was also evident in
South Molton. On a superficial level this seat, with Conservatives and
Liberals uniting in common cause against Socialism, appears to confirm
the success of realignment in the 1930s. Yet supporters of both parties
were unwilling to work together. The *Western Morning News* remarked
that the declaration of Lambert's election victory in 1935, judging from
the lack of 'enthusiasm and excitement, might have been the
announcement of the Parish Council Elections'. The Liberals regarded
their old enemies with suspicion, and the decision of the local
Conservatives to select a prospective candidate in 1933 had led to
further friction. Even in 1935 there was no real enthusiasm for the new
alliance:

> Liberals could not enter wholeheartedly in a fight behind a leader
> who was being supported by the Conservative Party, with whom
> they have been in conflict for over 40 years … The Conservatives,
> too, felt … uneasy in their efforts to help the candidate they had so
> desperately fought against in the past.[50]

Some Liberals were able to exploit this traditional hostility in those
constituencies where they were organized. *The Times* concluded during
the election campaign that while 'West Country constituencies are
expected to give a good majority for the National Government, there
are divisions where Liberalism is very lively. In several areas it is
anticipated that the Liberals will give Unionists a close run'.[51] This was
particularly the case in West Dorset where by 1935 the Liberals had a
more realistic chance of defeating the Conservatives than at any time
since before the First World War. In 1929 the presence of a Labour
candidate had divided the non-Conservative vote, but a combination of
straight fights in the thirties and a fall in the Conservative vote in 1935
significantly improved the Liberal position. George Chappell, the party's
candidate, conducted a 'vigorous campaign' in which he spoke at over
90 meetings in the 1935 campaign, and after the election the president

of the local Conservative association admitted that the Liberals had 'worked harder than we have'.[52] Another example was at Totnes where the party was well prepared for the election. It was reported that the Liberal Association was using the latest campaign methods, while the Devon and Cornwall Federation commented that the local organization had 'attained a high degree of efficiency' which enabled the Totnes Liberals to limit the fall in their support to a mere 151 votes in comparison with 1929.[53]

This vigorous defence certainly applied to the free trade issue. It was mentioned earlier that many former party activists in the region were transferring their allegiance to the National government on the grounds that the threat from Socialism was now more important than arguments over the extent of free trade. Nevertheless, other Liberals took a different line. Lord Bayford, the former Conservative MP for Wells (1924–9), commented on the 'curious' nature of the 1931 election when many of the contests in the region followed the 'old fashioned lines of 1906. We had the Big and Little Loaf and our west country agent Tydeman was not at all happy as to our prospects.'[54] Conservative candidates, particularly in the two western counties, still had to reassure voters in free trade areas by claiming that the government could be selective in introducing tariffs. Thorpe similarly found that only 55 per cent of Conservative candidates in the western peninsula and Severn regions (which covered Cornwall, Devon and Somerset) openly espoused the protectionist cause. In other traditional free trade areas, such as Lancashire and the West Riding, nearly 80 per cent of the party's candidates openly advocated tariffs, and Wales was the only other region in Britain where the figure was less than 60 per cent.[55] A vital factor for the continuing appeal of free trade was the survival of traditional values in the rural West which was outlined earlier. This veneration of the past was evident at Wells in 1931. John Thompson, the 70-year-old 'Liberal and Free Trade' candidate and former MP for East Somerset, personified this approach, and at one meeting he actually gave an election speech on the history of local Liberalism since 1868. Another interesting individual was John Coleby Morland, the 94-year-old chairman of the constituency party, who rejected claims that he had not moved with the times:

The Chairman described himself as one whose outlook as a Liberal

had remained the same from his beginning as an early Victorian. ...
He had never seen anything which led him to believe that the
reasoning which led Cobden and Bright to carry out their great Free
Trade campaign had any fallacy in it. He and his friends remained
as Liberals today ... because time had made no difference to their
beliefs.[56]

Free trade sentiment was especially strong in pastoral districts. This
was chiefly due to the belief of the local farming community that there
was a 'more hopeful outlook' for agriculture in the South-West which
meant that there was less reason to support tariffs. The secretary of the
Western Counties Agricultural Co-operative Association concluded in
December 1930 that they were much better off than farmers in other
parts of the country depending upon arable agriculture, and he called on
farmers to concentrate on beef, mutton and dairy produce.[57] Although
there were some indications by the following year that support for
protection was not restricted to arable farmers, there were reports
during the election that many farmers, particularly in the pastoral
Cornwall–Devon border area, were still supporting free trade. Indeed,
the Liberal agent for North Cornwall concluded after the election that
the farming community had 'remained in the main steadfast'.[58] The
electoral evidence also appears to confirm this view. In 1931 there was
an average swing in the region of 9.3 per cent to the Conservatives in
the thirteen seats that were contested by the Liberals in both 1929 and
1931. However, there was considerable variation, with the former
party's share of the vote in the three eastern seats of West Dorset, North
Dorset and Wells increasing by 11.1 to 15.1 per cent, while in the three
Tamar border divisions of North Cornwall, Barnstaple and Tavistock it
was only 3.0 to 7.7 per cent.

The small farmers still tended to favour free trade throughout the
early thirties. At the North Cornwall by-election the defeated
Conservative candidate remarked that he had been defeated by local
opposition to tariffs, while it was significant that even a Liberal National
like Lambert could argue in November 1932 that protectionism had
'injured the farmer in many respects, especially the stock raiser'.[59] Many
farmers were also irritated by the administrative problems created by the
government's agricultural policy. The local Liberals claimed that this was
a direct result of 'Tory Socialism' which could create 'conditions approx-

imating to servitude under a State-controlled "corporation" on the Italian model'.[60] Agricultural disenchantment therefore held out the prospect of a rural recovery of Liberalism. However, while many farmers were still critical of the government in 1935, over a range of issues from tariffs to tithes, agricultural reform had at least prevented further decline and led to a rise in farm prices and wages. Only individual candidates were able to exploit this complex situation. Sir Francis Acland certainly proved quite adept at championing the needs of local agriculture, calling for the radical reform of tithes and the setting up of a new Agricultural Commission which would encourage the dairy products of the South-West at the expense of sugar beet and wheat from East Anglia.[61] This enabled him to retain the support of a large number of farmers in his own constituency. Chappell was also able to construct a broad alliance of farmers, consumers and agricultural labourers in opposition to the local landlords who still dominated politics and society in rural Dorset. He claimed that neither the farmer nor the farm worker had really benefited from the government's agricultural policies, while the consumer was exploited in having to pay increased prices:

> Who was getting the benefits from the millions of pounds that were being expended upon [agriculture]? It would appear that the benefits were going into the pockets of the large landowners. I was very interested to read the names of those present at my opponent's adoption meeting. The names given comprised the chief officers of the West Dorset Conservative Association. They were the well known landowners in the division.[62]

This suggests, then, that the decline of Liberalism was not inevitable. On one hand there were definite signs of a reversal, with the party losing vital support in many constituencies to its opponents and with an ideology that appeared increasingly irrelevant. However, there are clearly plenty of other examples, particularly in rural areas, where the party was still was a vibrant force, able to retain many of its traditional supporters and mount a serious challenge against the Conservatives. What the party really required was a strategy that could maximize its electoral potential at a time when the national situation did not appear favourable. It is this area which now needs to be considered in order to understand the drift and paralysis of the period.

A Strategy for the Future

A political party is certainly at an advantage if it can depend on an effective means of achieving its aims. After 1929 the Liberals simply lacked credibility to pose as a party of government, and they had insufficient resources to even make an attempt at putting forward a large number of candidates. In these circumstances it seemed more realistic to adopt an alternative policy. What was interesting about this period was that many of the ideas put forward at the time were to be raised again in future decades. While the party was in no position to campaign as an alternative government, it was still possible to fight a vigorous narrow-front campaign in those seats where it had a good chance of victory. Such a campaign could be connected to local and regional issues. Many Liberals, however, still favoured a broad-front approach and the leadership's failure to encourage a more realistic approach after 1931 obviously did not help.

During the early part of this period conditions appeared promising for a change in approach. The *Liberal Magazine* claimed that the old idea of a majority government was 'gone for good', while the party's financial difficulties made a narrow front appear more attractive. A leading advocate for a new approach was Dingle Foot, son of Isaac and the party's prospective candidate for Tiverton. In *Contemporary Review* in May 1931 he accepted that the 'massed attack of 1929 [could] scarcely be repeated on the same scale'. Yet Foot claimed that a 'fierce guerrilla warfare' was still being carried on in many constituencies, and added that if at the next election the party could 'retain its quota of fifty seats it will have proved that it cannot be driven off the political map'. With a secure parliamentary base the Liberals could then consider the possibility of expansion. These fifty seats, according to Foot, were by 'no means unlikely', and if the alternative vote were introduced the party could expect to win even more seats. Many of the Liberals elected in 1929 had built up a personal vote in their constituencies, and this also applied to some of those candidates who had come second in the election. Foot concluded that this factor would help the party survive the expected swing to the Conservatives. But in order to justify their 'guerrilla warfare' the Liberals had to find a new role in British politics. Foot believed that the Irish Nationalists and the pre-war Labour party provided models that the Liberals had to study since both parties had attempted to 'justify their existence, not as potential ministries, but as minority parties'. He pointed out that this argument was one that the Liberals had not even attempted to make. During the previous decade they had concentrated on 'explaining why there should be Liberals on the Treasury bench', but voters now had to be 'told why there should be Liberals below the gangway'.[63] His comments were significant. The idea that the party could play an alternative role to that of claiming to be a party of government was one which many Liberals would return to in the dark years ahead.

An important aspect of that alternative role was to give more attention to local issues. After the 1929 election the five Liberal MPs in Cornwall decided to establish a so-called Duchy Parliamentary Committee to co-ordinate their activities for both local and national affairs. It was announced that the immediate priority of the group was to devise public work schemes to reduce unemployment, but the MPs also resolved to promote the wider interests of Cornwall, and key groups like the Cornish Farmers' Union took a keen interest in its work.[64] What was surprising, however, was that the Cornish MPs did not use their committee to rouse the nonconformist community by campaigning for Local Option. A key factor in the party's landslide in the county in 1929 had been the plan to introduce a Cornish Local Option Bill. While the local Liberals continued to raise the issue, such as in October 1930 when the Cornish Union of Women's Liberal Associations stressed the need for temperance 'at a time when the finances of the country were in so sorry a plight', the Duchy Committee made no attempt to put forward a local Bill. [65] The long-term problem for the party was that nonconformist issues were gradually becoming less important, and it was surely in the interests of the Liberals that temperance was kept firmly on the regional agenda. Nonetheless, the Duchy Committee could claim some successes, such as in March 1930 when the Cornish MPs forced the Labour government to abandon the previous administration's policy of including unemployed men from outside the region on public work schemes in Cornwall. By working together the five MPs could therefore consolidate their position by presenting themselves as a united group that was defending Cornish interests at Westminster.[66]

This discussion of local issues was not restricted to Cornwall. Day claimed that the Liberals were 'working to make life better and happier for the people' in rural areas like west Devon. That meant securing higher wages, building more houses and providing basic amenities like water for the 'working people' in the countryside.[67] Hore-Belisha declared in February 1930 that 'I will stand at the next election, as I always have stood as a "Hore-Belisha candidate" with a "Devonport policy first and last"'. He frequently combined local issues with criticism of the inactivity of the Socialists. Thus, the government was 'too slack' to support the building of a road bridge over the River Tamar to absorb unemployment, while its housing policy was not 'vigorous' enough to remove local slums.[68] This approach had enabled him to survive the Conservative landslide in 1924, and considering the fact that he had the largest Liberal majority in the region, 13.7 per cent, it was quite possible that he could have held his seat in 1931 if he had remained with the Liberals. Further evidence of this growing interest in a local role was demonstrated at the conference of the Devon Union of Women Liberals in 1930. Delegates concentrated on how party policy could benefit the region. One activist claimed that local holiday resorts were helped by free trade, while Lady Eleanor Acland declared that 'seaside landladies … should be thankful to the Liberals for their efforts on behalf of the consumer', particularly over the Coal Bill. It was also claimed that farmers had the NFU to 'state their case, but fishermen had no one, and it was for us to take up their cause'. This led to calls for a separate Ministry of Fisheries, a more efficient marketing system and a central market for the smaller fishing ports. Finally, the conference concluded that the party's plan to make planning compulsory for all local authorities would protect areas like South Devon from exploitation by the 'moneymakers'.[69]

Events at Westminster were to undermine this progress towards a new role for regional Liberalism. In the first place the Duchy Committee was to fail in its attempts to pursue a united approach because of growing differences within the Liberal parliamentary party. Even in 1930 their opponents claimed that instead of the 'Duchy Five' they were really the 'Duchy Three' (Runciman, Maclean and Jones) and the 'defaulting two' (Walters and Foot), while Runciman's defection to the Liberal National camp in the following year created further confusion.[70] The nature of the 1931 election also ensured the greater dominance of state issues. The formation of a National government, which could appeal to the electorate on the grounds of patriotism and anti-Socialism, undermined the position of the regional platform of the Old Left. Religious issues were relegated to the background, and it was only free trade, still

81

defended by the Liberals on the grounds of local economic circumstances, which counted as a significant factor at the regional level.

Furthermore, the move into opposition in 1933 led to calls for the party to campaign on a broad-front basis. In October of that year Samuel announced that when the next general election came there would be a 'powerful Liberal party, with at least 400 candidates in the constituencies'.[71] Other prominent Liberals like Ramsay Muir supported him. He stated that 'We have got to fight all along the line at the next election. We at headquarters see our way to fighting at least 400 seats.' Yet this idealistic view failed to take into account the decline of the party at the local level. By October 1934 Muir was admitting that if the Liberals even 'put up 400 candidates (which I think impossible), we shall forfeit at least 200 deposits', while two months later Sinclair was pointing out to Samuel that the party had less than sixty prospective candidates.[72] The Samuelite Liberals simply lacked sufficient finance, organization and candidates to effectively fight on a broad-front basis. Instead of formulating an alternative option the party continued to pursue this course until the autumn of 1935. Only then did circumstances force the party to accept reality, and a mere 159 Liberals eventually contested the election. Yet this was clearly not a *planned* narrow front since many of these candidates were supported by weak and impoverished organizations. Admittedly, the party leadership had its reasons for not adopting a new approach. In November 1934 Lord Lothian concluded that the broad-front policy was 'doomed to hopeless failure', and he suggested that the party should only contest about a hundred seats. Harcourt Johnstone, a Liberal whip, agreed in theory with this view. He accepted that it would be 'most improbable' to contest a large number of seats, but thought that 'we must try to keep up the bluff until the last moment'. Johnstone feared that if the party announced its intention to contest only a limited number of seats this would undermine the morale of local activists and result in the destruction of organized Liberalism.[73]

However, since the vast majority of constituency associations were already, as Cook put it, in a 'state of suspended animation', it would have been more realistic if the Liberals had concentrated their resources on target areas.[74] Such an approach would probably have benefited the party in the South-West. Although Samuel appeared to recognize the strategic importance of the peninsula when he declared that the 'Westcountry needs Liberalism and Liberalism needs the Westcountry', in reality the national party neglected what was one of the few regions that still had the potential of returning a large bloc of Liberal MPs. For example, the loss of financial support from party headquarters meant that the annual income of the Western Counties Federation fell from £3,091 in 1929 to just over £525 in 1934.[75] It was not just in financial terms that headquarters was failing to give support. In 1932 the Liberals launched a Free Trade campaign, but out of twenty-six meetings across Britain not a single one was held west of Bristol.[76] In August 1935 Allen asked Sinclair if he would address a party meeting in his constituency. Sinclair's secretary remarked that 'none of our eminent speakers has visited the Division for some years'. This seems surprising considering that Penryn & Falmouth was a marginal seat, and vulnerable to a 3 per cent swing from Conservative to Liberal. Sinclair agreed to visit the division at the end of October, but in the event it was cancelled because of the election campaign.[77]

The regional Liberals therefore found themselves fighting virtually on their own in 1935. Party workers, even in a Liberal seat like Bodmin, were dependent on posters and leaflets from local branches. The Conservative and Labour candidates, in contrast, had 'almost unlimited quantities of propaganda from their respective party headquarters'.[78] Many local parties were simply in no position to contest the election. This was evident on nomination day when only eighteen candidates came forward instead of a possible twenty-seven. The Liberals did not contest a single seat in Plymouth, but this was understandable in view of their low poll in Sutton and Drake in 1929. Without Hore-Belisha's personal vote the party's prospects seemed equally poor in Devonport. More surprising was the failure to put forward candidates in rural seats like Honiton and Tiverton where the Liberal vote had been in excess of 40 per cent in 1929. Until nomination day there was confusion over the number of seats to be contested, and the candidates for five constituencies (South Dorset, East Dorset, Bridgwater, Camborne and Torquay) only came forward at the eleventh hour.

The failure of the Liberals to consolidate their position in the localities reflected the wider difficulties that they experienced in adjusting to third party status. Many leading activists still regarded politics purely in terms of major international and domestic issues, which meant that they were unable to adopt an alternative role based on low politics.[79] When Samuel had first moved into opposition he had assumed that a broad front would enable the party to return to its traditional *raison d'être*: a Liberal government. In May 1933 he declared that the country would 'definitely have the chance of returning a Liberal Government', while even a year later he argued that the 'present task is clearly to build up again a powerful and united Liberal Party'. By 1935, however, he could only claim that the party was a 'most useful factor' in protecting Britain from 'idle Toryism' and 'subversive Socialism'.[80] There was insufficient time during the election to convince the electorate of the possible benefits of such a role and it resulted instead in confusion. Allen, for example, explained his defeat on the grounds that the party had so 'few candidates in the field'. An early decision to fight only a limited number of seats would have enabled the party to have developed convincing reasons for voting Liberal, but all that Allen could claim was that a 'strong opposition was essential in the next House of Commons'.[81] With only 159 candidates the demoralized Liberals could not even aspire to be an effective opposition.

Another option, which would probably have enabled the Liberals to benefit from their survival as the second force in the region, was to have concentrated on the creation of an electoral alliance with Labour. The idea of an anti-Conservative agreement appeared more promising, particularly after the disastrous election performance of Labour in 1931, and many Liberals echoed Lloyd George's call for a pact or even a new Radical party.[82] Sir Francis Acland's narrow victory in a straight fight in the North Cornwall by-election in 1932 demonstrated the potential benefits. F.E. Church, the Labour candidate in 1929, said that it was impossible for Socialists to vote for a capitalist candidate, and the local Labour party advised its supporters to ignore the contest. However, many Socialist supporters were still willing to vote Liberal. Although the Samuelites were participating in the National government, the chairman of the Kilkhampton branch pledged his support and two of Acland's nomination papers were signed by Labour members. Church admitted after the election that 'large numbers of Labour voters had gone over to the Liberal candidate'.[83] The absence of Labour candidates would certainly have improved the morale and vigour of Liberal activists in 1935. A party activist in Wells had to appeal to her fellow Liberals 'not to feel any discouragement on the question of the split progressive vote', while a post-election report by the Devon and Cornwall Federation concluded that in many constituencies the 'advent of a Labour candidate' had greatly discouraged party supporters.[84]

Once Samuel had defected from the government side of the House of Commons there was an opportunity for a united opposition. Some prospective Liberal candidates in the South-West, such as Sir Francis Acland and Ronald Haylor at Totnes, had actively attempted to form an anti-Conservative alliance in their constituencies during the two years leading up to the election.[85] The main Labour advocate of co-operation was A.L. Rowse. At the Liberal Summer School at Oxford in August 1934 he expressed his support for regional pacts between the two parties. Cornwall, he believed, was an ideal area for such an agreement, with Labour supporting the Liberals in Bodmin, St Ives and North Cornwall, while the Liberals would stand down in his favour in Penryn & Falmouth. He even agreed that Liberals should serve in a future Labour-led government. The *News Chronicle* subsequently published articles by Rowse and Samuel on the subject. While Samuel welcomed the idea of co-operation in principle, he thought that the Labour party's commitment to nationalization was a major obstacle. Both men agreed that there was no immediate prospect of a 'common platform', but Rowse believed that the centre-left had to unite in defence of freedom and democracy.[86]

In 1935, however, Labour even put up candidates in seats like Wells and Totnes which it had not contested since 1929, and the Liberals enjoyed straight fights in only three divisions (West Dorset, North Cornwall and Barnstaple). The inconsistent stance of Liberal activists in the region was partly responsible for Labour's reluctance to support an alliance. A good example was Alfred Browning Lyne, chairman of the Bodmin Liberal Association, who proved totally inconsistent in his choice of partners In November 1931 he was already discussing the future possibility of a Liberal–Labour combination, and in 1934 he supported Rowse's idea of regional opposition pacts. However, only a few months before the general election he was suggesting that the Liberals should give 'active and helpful support to the National government, while not being out and out supporters'.[87] Such statements ensured that the party lacked a definite position on the political spectrum, which enabled Labour activists to claim that the Liberals had proved 'again and again to be the enemy of Labour'. While there was respect for Lloyd George, the new Liberal leadership was seen as conservative and pro-establishment. As one Labour member from

North Cornwall put it, the Liberals had simply lost all credibility as a party of principle:

> During the 1910 election Asquith was able to declare 'what I said in 1900, I repeated in 1906, and I am saying the same today' … Samuel declared in 1929 that 'Pacts with the Tories have a habit of defeating themselves', yet in 1931 he entered again into such pacts and his subsequent career has meant the adoption of … 'gentlemen's agreements' to give his actions some semblance of consistency.[88]

Conclusion

The early 1930s form a period of almost total confusion for the Liberal party. An inability to sustain a unified approach to the party's relationship with the second Labour administration was repeated after 1931 by divisions over the issue of whether to participate in the National government or move into full opposition. When the decision was finally taken by Samuel to move into opposition it was simply too late for the party to carve out a sufficient niche for itself as a major player in British politics. Moreover, the paralysis of the Old Left after 1929 prevented the Liberals from adjusting to a junior role in a three-party system. While the issues which had sustained the brief revivals of the 1920s now had less relevance at the national level, a more conducive environment still existed in rural areas like the South-West. But a lack of leadership at Westminster, which in view of the difficulties confronting the party was perhaps understandable, ensured that a more imaginative strategy was not implemented.

4

Advance and Retreat: 1936–1945

Introduction

The landslide victory of Clement Atlee's Labour party in 1945 was to sweep away much of the remnants of pre-war Liberalism. At the previous election of 1935 only twenty-one Liberals had retained their seats, but in the first post-war contest that figure was reduced even further to just twelve MPs, with even their leader, Sir Archibald Sinclair, losing his personal stronghold of Caithness & Sutherland. In the South-West the Liberals were to retain their two seats, the loss of Barnstaple compensated by a gain in North Dorset, but it was Labour with six seats and a vastly increased share of the vote, up from 21.5 to 33.5 per cent, that now became the local alternative to Conservatism. The absence of a general election for nearly ten years raises the intriguing question as to the timing of political change. Did the late 1930s merely represent a twilight period on the road to disaster in 1945? Alternatively, could it be said that the pre-war years offered an opportunity for reconstruction that was only lost because of the impact of the Second World War? By focusing on three specific areas; the debate over Liberal–Labour co-operation; organization and strategy; and, finally, changes in image and policy, it will be suggested that the years leading up to the outbreak of war held out the prospect of a recovery, at least in rural Britain, which was only undermined by events during the early 1940s.

'Popular Front in the West'

The idea of a Popular Front was supported by a variety of groups and individuals after Baldwin's victory in 1935. Widespread concern over the National government's foreign policy meant that Conservatives like Winston Churchill and Ronald Cartland believed that some sort of alternative coalition, which included Labour and the Liberals, was needed, while far left groups like the Communists were prepared to work with capitalist parties.[1] The Liberal assembly at Bath in 1936 voted to co-operate with other parties, and two years later Vernon Bartlett, the Independent Progressive candidate at the Bridgwater by-election, received a letter of support from thirty-nine Labour MPs. Sir Stafford Cripps, the leading left-winger, concluded in January 1939 that an 'effective victory by the Labour party alone is highly improbable at the next election'. When he launched a National Petition Campaign to obtain an alliance of the 'Parties of peace', the Popular Front issue was placed firmly on the political agenda.[2]

Yet historians tend to conclude that there was no real possibility of realignment at Westminster. According to Cook, the prospects for an alliance had 'completely faded by 1937'. De Groot has claimed that leaving 'aside the inevitable revolt among the Liberal right that … a pact would have caused, it was inconceivable that Labour would have found any justification for throwing a lifeline to the Liberals'.[3] There is plenty of evidence to support this view. For example, in November 1938 the NEC of the Labour party concluded that a Popular Front would be 'politically unsound, electorally disadvantageous and governmentally impossible'. Furthermore, even if a national alliance had been formed it was unlikely to have been of any direct benefit to Labour. A significant proportion of Liberal supporters, in the absence of a candidate from their own party, would either abstain or vote for the government, and it was actually in Labour's interests for the Liberals to *increase* their number of candidates in order to divide the Conservative vote.[4] The Labour conference in 1939 appeared to conclusively reject the idea when delegates, after expelling Cripps from the party, defeated a Popular Front resolution by 2,360,000 to 248,000 votes.[5]

Even the Liberals were uncertain about the benefits. Aside from the fact that many activists were reluctant to work with the Labour party because of its apparent commitment to state Socialism, there was also a strong regional dimension to the Liberal party's internal debate. In rural constituencies, especially in Southern England and the Celtic fringe, the Liberals would have been the main beneficiaries of an anti-Conservative alliance, and they regarded the presence of Labour candidates purely in terms of their nuisance value. However, Labour was the dominant party in the industrial seats of the North of England. Liberal activists in this type of constituency tended to regard the Socialists as their main opponents, and were naturally opposed to the idea of a national agreement that was not in their interest. It was understandable that the Liberal leadership often seemed to adopt a cautious approach. In February 1937 the national executive decided that Labour would have to make the first move in the direction of an alliance. Sinclair was adamant that the party had to 'maintain its full independence and integrity in the eyes of the public', and he never had the 'slightest intention of grovelling to the Labour Party and begging for a place under their umbrella'.[6] De Groot has concluded that the Liberal leader was unwilling to waste the opportunity for a revival of independent Liberalism for the 'transitory gains offered by a Popular Front'. Even on the eve of the Second World War, his idea of co-operation was restricted to a by-election pact that would unite the protest vote against Chamberlain's foreign policy.[7]

Nevertheless, a pact between the main opposition parties was still likely in 1939. Sinclair's position was more complex than the above views suggest. He was in favour of more than just a by-election agreement, and his caution was due to a belief that if the Popular Front was going to be successful it required the right circumstances. There had to be a consensus within the party, while a Liberal revival, especially at by-elections, was the 'best possible argument to convince the Labour Party and the dissident Conservatives that co-operation [was] necessary'. By December 1938 Sinclair believed that the 'fact that we are now in a crisis and that the whole party, with a small number of exceptions', was willing to support co-operation made the task easier. The party's success in holding North Cornwall on 13 July 1939 and the rise in the Liberal vote at the Holderness and Hythe by-elections (15 February and 20 July 1939 respectively) were also encouraging to Sinclair.[8]

It would be a mistake to discount the possibility of Labour support for an agreement. In February 1939 Frank Darvall, Liberal prospective candidate for East Dorset and a member of the national Party Council, was 'assured by Labour friends ... that the Labour leaders, while opposed [to] Cripps' proposals, are not opposed to constituency arrangements'. Darvall claimed in private correspondence to party headquarters that if the Liberals refrained from supporting Cripps and considered more 'definite' proposals in regard to local agreements there would be a good chance of an 'arrangement'. The party therefore adopted a cautious approach to Cripps' petition campaign in order not to antagonize Transport House.[9] There is certainly evidence to suggest that a number of senior figures in the Labour party were more in favour of an alliance than they indicated in public. Hugh Dalton, for example, gave his personal support to party members involved in local pacts. Although he was highly critical of Cripps' campaign, his real fear was that such a high-profile approach would prevent constituency agreements. Despite Dalton's concern, it was significant that Labour's 1939 conference confirmed that local pacts were still possible. A resolution was put before the conference that called on the party to impose candidates in seats where divisional parties withdrew in favour of other candidates, but this led to criticism from other delegates who argued that local pacts were 'entirely different' from a national alliance. The resolution was then withdrawn because the NEC did not want the party to become 'too rigid on matters of this character'.[10]

Developments in the South-West also suggest that the Popular Front idea had more success at the local level. Within the Labour party, as Pimlott concluded, it was 'those without roots in the trade union movement … who were most inclined to support an alliance', and it was precisely these individuals, such as A.L. Rowse, prospective Labour candidate for Penryn & Falmouth and a key figure in the emergence of a regional alliance, who provided the leadership for Labour in the South-West.[11] In addition, the weakness of Labour, combined with the dominance of the National government, created a general consensus that there was 'no point in Liberals and Labour fighting each other in this part of the country'. The two Liberal Federations recognized the importance of obtaining straight fights with National government candidates, while in July 1939 Rowse claimed that even Transport House was in favour of an 'arrangement' in the South-West. This level of support, from both the national and regional level, therefore created a favourable climate for local pacts.[12]

It was the so-called 'miniature general election' of 1937 that provided the first test of this regional move towards realignment. In the summer of that year there were three by-elections: Plymouth Drake on 15 June; St Ives on 30 June; and North Dorset on 13 July. In the two earlier by-elections a *quid pro quo* was arranged, with every effort made in Drake to 'get Liberal support in return for Labour support' at St Ives. The Labour candidate for Drake produced a pamphlet targeted at progressive voters, while Liberals like John Foot addressed his election meetings.[13] In 1937 Walter Runciman, MP for St Ives, was elevated to the House of Lords. The Liberal Nationals selected Alan Beechman, a former president of the Union of University Liberal Societies, as their candidate, while the independent Liberals invited Isaac Foot to contest the election. Foot had the support of local Labour members, and he received a letter from Rowse who described him as the 'inheritor of the tradition of Cornish Radicalism'.[14] Similarly, in North Dorset the Liberal candidate advocated the idea of a progressive government in order to appeal to Labour supporters. But the opposition parties enjoyed rather mixed fortunes (see Table 4.1). Liberal headquarters concluded that the Drake by-election 'proved the impossibility of shepherding the Liberal vote into the Labour pen'. The St Ives and North Dorset results, however, confirmed that Labour voters would support an independent Liberal, and the National government came close to defeat in both constituencies.[15]

The Bridgwater by-election on 17 November 1938 was a sensational triumph for Popular Front supporters throughout the country. Since January of that year the local opposition parties, encouraged by Richard Acland, had been working towards an agreement. When the Conservative MP resigned the seat after his appointment as a High Court Judge,

Table 4.1: Parliamentary by-elections in the South-West, 1937–1939 (percentages).

	1935				By-election			
	National	Liberal	Labour	Other	National	Liberal	Labour	Other
Drake	58.3	—	41.7	—	58.8	—	41.2	—
St Ives	—	—	—	—	50.4	49.6		
North Dorset	50.1	37.9	5.2	6.8*	51.1	48.9	—	—
Bridgwater	56.8	23.4	19.8	—	46.8	—	—	53.2
North Cornwall	48.7	51.3	—	—	47.8	52.2	—	—

* An Independent Conservative candidate stood at North Dorset in 1935.

the Liberals invited Vernon Bartlett, a journalist and broadcaster, to stand as an Independent Progressive. There was a 'hard core' of Labour activists who were opposed, but on 5 November the local Labour party finally advised its supporters to vote for Bartlett.[16] In the event he won the seat from the Conservatives with a majority of 2,332 votes. The crucial factor in Bartlett's success was the rise in turnout (72.7 per cent to 82.3 per cent), which enabled Popular Front enthusiasts to claim that a united opposition would be more likely to attract the 'floating vote'. Local Conservatives, naturally shocked by Bartlett's victory, were concerned that this result would lead to a regional Popular Front that would undermine their supremacy in the four counties. As Frank Trethewey, the Liberal agent for Tavistock, remarked, 'every West of England seat could now be taken from the Tories'.[17]

Bartlett's success certainly increased the demands for co-operation. Sir Francis Acland described the result as a 'good example of what can be done if all working-class people, putting it broadly, will work together', while Rowse called on the government's opponents in Cornwall to 'follow the Bridgwater lead'.[18] It was not long before constituency associations throughout the region were copying this example. On 19 November Totnes Labour party passed a resolution calling for the local Liberal and Labour parties to adopt an Independent Progressive candidate, while four days later it was reported that another pact was being discussed in Exeter.[19] In December 1938 Weston-super-Mare DLP decided to co-operate with the Liberals in support of a joint candidate at the next election, while Taunton DLP were prepared to stand aside and support any 'first-class candidate' proposed by the Liberals.[20] During the same month R.H. Baker, the prospective Labour candidate for the marginal seat of Bodmin, resigned in favour of John Foot, the Liberal candidate. The pro-government *Western Morning News* admitted that Foot could feel 'justified in feeling his prospects greatly improved'. In a letter to Walter Layton, the chairman of the *News Chronicle,* Rowse revealed that he had been partly responsible for Baker's withdrawal and that he was working towards another agreement in Camborne.[21]

The North Cornwall by-election on 13 July 1939 provided another stimulus. This election was caused by the death on 9 June of Sir Francis Acland who had already announced his intention of resigning at the next election on the grounds of ill health. The new Liberal candidate was

Thomas Horabin, a 42-year-old business consultant, while E.R. Whitehouse was again selected as the Conservative candidate. Given the fact that Acland had held North Cornwall with only a narrow majority in 1935, the Liberals could well have been defeated if C.N. Wakley, the prospective Labour candidate, had contested the seat. Although Wakley wanted to stand in the by-election, party headquarters in London made the surprising announcement that the party would not be fielding a candidate. The political correspondent of the *Western Morning News* concluded that this intervention from the national party pointed to a 'tacit understanding to support the Liberals'.[22] Horabin's eventual victory, with a slightly increased majority, was hailed as a 'magnificent' victory for the Popular Front. Labour members and dissident Conservatives signed his nomination papers, while senior officials of the local Labour party actively supported the Liberal campaign. Whitehouse concluded that he had been defeated by a 'solid block of Opposition' consisting of 'all parties who opposed the National Government'.[23]

If there had been a general election in 1939, then, the National government would probably have been confronted by a united opposition in the majority of seats in the South-West. Although some local Labour parties, such as South Dorset and Tavistock, appeared reluctant to come to an agreement with the Liberals, the general trend was towards co-operation.[24] Although the Liberals, still entrenched as the main centre-left party in rural areas, were the obvious beneficiaries, it is difficult to predict how far this process would have restored their fortunes. A swing on the scale of Bridgwater would have led to a repeat of 1923 when the Liberals had won eighteen seats in the region, but this was unlikely because the other four by-elections had indicated that the National government was still quite popular (see Table 4.1). Nevertheless, the government's position was now vulnerable in a number of rural seats, such as Bodmin and North Dorset. Even a small swing of votes would have created a secure bloc of Liberal seats in the region for the first time since 1929.

The Second World War effectively removed this opportunity. Political changes at Westminster, symbolized by the creation of an all-party coalition under Winston Churchill in May 1940, naturally undermined the momentum for a Popular Front. Labour and the Liberals fought the 1945 election as rival parties, and there were very few constituencies where the Socialists allowed the Liberals a straight fight against the Conservatives. This meant that in the rural backwaters of Britain, where the Liberals could still poll a respectable vote in 1945, the swing against the Conservatives was not translated into parliamentary victories. Although the National parties suffered a major defeat in 1945, it might have been even greater if the opposition vote had been united since 97 of their 213 MPs were returned on a minority vote. The South-West was a good example. Only two seats in the region (North Cornwall and North Dorset) were not contested by Labour and the Liberals emerged as the victors. But in former Liberal strongholds, such as Tavistock and St Ives, the National parties were returned on a minority vote, and in terms of seats the anti-Conservative parties were not so successful as they had been in previous centre-left landslides.

Table 4.2: Parliamentary results in the South-West for selected elections.

Election	Conservative	Liberal	Labour	Other
1906	6	28	—	—
1923	8	18	1	—
1929	16	8	2	1
1945	18	2	6	1

The danger of a split in the opposition vote was recognized before the election. T.H. Keast, the chairman of Bodmin Labour party, predicted a few months before that 'we are again to see enacted the European pre-war tragedy of the forces of progress fighting among themselves', while this concern led the former chairman of Bideford Labour Party to sign the nomination papers of Mark Bonham Carter, the Liberal candidate for Barnstaple.[25] Even the Communists were still in favour of a Popular Front. Isabel Brown resigned as their candidate for Plymouth Sutton in favour of the Labour nominee, and at a meeting of the Redruth Communist party she called on Labour candidates in rural seats to stand down as Cornwall and Devon had a Liberal tradition.[26] An alliance on the centre-left of British politics was also one of the objectives of Radical Action, a ginger group within the Liberal party. Horabin was one of its leading members, and he played a key role in attempts to obtain a pact. In his own constituency of North Cornwall he demonstrated the potential benefits of such a strategy by forming an alliance with other left-wing parties, and in 1945 he was actively supported by the divisional Labour party. Horabin accepted that a swing to the left had taken place in Britain during the war, but he believed that this opportunity would be lost if the anti-Conservative parties failed to form a 'Coalition of the Left'. Before the election he claimed that the group could, as Baines put it, 'forge local deals with Labour, elect fifty MPs and act as a pressure group to force a Labour government to carry out fundamental change'.[27]

This obviously raises the question as to why some type of Popular Front was not formed in 1945. There is no doubt that there was opposition to a pact from the national level. When Keast and his supporters in Bodmin called on the divisional Labour party to support John Foot, Transport House responded by disaffiliating the town branch.[28] Yet the North Cornwall and North Dorset examples suggest that a certain amount of independence still lay with local parties. Timing was possibly of crucial importance in some seats. In 1945 more members of the armed services stood as Liberals than for any other party, but armed servicemen were released for only the three weeks preceding polling day and the wives and sisters of service candidates were 'virtually fighting the election' during the early stages of the campaign. In many cases, such as Bodmin, a Labour nominee would probably have been adopted before the Liberal candidate returned home, and having committed themselves to contesting a particular seat it was unlikely that the party would be persuaded to withdraw.[29] Horabin, in contrast, had remained active in politics throughout the war, and had established himself as a prominent Radical at the national level. Even in 1942 local Labour activists were declaring that they would support him at the next election.[30]

Perhaps the underlying reason for the failure to create a Popular Front lay with the Liberals themselves. Before the Second World War there had been a growing realization amongst leading Liberals that the party could only hope to share power in a coalition, but by 1945 many activists were convinced that they were in a stronger position than at any time since the 1920s.[31] The party therefore reverted to its old stance of acting as an independent force, which at least appealed to many Liberal activists. Gorley Putt, prospective Liberal candidate for Torquay, found that the 'old Liberals' were more concerned to 'flatter themselves as a happy band of brothers than to win over supporters from the big battalions. They combined pride in the Liberal big battalions of 1906 with a sense of moral outrage at anything but very small hand-picked battalions today'.[32] When this independent role was combined with the party's vague 'middle of the road' image, it was perhaps not surprising that Labour was unwilling to form an alliance with the Liberals. The *New Statesman* concluded that the Liberals were 'divided between disguised Conservatives and Socialists who were too timid to face the logic of their own thinking'.[33]

The party leadership must therefore be held largely responsible for failing to create the right conditions. In the late 1930s Sinclair had played a key role in forming a consensus in favour of inter-party co-operation. By the early 1940s, however, he favoured a continuation of the Churchill coalition, and this created tensions within the party, particularly at the 1943 Assembly, over the whole issue of pacts with other parties. From an electoral perspective it was surely in the interests of the party's national leadership to have maintained the momentum towards a Liberal–Labour alliance in rural areas like the South-West, particularly as Labour also appeared weaker at this time. By 1945 it was simply too late for individuals within the party to call on Labour candidates to withdraw since the Socialists were already preparing for the election.

Organization and Direction

Developments during the war had a wider impact on South-West Liberalism. In September 1939 the party appeared to be in a stronger position in the region than at any time since the late 1920s. An early adoption of candidates and the prospect of an immediate election, due by 1940 at the latest, had provided a stimulus for organizational improvements. The wider framework also seemed more positive since the national party had accepted the principle of 'concentration' on target seats, while Sinclair's leadership provided a clear sense of direction. Yet the war effectively removed these advantages. Liberal organization at the local level was considerably weakened by 1945, while Sinclair, who became Secretary of State for Air in May 1940, was unable to provided effective leadership. Above all, the party lacked an obvious political role. The Liberals were in no position to campaign as a party of government, but they lacked an alternative vision that could convince a wider section of the electorate that Liberalism was still a credible and relevant force.

The 1935 election had revealed that there was an urgent need for reorganization within the party. Although a commission on organization was appointed under the chairmanship of Lord Meston, the conventional view amongst historians is that the report concentrated too much on the national level. Cook claimed that Meston failed to 'pay much attention to the constituencies—the weakest part of the party', and this view has been supported by Baines who concluded that the party's 'strength in the constituencies continued to decay' after 1935.[34] However, the situation was certainly more positive in the South-West at this time. Following the reforms introduced at the national level, the Devon and Cornwall Federation announced its own plans for reorganization. Mass meetings were held and local parties were placed on a firmer footing, while John Day, the treasurer of the federation, explained that this was just the 'first stage in a scheme to put Liberal candidates in every constituency in Devon and Cornwall'.[35] Although there were setbacks, such as in Exeter, it was evident by 1939 that a great deal of progress had been achieved. Apart from the eight seats that had been contested in 1935, the Liberals also had candidates for St Ives, Tiverton and Honiton, which would have meant the largest number of candidates since 1929. This was in contrast to the previous election when the party had entered the campaign in total confusion with only a small number of definite candidates.

Admittedly, in some constituencies in the eastern counties there was likely to be a repeat of 1935 when candidates were selected at the last minute. The secretary of the Western Counties Federation reported in June 1939 that some local parties 'hoped it might be possible to run a Liberal candidate when the occasion arises'.[36] Even so, with the exception of Frome and South Dorset, the party appeared to be better prepared. In East Dorset, where the Liberals had entered the previous election in total confusion, the party enjoyed more energetic leadership in the latter half of the decade from Darvall. It is significant that when he resigned in July 1939 to contest the Hythe by-election, another candidate was immediately selected in order to maintain enthusiasm.[37] In 1938 the Yeovil Liberals appointed a younger agent who developed an efficient organization, while Brown encouraged his supporters to adopt 'new methods of appeal, new kinds of meetings and publicity'.[38]

Similarly, the West Dorset Liberals made 'encouraging' progress in organization and finance. Their Conservative opponents, in contrast, were faced with a decline in both members and income.[39]

Candidates have traditionally played an important role in the region because organization and enthusiasm have required an individual on which to focus. In that sense the election debacle of 1935 actually assisted reorganization because it revealed the need for improvement. Thus, in 1936 the secretary of the regional federation reported that in Camborne and Torquay the contest had had a 'stimulating effect and they have started to prepare for the next one'.[40] Developments in Bodmin also pointed to the role of the candidate. When Isaac Foot formally stood down as the party's prospective candidate in July 1937 in order to concentrate on St Ives, it was not until the following year that the local party selected one of his sons, John Foot, as his successor. Although he benefited from his family connections and it was emphasized that he was following in the 'path of his father', he proved to be an able candidate in his own right. Enthusiasm was apparently 'beginning to wane' in the division, but John Foot launched 'an intensive campaign which breathed new life into a declining organization'. An example of his success was the progress made by the Young Liberals. The 1939 report of the Liskeard branch concluded that there was now a 'healthy financial position, an increase in membership and a record of achievement to be proud of'.[41]

A general acceptance of the need for some form of planned narrow front created a positive framework for this regional revival. In June 1938 at a meeting of leading party members in London it was 'agreed that there ought to be a real measure of concentration' upon about forty seats which the party would 'resolve to win' at the next election. Those individuals who attended the meeting recognized that this new approach would threaten the 'national character of the Party', and it was therefore decided that this new plan had to be kept 'strictly confidential'.[42] Advocates of a narrow front were helped by the attempts to form an alliance with Labour. The logic of an electoral pact was that the party would only contest a limited number of seats, and the objective of a 'Progressive Government' provided a credible reason for electors to still vote Liberal. In February 1939 Darvall and the secretary of the Liberal Party Organisation discussed the possibility of negotiations with Labour over the question of which seats the two parties would contest. Darvall said that the party would in any case be in no position to contest a large number of seats, and it was essential to avoid a repeat of 1935 when the party had talked of sufficient candidates to form a government but only produced a mere 159:

> If no arrangement proves possible it will still be wise for us, having regard to the candidates, agents, speakers and money at our disposal to fight not more than 200 seats … [We] should make a virtue out of necessity and instead of appearing to aim at hundreds of candidates … we should announce in advance that we were nominating only a limited number (in order not to split the Opposition poll) and were aiming at 100 Liberal MPs and a Progressive Government.[43]

Such a view fitted in with Sinclair's belief that the old *raison d'être* of a Liberal government had to be a long-term objective. As Cowling remarks, his immediate aim was to bring the 'Liberals out of their hibernations'.[44] In order to achieve this objective the party had to demonstrate its potential strength in by-elections, and then strengthen their position in the House of Commons at the next election. Sinclair saw the North Dorset by-election as 'our big opportunity'; while at the general election target seats like West Dorset had 'to be won at all costs'.[45] Apart from concentrating the party's limited financial resources on such seats, it was decided that headquarters should ensure an 'adequate supply of good speakers' who could generate a sense of enthusiasm for the Liberal cause. This had been demonstrated in the St Ives by-election. At the beginning of the campaign Foot found a 'general indifference' on the part of the electors, while he had to 'start practically with no organization'. By the end of the campaign visits by individuals like Viscount Samuel and Viscount Clifden had helped Foot to attract large and enthusiastic crowds, and this was repeated in 1939 when Horabin's by-election campaign could depend on a constant supply of prominent speakers like Bartlett, Sinclair and Lloyd George.[46] The party was also in the position to organise its biggest autumn campaign since the late 1920s, with Sinclair preparing to make a 2,000 miles tour of England in October 1939 supported by a convoy of cars, loudspeakers, MPs and candidates.[47]

Following the outbreak of war, however, the three principal parties decided to postpone municipal elections and the next general election for the duration of the war. Without the stimulus of open electoral rivalry there was a considerable reduction in political activity, while the work of local political associations was further hampered by the war effort. According to Churchill, this gave an advantage to Labour in 1945 since Conservative activists, particularly agents, had either joined the armed services or were fully involved with war work. Labour, by comparison, could rely on a solid nucleus of trade union supporters who had remained at home in reserved occupations. Historians of the period have been divided over the issue. Addison claimed that Labour did not have any great advantage over the Conservatives. Only a 'very few' Conservative associations were 'inactive' since headquarters had encouraged branches to concentrate on war work, while by 1945 the party actually had a greater number of full-time agents than Labour. Jefferys, however, has concluded that Labour was able to seize the advantage since the party's 'reliance on trade unionists permitted a much high level of activity'.[48]

The state of the Liberal organization was not considered in this debate. While this is not really surprising in view of the fact that the party was no longer a serious contender for government, it could be argued that good organization was even more essential to a third party. Labour and the Conservatives could both rely on the support of a significant section of the electorate, but the Liberals could only claim to be a major force in a limited number of scattered constituencies. An effective organization was a key factor in preventing these seats from being assimilated into the national political culture. Apart from disseminating propaganda, which could counteract the growing tendency to consider politics in terms of the conventional Left/Right divide, the mere presence of such an organization would constantly remind voters that, despite its national weakness, the party was still a credible force at the local level. Yet, so far as the South-West was concerned, the war years witnessed a general collapse of Liberal organization. One of the positive developments of the late 1930s had been the decision of party headquarters to provide some financial assistance for the regional federations. In September 1939, however, the party announced that it was ending this support for the duration of the war. The Western Counties Federation had to close the regional offices of the party in Bristol, and terminate the employment of paid officers. Financial restrictions meant that the federation was unable to provide effective supervision of local associations. By February 1940 the area secretary was already warning that there was a danger that organization in some constituencies would 'drift' if essential activity was ended.[49]

Individuals had always played a significant role in generating enthusiasm and interest in the work of the constituency organization. Yet many of the candidates that were adopted in the late 1930s were in their twenties and thirties, and on the outbreak of war they were called up for active service in the armed forces. By February 1941 the secretary of the Western Counties Federation reported that Chappell in West Dorset was the only candidate in the east of the region who was not engaged in some form of national service.[50] It was only to be expected that local branches of the party would become inactive. An example from the far west suggests that meetings were extremely infrequent during the war years. John Foot served as an army officer during the war, and he made only a few visits to Bodmin after 1939. In these circumstances there was no incentive for the association to hold regular meetings, and the executive committee apparently did not hold a single meeting between February 1941 and May 1945.[51] Visits by national politicians were also rare during this period. At the end of 1944 Wilfred Roberts, the Liberal MP for North Cumberland, called on Sinclair to participate in a national campaign, but the Liberal leader refused this request on the grounds that Churchill and Attlee were not addressing party rallies. Roberts replied that the other parties had a number of well-known personalities who could speak at meetings, and he warned that there was a danger that the 'memory' of Sinclair's leadership before the war could fade if he did not 'give more of a lead in future'.[52]

In the event, however, it was not until the election campaign that the Liberal leader took an active role in party politics. Although Sinclair visited the South-West as part of his election tour of Britain, local Liberals probably obtained little benefit from his visit. His two-day tour of the region was described as a 'whirlwind affair' by the local press since instead of concentrating on the party's key seats, he attempted to visit as many constituencies as possible. When he arrived at Torquay, 'half asleep with fatigue', he began by praising Putt as the 'fine young candidate for Newquay'.[53] Brief visits during an election were obviously no substitute for a long-term publicity campaign. But this was just a typical example of the party's failure to formulate a wartime strategy.

The disruption caused by the war effort presented major problems for a third force like the Liberals, and the national party should have ensured that its position was maintained at the local level. Although it must be acknowledged that Labour and the Conservatives also experienced problems at this time, it could be said that the task of the Liberals was easier in the sense that they just had to concentrate on a limited number of seats. National headquarters could at least have ensured that those basic requirements for victory, such as good candidates, competent agents and effective organization, existed in the party's target seats.

The general weakness of Liberal organization became obvious by 1945. When Putt visited the Torquay division at the end of the previous year he was only able to meet a small number of local 'worthies' since 'party activity had dwindled away'. During the first few months of 1945 he had to spend his brief periods of leave from the Royal Navy in a desperate attempt to establish new ward branches.[54] The party suffered from weak organization even in those seats where it had survived as a major force. In 1935 the Tavistock Liberals had come a good second to the Conservatives, but only forty party stalwarts were present in 1945 when Isaac Foot was adopted as the party's candidate. The local party also experienced serious problems in raising sufficient money to contest the seat.[55] Totnes Liberal Association had 'attained a high degree of efficiency' in the 1930s, but it became virtually moribund after the outbreak of war. In March 1945 the president called on members to revive the party's organization throughout the division. It is evident that this appeal was not heeded since voters in the South Hams district did not even know that a Liberal was contesting the seat.[56] Admittedly, there were some associations that remained relatively active. A new agent was appointed in North Cornwall in February 1944, and he was able to build up an 'efficient machine' throughout the division, while it was curious that in Tiverton, a seat which had not been contested since 1929, the local party held frequent debates on political issues during the war. Yet the secretary of the Western Counties Federation provided the most appropriate conclusion on the general state of the party's organization. He remarked after the election that the party's agents were 'either brought out of retirement, or new and inexperienced and in no case had they had sufficient time to get to know their constituencies properly. Organization in most divisions was scanty, and helpers generally scarce'.[57]

This collapse in organization effectively undermined the party's new electoral policy. The pre-war goal of Liberal participation in a Progressive government was abandoned since party activists were in a more idealistic mood at the end of the war. Opinion polls pointed to a new revival, while Liberal prestige was enhanced when Sir William Beveridge joined the party in September 1944 and in the following month held Berwick-upon-Tweed in a by-election. This encouraged the Liberals to campaign as an alternative government. A meeting in 1944 between Putt and Sir Percy Harris, the party's Chief Whip, provides a revealing insight into Liberal thinking. Putt was told that the party was 'struggling to assemble a stage army of new candidates' in time for the next election. Harris admitted that the party's prospects were poor in the vast majority of these seats, but he believed that it would 'encourage ... lonely pioneers at other more favoured places in the battle line':

> The great need of the hour would be a sufficient body of candidates in unwinnable constituencies, whose sacrificial presence was deemed to offer a specious affirmative to the one question the front-line candidates ... would otherwise be unable to answer. That question was simply: 'Yes, oh yes—but can you people form a government?'.[58]

But the party was simply in no position to achieve its aim of 600 candidates. Only 307 Liberals came forward by nomination day, and this meant that, as in 1935, the party lacked a clearly defined role in British politics. The number of Liberal candidates was really too small for the party to claim that it could form a government, while yet again there was insufficient time to create a secure electoral niche. A few candidates, such as Isaac Foot, claimed that the party could still theoretically form a government if sufficient voters supported the old cause, while radicals like Horabin and John Foot expressed their preference for a Labour-led administration. Most Liberals, however, tended to appeal for support on the grounds that they could 'hold the balance' in a hung parliament, but the prospect of stalemate merely strengthened the Left/Right divide which had so often undermined Liberalism in the past. Sinclair, whose effective absence from party politics had caused this lack of direction, could only tell voters in the South-West that he reserved 'complete freedom of action for the Liberal Party to decide for itself' whether to support a Conservative or a Labour administration.[59] Such a statement was perhaps necessary for a 'middle of the road' party that was attempting to attract votes from the two main parties, but it reinforced the claims of its opponents that a hung parliament would produce confusion and weak government. Once again the political events of the Second World War had placed the Liberals at a disadvantage.

Liberalism and the Region

Finally, consideration should be given to the changing fortunes of the south-western Liberals within a social and economic context. On the eve of the war it appeared that the party was finally developing a new role. Sinclair was keen to develop the image of modern Liberalism, and the party was targeting key groups like non-unionized workers, pensioners and farmers. This line had particularly relevance at the local level because of the electoral significance of such groups. By 1939, with remarkable similarity to developments in the 1950s, the Liberals were combining the grievances of target groups and presenting the party as the voice of the countryside. Yet the political vacuum of the early 1940s meant that the Liberals lost this distinctive image, while demographic change in the South-West, including the presence of evacuees and wartime labour forces, further undermined their electoral position

When Sinclair became Liberal leader in November 1935 he set out to provide the party with a clear sense of direction. In contrast to the paralysis and confusion of the early 1930s, he outlined a two-stage approach to policy formulation. From 1935 to 1937 the party would concentrate on the 'exposition of the fundamental principles of Liberalism', such as peace, freedom and employment, which would impress upon the public a clear idea of what the party stood for. After 1937 'Hitler's preparations for whatever he intends to do' would be complete and this would lead to a 'new situation' in regard to foreign affairs. In addition, during the years running up to the next general election there would be a 'real need of a re-statement of Liberal policy, putting so much cutting edge on it as we can'. The key factor in his approach was his emphasis on the party's image. He concluded that the disaster of 1935 had occurred because the electorate did not 'believe in Liberal principles' and had little faith in the party's ability to 'carry any of its proposals'. The party had a variety of policies contained in the

Liberal Way and *Liberal Address to the Nation,* but they had been 'too diffuse' for a 'fighting policy'.[60]

This view was reinforced at the regional level. For example, James Brown, the party's candidate for Wells and representative of the National League of Young Liberals on the Liberal Party Council, believed that the party should give more attention to the public's perception of British politics. Brown stated that many 'people with no party ties had a rough idea' of what Labour and the Conservatives stood for, and what the Liberals 'needed to do was to set up a clear idea of what Liberalism meant'. The basic problem was that their opponents and the press had 'built up in ... people's minds' the idea that the party stood for one thing only—Free Trade—while at the same time 'the whole doctrine of Free Trade was derided'. The party had also elevated proportional representation to the 'first place' in the Liberal programme instead of emphasizing social and economic issues that appealed to the electorate. Brown believed that they had to concentrate instead on concern over poverty and the problems facing the rural community, while slogans such as 'Ownership for All' and 'The Fight for the Disinherited' would be used in order to 'impress the Liberal aim on people's minds'.[61]

Moreover, the Liberals were determined to change their image as a party of the past and win over the support of younger voters. In a move which was to be repeated some twenty years later with Grimond's New Liberalism, policy statements attempted to project a modern image, with titles like *Liberal Policy for Today's Needs* and *The Modern Mission of the Liberal Party.* Another example was the *Liberal Charter for the Under-Thirties,* which advocated such policies as reform of the education system, government investigations into 'blind-alley jobs' and the 'opening up of the professions'.[62] In order to present a fresh and radical image at Westminster the party encouraged younger members to become candidates. The South-West was an ideal area in which to implement this plan because of its considerable number of winnable seats. In February 1938 Brown said that in the 'West of England ... there were at least six men and women of his own generation [such as Frank Byers (North Dorset) and Philip Hopkins (Bath)] who had been adopted ... during the past few months, and more were coming'. Headquarters even suggested that a seat in the South West could be found for Jo Grimond, the party's future leader.[63]

This emphasis on a modern image could theoretically have caused further divisions. As the secretary of the Devon and Cornwall Federation remarked, the 'trouble with the older Liberals [was] that in the realm of economics' they believed that there was 'one simple remedy—Free Trade', while younger activists argued that it was the 'duty of the state' to tackle social and economic problems. In the event, however, the party remained reasonably united over domestic policy. This was partly due to the fact that, as Rowse commented, the 'greater portion of the reactionary Liberals' were already voting for the National government parties, and the majority of those who remained were prepared to support more interventionist policies.[64] Above all, the Liberals proved more adept at focusing on issues which both fitted in with the party's traditional ideology and yet could prove popular with voters. In 1937 the party launched a campaign pointing out how tariffs had led to an increase in the cost of living, and a nation-wide petition collected 800,000 signatures throughout Britain. At a meeting of federation secretaries it was stated that the petition had received an 'enthusiastic reception' from Cornwall to Somerset.[65] The state of the Old Age pension was another rallying cry that had a nostalgic association with pre-war Liberalism, while it was considered 'practically the only domestic question that aroused any interest' in 1939. It certainly emerged as one of the main issues in the North Cornwall by-election, and the Liberal agent told Sinclair that Horabin's 'stand for larger Old Age Pensions has been a good one to gather support'. Indeed, the Liberal victory forced the government to hold an inquiry into the subject.[66]

Another issue of particular significance for South-West Liberalism was the growing discontent of the agricultural community. Many farmers had already been critical of aspects of government policy earlier in the decade, but a fall in agricultural prices, a rise in the cost of feeding stuffs and the continuing 'drift from the land' had made matters worse. Furthermore, while agricultural legislation continued to be introduced in the late 1930s, it could be said that the National government under Neville Chamberlain did not appear to represent agricultural interests in the same way that his predecessor had done. Whereas Baldwin had been able to evoke an image of rural England, Chamberlain with his Birmingham connections symbolized the importance of manufacturing industry and urban society. By the winter of 1938–9 local branches of the NFU were seriously discussing the idea of backing Independent or opposition party candidates in protest at the perceived indifference of central government. As Charles Smith pointed out in the *Fabian Quarterly* in 1939, this 'situation was extremely dangerous' for the Conservatives because they relied on the traditional loyalty of the rural seats to win a majority in the Commons.[67]

Agricultural discontent was very much in evidence at the Bridgwater by-election in November 1938. Historians have usually assumed that Bartlett's victory was due to public revulsion against the Munich agreement. Maclean suggested that it was probably a 'rare case in British electoral history of a by-election whose unusual result can be traced to a foreign policy issue', while Eatwell concluded that it could really only be interpreted in 'terms of opposition to Neville Chamberlain's foreign policy'. These views were supported by Bartlett's claim that the 'country people [were] passionately interested in foreign affairs and frankly bored by the agricultural part of his speeches'.[68] However, it was understandable that Bartlett should emphasize the importance of foreign affairs because he wanted to use his victory to change government policy on this issue. While Munich should not be ignored, more attention must be given to the agricultural vote. Opposition to the government amongst members of the Somerset NFU was steadily growing during the weeks leading up to the election, while the Conservative candidate, frequently on the defensive over the issue, had to appeal to the farming community to 'support the Government, vote Conservative and go on grumbling'. Smith also claimed that discontent over the state of agriculture had contributed to Bartlett's victory, while the *News Chronicle* pointed out that the main group to go over to Bartlett was the farming community in the western part of the constituency. In addition, the local press reported that while farmers and farm labourers 'might talk about foreign politics, they were much more interested in the Government's agricultural policy'.[69] Brown concluded that the Bridgwater result indicated that the farmers could well desert the Conservatives at the next election:

> There was once a tradition that the Conservative Party stood for the agricultural section of the community. They never did very much about it, except to make vague promises to the farmer ... Country folk are supposed to be Conservative by nature, and

despite the ineptitude … of successive Conservative Governments this impression remains. Now at long last, things are changing. The farmer is turning.[70]

The Liberals were eager to establish themselves as the new champions of the agricultural community. Wilfred Roberts, the party's parliamentary spokesman on agriculture, argued that on electoral grounds alone the 'agriculturalist must … receive attention [if his] old association with the Conservative Party [was] to be broken'.[71] The Liberals believed that they were in a natural position to exploit any discontent because they still remained a significant force in many rural seats, especially in the South-West. Apart from developing policies that would favour the dairy farmers and pig producers of the region, the party exploited local discontent over the Tithe Redemption Act of 1936. The president of North Cornwall Liberal Association informed Sinclair that one of his 'farmer friends [was] of the opinion that if Liberals were to adopt the policy of removing the burden of the tithes … and placing it upon the general Taxpayer it would win the next General Election'. Both men naturally understood that tithes would not have the same appeal at the national level, but they also realized the benefit of exploiting the issue in rural seats. During the North Cornwall by-election Horabin argued that the 'Tithe should revert to be a National Charge', and his 'clear position' won him the support of the farming community.[72]

The Liberals also attempted to project a wider image as the party of the countryside. In a move foreshadowing developments in the 1950s and 1960s the party's candidates exploited the grievances of interest groups in the region. This was encouraged by Sinclair who had established a reputation as a good constituency MP for his own rural seat of Caithness & Sutherland by raising local issues and considering how parliamentary legislation 'affected the local people and might influence their voting pattern'. As party leader he used the same technique on a wider level, and before speaking in a constituency asked for information on particular issues concerning the local community.[73] In the North Dorset and St Ives by-elections in 1937 the party had campaigned on local issues and championed the cause of unorganized groups like fishermen and agricultural labourers. A national report concluded that these by-elections had shown that issues like holidays with pay and the improvement of working conditions appealed especially to unorganized workers who were 'ignored by the Labour Party'.[74] This provided a distinctive role for the party in areas like the rural South-West where trade unionism was generally weak. By 1939 the party was able to present a package of measures targeted at rural voters, and Brown could claim that the countryside was no longer the 'private concern' of the Conservatives:

> To prevent the present drift from the land, we will not only ensure better wages, but will also provide … more opportunities of obtaining smallholdings at fair rents. The holidays with pay scheme must be applied to all … There must be provision for free transport to hospitals and consultation with specialists. The countryside needs more district nurses. Rural education must be improved … In a sentence we intend to give some meaning to the phrase 'England's green and pleasant land'.[75]

However, the party's unity and progress over policy formulation was undermined during the early 1940s. De Groot has argued that with Sinclair committed to his work at the Air Ministry after 1940, the 'rank and file of the party wandered erratically in various directions'.[76] The libertarian wing of the party wanted to emphasize the need for free trade and private enterprise, while the radicals advocated collectivist ideas like the nationalization of public utilities. By the time of the 1945 election the party was unable to devise an acceptable compromise, and its campaign pamphlet, *The Radical Programme of the Liberal Party,* did not even mention the nationalization issue. Younger Liberals believed that the party's subsequent policies were 'dry, unimaginative and unattractive', and by failing to tackle contentious issues the party certainly lost the opportunity to present a distinctive image.[77] It was also significant that the radical wing, the main catalyst for new ideas in the late 1930s, was now weaker. Sir Richard Acland and his supporters moved far to the left of official Liberalism with the creation of Common Wealth in 1942, while many younger activists served with the armed forces. This ensured that Radical Action, rather than acting as a positive force that could take the lead on party policy, effectively became a disgruntled opposition to mainstream Liberalism.

In addition, by 1945 the party had lost its potential role as the voice of the countryside. While six years earlier the Liberals had appeared the likely beneficiaries of rural discontent, agriculture was obviously of central importance in wartime. At a meeting of the Cornish branch of the NFU in May 1945 the former chairman declared that there was 'no subject on which there was such general agreement among all parties ... as there was in regard to agriculture'. Another farmer echoed this view by claiming that the 'best policy' was to place agriculture above party politics.[78] The need to increase agricultural production had also led to a rise in union membership in rural areas in the eastern counties, and in 1945 it was reported that the National Union of Agricultural Workers had given a 'good deal of support' to Labour in rural seats like West Dorset. Even the party's traditional supporters from the farming community were no longer as loyal as they had been in the past. It was reported that many small farmers were now looking to Labour, while several Liberal farmers in North Cornwall signed the nomination papers of the Conservative candidate because they were opposed to Horabin's support for land nationalization.[79]

Since agriculture was at this stage no longer regarded as a controversial issue, it was left to the individual candidate to appeal to

Figure 4.1: Grandson of a Liberal Prime Minister: Mark Bonham Carter (MP for Torrington 1958–59) and party members at Barnstaple in 1945.

the farming community on personal grounds. It is perhaps significant that Frank Byers, who captured the rural seat of North Dorset, was apparently the only Liberal candidate in the region who had any practical experience of the industry. The other parties, in contrast, had a number of candidates who were involved in farming. For example, the Conservative candidate for Tavistock was presented as 'a man of Devon, a man interested in agriculture [and] a man of wide experience'.[80] In West Dorset Chappell was forced to resign as candidate shortly before the 1945 election because of ill health, and the local Liberals had to make a last-minute decision to adopt George Newsom, a barrister from London. In these circumstances farmers were more likely to vote either for Digby, a Dorset landowner, or for John Kane, the Labour candidate, who was a local dairy farmer and a member of the NFU.[81]

But increasing evidence of social change in the region suggests that there were wider problems for rural Liberalism. Even back in 1935 Isaac Foot was lamenting that the 'habits of the countryside have undergone ... revolutionary changes. The contained life of the village has been broken in upon by the convenience of motor cars and other modern transport ... The local "character" tends to disappear; habits, clothing, speech becomes more generally assimilated'.[82] It was this sense of isolation from the outside world that had assisted the survival of the Liberal party. External influences, such as class politics, were of secondary importance to local issues, while loyalty to the Liberal cause was regarded as a venerated tradition. Yet traditional party loyalties were not so strong in 1945 as in pre-war elections. The *Express and Echo* remarked that in Devon there was a 'notable change [as] compared with previous elections. Instead of being unswervingly "Party" in their attitude, quite a large proportion of those attending meetings had an examining frame of mind.' Similarly, the *Wells Journal* and the *Mid-Devon Advertiser* commented on the marked absence of party colours.[83] A decline in traditional voting was more of a problem for the Liberals than for the other parties since it was one of the few reasons why voters were still likely to support the party. The majority of voters, particularly in rural areas, remained loyal to the party that they had always supported, and this helped to ensure the survival of Liberalism. The *Cornish Guardian* concluded that what actually happened in 1945 was that while there was an increase in the number of 'floating voters', most people still supported the party which they had been 'brought up in since childhood'.[84] Nevertheless, even the limited decline in traditional voting posed a serious problem for the Liberals, which was exploited by the Labour candidate for Wells who declared that Liberalism could make no relevant contribution to modern British politics:

> Liberalism was dead or so near dying as made no difference. No-one could equal the old Liberal leaders such as Cobden, Bright, Gladstone and others as reformers, and he was quite certain if they were alive to-day they would be leaders of the Labour Party.[85]

In addition, the old Liberal–Nonconformist agenda appeared less relevant. Back in the immediate pre-war period the Liberal party was still regarded by many people in the South-West as the natural champion of nonconformist interests. Isaac Foot's campaign at the St Ives by-election in 1937 was supported by leading nonconformist ministers like the Rev. Henry Carter, while a national inquest into the result concluded that his decision to make 'absolutely no compromise on … Temperance' had appealed to voters.[86] On a superficial level little had changed during the war. For example, in November 1944 the Newton Abbot and District Temperance Council was still able to hold a 'successful series of meetings' in South Devon. Mrs Brown, one of the guest speakers, claimed that a 'huge amount of money was being wasted' on alcohol rather than being spent on the war effort and reconstruction, and she added that the movement had a new task in opposing the granting of licences in blitzed areas. Nevertheless, Brown had to admit that most people were indifferent to the ideals of temperance. She was concerned that even some Free Church ministers believed that the 'need for Bands of Hope had passed', and emphasized the need to attract the support of the younger generation. Similarly, in May 1945 a minister in Devon lamented that temperance was being 'overlooked in these days'.[87]

Only in the rural heartland of Liberalism centred on the Cornwall–Devon border was religious nonconformity still a force to be reckoned with. Both Conservative and Liberal activists in Bodmin regarded the temperance issue as a major dividing line between the two parties in 1945, while the Rev. Richard Ryke, ex-president of the Methodist Conference, was symbolically on the Liberal platform at one of Mark Bonham Carter's meetings in Barnstaple. Many Methodist preachers publicly campaigned for Isaac Foot in Tavistock, and it was quite common for nonconformists to carry bibles to Liberal meetings.[88] Temperance was still an election issue in North Cornwall. The Conservative candidate was opposed to the cause, but Horabin promised local Methodists that he would support their demands for Local Option and a change in the law so as to prevent the registration of 'new undesirable clubs'.[89] Liberalism, sustained by the strength of religious non-conformity, therefore remained a major force in all four constituencies after 1945.

Finally, consideration should be given to the way in which changes in the composition of the electorate had an impact on the election results. A general election had not been held since 1935, and natural demographic change was obviously greater than it would have been for the normal four to five year period between elections. Electors under the age of 30 had not had the chance to vote in an election before 1945, while many older voters, who were perhaps more likely to remain loyal to the Liberals, had died since the last election. The family voting tradition probably limited the full effect of demographic change in isolated rural areas like the Cornwall–Devon border, but Labour apparently obtained the support of the majority of younger voters in seats like Penryn & Falmouth.[90] Moreover, the disruption caused by the war had quite a major impact upon the nature of the region's electorate. In Plymouth many residents had left blitzed areas in the city for accommodation elsewhere, and the total electorate of the city had declined by 21,371 in comparison with 1935 (see Table 4.2). This factor assisted the Labour party to capture all of the three Plymouth divisions since many of those voters who had left the city were residential voters who tended to support the Conservatives. Labour, in contrast, benefited from the fact that the number of workers employed in the Royal Dockyard, the city's main industry, had remained steady. Elsewhere in the South-West there had been a significant increase in the number of voters. This was particularly the case in individual constituencies like Weston-super-Mare (+20,670), Frome (+17,372) and East Dorset (+16,748).[91]

During the war a considerable number of evacuees from urban areas, particularly London, had moved to the region. While some families had returned home by the time of the general election, there were reports in rural constituencies like Barnstaple (+9,290) and North Cornwall (+7,842 since June 1939) that 'many evacuees' who were left behind cast

113

their votes in the South-West. There were also many factories in the region which were engaged in production for the war effort, and labour forces had been moved to the South-West from other areas of the country. This was particularly the case in Barnstaple, Tavistock, where the electorate had increased by 13,029 since 1935, and the Somerset constituencies of Frome, Yeovil (+10,792), Bridgwater (+10,529) and Taunton (+9,244).[92]

Table 4.3: A comparison of the South-Western electorate in 1935 and 1945.

	1935	1945	Change	Average per seat
Somerset	336,286	419,696	+83,410	+11,916
Devon	288,412	340,703	+52,291	+8,185
Dorset	173,098	198,988	+25,890	+6,473
Cornwall	181,848	202,842	+20,994	+5,249
Plymouth	139,089	117,718	–21,371	–7,124

Political observers concluded that the majority of these temporary voters supported Labour. For example, in 1935 the Liberals had come second in Yeovil with 12,482 votes (33.1 per cent), while Labour was still in third place on 7,567 (20.1 per cent). However, several thousand workers had moved to the area during the war because of the importance of the Fleet Air Arm base at Yeovilton and the Westland defence industry, and the vast majority of these new residents backed Labour in 1945. This view is supported by the election results. The combined fall in the Conservative–Liberal vote was only 2,250, but Labour attracted an extra 9,074 votes. Although the Liberals, on 11,057, remained a significant force, Labour was now established as the main alternative to the Conservatives.[93] The movement of industrial workers to the region also encouraged the growth of the trade union movement. Thus, there were three branches of the Amalgamated Engineering Union in Cornwall before the war, but this had increased to nine by August 1944. This expansion was particularly dramatic in the Camborne area where a a number of factories had been established for the duration of the war.[94] This growth in trade unionism provided a stronger organization for the socialists. At the AGM of the divisional party in Totnes in March 1945 there was a record attendance of trade union members, while the presence in Yeovil of 9,000 wartime workers meant that Labour was well prepared for the election campaign.[95] It could therefore be said that these developments challenged the isolated world of the South-Western peninsula, and it was only to be expected that such change would assist the rise of Labour.

Conclusion

By 1939 it appeared that the Liberals had finally consolidated their position in the rural South-West. The momentum in favour of a Popular Front improved the morale of regional activists, while in making a strong appeal to youth the party was ensuring its survival in the future. In addition, with Labour failing to make any real progress, partly because of the general weakness of the trade unions, the Liberals still had a role as the voice of farmers and labourers in the countryside. The war years removed the possibility of a recovery. Sinclair's effective absence from party politics meant that the Liberals lost the initiative, which created divisions over policy formulation and led to an independent challenge by Labour in those rural constituencies where the progressive vote needed to be united in order to defeat the Conservatives. In retrospect, then, this case study of the experience of the South-West suggests that the pre-war years form a neglected but fascinating period in the history of organised Liberalism that deserves further investigation.

5

Crusade for Survival: 1945–1950

Introduction

During the late 1940s the Liberal party under its new leader, Clement Davies, attempted to stage yet another recovery. Although the third force was able to field sufficient candidates in 1950 to campaign as a party of government, the general election of that year proved to be another disaster. This chapter is based on an investigation into the reasons for the failure of this approach within the context of national and regional developments. Many Liberals were convinced that they would win the next election by just improving their organization and contesting 600 seats. Credibility, however, depended on more than just an increased number of candidates, and the broad-front approach actually focused attention on the party's increasingly precarious position. With the Liberals campaigning as a party of government there was also little attempt to address local factors. The Labour party, formerly a minor force in much of the rural South-West, appeared to be finally benefiting with the Conservatives, albeit to a lesser degree, in a rather late realignment of regional politics. Above all, growing evidence of the emergence of a new regional agenda in the far west, a process which was to assist the revival of Liberalism in subsequent decades, was actually ignored by the Liberals but incorporated into this new Westminster-focused alignment.

'Time we had the Liberals back'?

Following their poor showing in 1945 the Liberals embarked upon another crusade to convince voters that they were a credible alternative government with a declaration that they would fight the next election on a broad-front basis. In the event the stated objective of 600 candidates proved too ambitious, but the Liberals were able to contest 475 constituencies in 1950. However, the election was to prove that this plan was seriously flawed. The party's organization was still too weak to support a broad front, while its poor showing in parliamentary by-elections and opinion polls after 1945 undermined the party's attempts to portray itself as a serious contender for power. Yet reorganization during the late 1940s had convinced the Liberals that they were in a position to put forward a large number of candidates. A Reconstruction Committee was appointed, and its report, *Coats off for the Future*, was presented to the party's annual Assembly in 1946. It envisaged a 'grand revivalist campaign, infused with the evangelical passion of a crusade'. The committee advocated a thorough reform of Liberal organization. At the national level this included the appointment of a managing director of the party's organization, more professional staff and a publication department organized on a commercial basis. *Coats off for the Future* also recommended three ambitious stages for the revival of the party at the local level:

(1) Immediately: launching of a Liberal Foundation Fund leading up to foundation Day ... This should result in a re-awakening.
(2) Within eighteen months: ... commando raids on derelict constituencies, campaigns on vital national issues and by-election fights.
(3) Within three years: a national crusade would then have a real impact on the country.[1]

The 1950 election was to demonstrate that the party's organization was still weak, but there were definite signs of improvement in some seats in the South-West. Torquay Liberal Association claimed that its organization was better than at any time for the past fifteen or twenty years, and F.K. Way, the political correspondent of the *Western Morning News*, confirmed that the local Liberals had far less difficulty raising campaign funds than their Labour opponents.[2] In 1947 a new Liberal agent was appointed for Bath. Within two years he was able to increase the membership of the constituency party by 300 per cent, and the treasurer claimed that it was the 'most successful year the association had ever had'.[3] Similarly, Isaac Foot believed that the party's campaign in 1950 compared favourably with the previous election:

> In 1945 when he was a candidate for the Tavistock Division, there were only 40 veterans at the adoption meetings. They had great difficulty in raising the money. This time there were ... 400 people [and] they raised £560 in ten minutes. In Wells he had difficulty in getting into a Liberal meeting. There were nearly 1,000 people there and they raised £530 during the night.[4]

Many Liberals believed that they had a 'very hard core' of support in the South-West which would provide the basis for a revival. The party was still a major electoral force in the region with 18.8 per cent of the vote in 1945, and an even higher average vote per candidate of 25.7 per cent. The party had experienced a setback when Thomas Horabin, MP for North Cornwall, resigned the Liberal whip in 1947 and defected to Labour in the following year. Nevertheless, party activists were encouraged by their belief that the scale of the Conservative defeat was so great that the future lay between Liberalism and Socialism. Gerald Whitmarsh, who had defected from the Conservatives in 1939, believed that his old party would never recover from the Labour landslide of 1945, and that in future the Western world, especially the Anglo-American democracies, would be ruled by 'Liberal' parties.[5] The Liberals also had some success in attracting recruits from the other political parties. Lord Milverton defected from Labour in 1949, and he played a prominent role in the Liberal campaign in the South-West. At least five out of the party's twenty-four candidates in the region in 1950 had backed other parties in the previous election. Alfred Cann (Devonport) and Henry Townend (Torquay) were recent converts from the Conservatives, while Elizabeth Rashleigh (Torrington) was a Liberal National until 1946. Leon Maclaren (Yeovil) was the son of a former Labour MP and had himself contested Westmorland for Labour in 1945. Another high-profile recruit was 34-year-old Anthony Marreco, the party's candidate for Wells, who had been a junior counsel at the Nuremburg trial and a former Labour supporter.[6]

Developments at the national level resulted in a number of recruits from the Liberal Nationals. The Wooton–Teviot agreement in May 1947 effectively ended any pretensions that the Liberal Nationals

(National Liberal after 1948) had of being an independent force. Under the terms of the agreement combined associations of Conservatives and Liberal Nationals were formed under a 'mutually agreed title', while in those constituencies where only one of the parties had an organization it would offer membership to all those who were opposed to Socialism. However, relations between the two parties had always been difficult in the Liberal National seats of St Ives and South Molton, and even in 1950 the local National Liberals retained a 'sturdy independence'. Many Liberal National activists, particularly in South Molton, refused to join a combined association and returned to the Liberals, while there were reports in 1950 of some Conservatives abstaining rather than voting for the sitting National Liberal MP.[7] There was even a possibility of a regional merger of the two Liberal groups. Speculation arose in February 1946 when a number of leading Liberal Nationals attended a rally in Torquay organized by the Devon and Cornwall Liberal Federation, while a month later a resolution was passed at a conference in Plymouth recommending the union of the Liberal Federation and the equivalent Liberal National organization.[8]

Finally, the party was able to put forward candidates in twenty-four out of the twenty-six seats in the region in 1950. This was the highest number of Liberal candidates since 1929, and by itself convinced party supporters that they could stage a recovery in the four counties. Even in seats where the party eventually came third in 1950, such as Totnes and Honiton, local Liberals seemed genuinely convinced during the campaign that they would win. This optimistic view prevailed at party headquarters in London. Lord Moynihan, chairman of the Liberal Party Organization, claimed that there was a 'real resurgence of Liberalism' in the region, while Edward Martell, deputy chairman of the national Liberal Central Association, predicted that North Cornwall, St Ives, Bodmin and North Devon would be captured. The party also expected victories in Torrington, Totnes, Tavistock, Torquay and Honiton.[9]

Despite this optimistic background, the eventual result in 1950 proved to be a disastrous setback as the Liberal party's representation in the House of Commons actually dropped from twelve to a new low point of nine. The Conservatives emerged as the real victors of the election in the South-West, winning three seats from Labour, two from the Liberals and one from the Independent Progressives, while losing only one seat to Labour because of boundary changes (see Table 5.1).

119

It had been widely expected that Frank Byers would hold his North Dorset seat for the Liberals, but he was narrowly defeated by ninety-seven votes. The party failed to win any new seats, and this meant that for the first time not a single Liberal MP was elected from any of the four counties. Indeed, with the exception of Byers and Dingle Foot, 3,072 votes behind the Conservatives in North Cornwall, no Liberal had even come within striking distance of victory. The party had only come second in a further three seats in the region: North Devon, Bodmin and Torrington. Once again it had been confirmed that the Liberals were now only a significant force in a few rural divisions of Cornwall and Devon, although even there they could not win any seats. Apart from North Dorset and Wells the party polled less than a fifth of the vote in every seat that it contested in Dorset and Somerset, while in urban Plymouth both candidates lost their deposits.

Table 5.1: Election results in the South-West in 1945 and 1950.

	1945		1950		Change	
	Seats	%	Seats	%	Seats	%
Conservative	18	45.8	23	47.9	+5	+2.1
Labour	6	33.5	3	34.1	−3	+0.6
Liberal	2	18.8	—	17.3	−2	−1.5
Other	1	1.9	—	0.7	−1	−1.2

While the Liberal share of the vote appeared to compare favourably with the previous election, an increase in the number of candidates and the redistribution of seats in 1948 makes it difficult to assess the actual decline in the party's vote. Local observers believed that there was a modest improvement in Liberal fortunes in a few constituencies. The *Western Morning News* concluded that Rashleigh did 'well to take the Liberals into second place' at Torrington, while charismatic candidates at Truro and Totnes made some progress.[10] Nonetheless, in the region as a whole the party fared worse than in 1945, especially in those constituencies where it had a reasonable chance of victory. For example, in the first post-war election the party had polled over 30 per cent in

Tavistock and Bodmin. Despite favourable boundary changes in both constituencies, the Liberals were forced into third place in Tavistock and John Foot's share of the vote in Bodmin fell from 38.0 to only 29.5 per cent. The election, far from heralding a Liberal recovery, left the Old Left struggling to survive as a credible force even in its few remaining strongholds.

But the so-called 'Day of Disillusionment' after the election was only to be expected, since at no time between 1945 and 1950 did the Liberals look like making a significant impact on public opinion. The party's highest vote in a parliamentary by-election was only 25.3 per cent at Bermondsey (Rotherhithe) in 1946, while its vote was lower in every three-cornered by-election compared with 1945. National opinion polls also suggested that Liberal support was actually less in 1950 than it had been in the previous election (see Table 5.2). The cumulative effect was to convince the general public that the idea of a Liberal government was simply not credible. Although the party was better placed in the rural South-West than in many other areas, the 'wasted vote' argument was still used with devastating effect in potentially winnable seats like Bodmin and North Devon. Liberal spokesmen, such as the secretary of the Taunton Liberals, claimed that the start of the election campaign was the 'signal for a mass onslaught' by the Conservatives on the party's lack of credibility.[11]

Table 5.2: Annual average of Liberal support according to Gallup, 1945–1950.

1945	13.8 %	1946	12.0 %	1947	11.3 %
1948	9.5 %	1949	12.0 %	1950	10.0 %

The subsequent 'squeeze' of the Liberal vote was so successful because of a polarization of political opinion on class lines. A post-election report by the national secretary of the Labour party concluded that industrial workers had voted Labour more strongly than ever before, but the party had lost the support of middle-class voters.[12] The Liberal candidate for Taunton concluded that Britain was faced with 'two irreconcilable forces, both of which fear each other', and the evidence certainly suggests that voters really did *fear* the 'other side' winning the election. A survey in Bristol North-East found that over two-thirds of those electors who gave reasons for supporting Labour did so on the grounds that they dreaded a return to unemployment and the financial hardships of the 1930s.[13] Yet Conservative voters believed that a Labour victory would turn Britain into a Socialist state. In some Conservative areas in the South-West there was a turnout of over 90 per cent in order to stop the Socialists, and this polarization of the vote ensured that the Liberals had little success in exploiting the particular concerns of the *petite bourgeoisie*, with many small traders and farmers defecting to the Conservatives.[14] In these circumstances, then, the party's claim that it would be able to form the next government was hardly realistic.

Although many Liberals tended to be optimistic, at least in public, it is evident that some candidates were less confident over their prospects by the end of the campaign. Thus, the candidate for Tavistock was asking voters whether they wanted the party to disappear from the House of Commons and for politics to degenerate into a dogfight and unashamed class war.[15] The following extract from the adoption speech of Grant Cameron, the Liberal candidate for South Dorset, indicates the curious combination of defeatism and delusion that characterized the party's campaign:

> Mr Cameron said he was confident that this was going to be a successful election for Liberals, whether they won the seat or not. They were fighting not only to win South Dorset, but to become the next Government … One thing was certain, that whatever the outcome of the election, Liberalism in Dorset must carry on.[16]

It was also difficult to convince voters that Liberalism represented a distinct and relevant alternative to the two main parties. Once again the problem was not that the party lacked policies. The Liberal manifesto in 1950 proposed a variety of measures including family allowances for the first child, an end to peacetime conscription, greater European co-operation (including the idea that European currencies should be convertible) and co-ownership in industry. Activists at the local level claimed that their party was campaigning on nine fundamental issues (free trade, devolution for Scotland and Wales, abandonment of conscription, co-ownership, proportional representation, the outlawing of monopolies, tax reform, taxation of site values and support for a World Federation) which distinguished the party from its opponents.[17] Yet these policies were insignificant compared to the supreme issue of whether Labour should be given a second term in office. Conservative policies like *The Industrial Charter* (1947) had been produced with the intention of changing that party's reactionary image. Although Labour voters were still suspicious, this new image was likely to appeal to moderate Liberals and floating voters. The Liberals warned that 'if the Tories came to power and there was a big dose of unemployment, there was going to be industrial trouble, and that brought in the Communists'. But F.K. Way concluded that the regional electorate believed there was little difference between the two anti-Socialist parties, especially since the Conservative candidates tended to emphasize Liberal themes like freedom and decentralization.[18]

Moreover, the controversial nature of some of the Liberal party's distinctive policies tended to alienate voters. The *Manchester Guardian* argued that the party's approach to policy formulation was in danger of 'over-elaboration, for it is easy create misunderstandings and to tie candidates unnecessarily'.[19] A good example of this problem can be seen in the party's attempt to win the women's vote by advocating equal pay for equal work. The Liberal candidates for Poole and Taunton even held special women's meetings during the election, but it was obvious that female members of the party were divided over the issue of equal pay. This was clearly demonstrated by a leading member of the Taunton Women's Liberal Association, who took the line that 'Quite frankly, we want to see women in the home. We do not think it is a good thing for women with small children to be so strongly encouraged to go back into factories, at the expense of their own health, their children and families'.[20] Other candidates in the South-West did not even discuss the party's equal pay proposals. The *Western Morning News* invited Rashleigh, the region's only female Liberal candidate, to write an article on why women should vote for Liberalism. Rashleigh made no mention of equal pay, and instead showed how the party's policies would benefit the family. Her emphasis on issues like the removal of purchase tax, the right of council tenants to buy their own home, conscription and education indicate that she saw the political interests of women purely in terms of their traditional roles as housewife and mother.[21] In the event the party's bid to attract the female vote failed, with local observers concluding that concern over the cost of living had led to an above-average swing of women voters to the Conservative cause.[22]

The party did not even obtain much benefit from reorganization in the late 1940s. Finance and organization were still insufficient to field a large number of candidates properly, and less than sixty of the party's 527 constituency associations were 'up to election standard'. In October 1949 the Liberals had only selected about 200 candidates, but during the election there was, as Cook put it, a 'flood of inexperienced candidates [rising from 329 in January to 475 by nomination day] who seriously weakened the party's image'.[23] The West Country did not remain immune from these problems. In November 1948 Mrs Brinsley, an organizer from the Women's Federation, gave a gloomy report of organization in the Honiton division. Brinsley had been provided with a list of party members in the Exmouth area, and she attempted to set up an executive committee as a nucleus for a new women's branch. Yet out of the sixty people she contacted only about six were interested, and even then she was unable to obtain any definite promises to serve on the committee. Many on the list were 'too old or decrepit to do any active work … and quite a few were Conservatives of many years standing'.[24] Similarly, the *West Briton* reported in 1950 that there had been 'very little' Liberal activity in the Camborne area since the previous election. The constituency party did not even have a full-time agent, and the candidate had to appoint his own agent who arrived from London after the election campaign had commenced. In the adjacent constituency of Truro the local association was also inactive, and it was not until six weeks before the election that the party made any attempt to reorganize.[25] This was in stark contrast to the Conservative organization in the four counties. As Way remarked, the 'old costly complacency of the 1945 era has gone and in its place has come an efficient election machine'.[26]

The Liberals may have had greater success if they had concentrated more on local government. By contesting municipal elections on a regular basis this would have improved the party's organization, while local victories could have increased its credibility in individual constituencies. Yet in the South-West there was still a general reluctance, especially in rural areas, on the part of both Liberals and Conservatives to contest municipal elections on a party basis. Labour's perseverance in contesting seats on rural and urban district councils eventually forced the Conservatives to either put forward their own candidates or support Independents. The Liberals, however, remained opposed to party politics in local government. Individual members of the party continued to play an active role, but in rural areas this was invariably as Independents. Thus, the president of the North Cornwall Liberals captured a seat in the 1946 county council elections, but it was reported that he stood on 'strictly non-party lines'.[27]

When the Liberals did contest local elections this was usually in the larger urban centres where the party was no longer a major force. Plymouth was the classic example. During the 1930s the Liberals had an electoral agreement with the Conservatives, and this enabled them to retain a strong presence on the city council. Labour's landslide victory in the 1945 municipal elections was a blow from which the Liberals never recovered. In 1947 the party only fought the seats that they were defending, but all three candidates came third. By 1950 the party had lost its last seats on the council. The basic problem confronting the Plymouth Liberals was that they lacked a distinct position on the political spectrum. From 1945 onwards the Liberals fought as an independent party, but this meant that they did not share in the Conservative revival. Yet their close association with the Conservatives during the previous decade meant that they were unlikely to attract many Labour votes.[28]

Table 5.3: Party representation on Plymouth City Council, 1938–1947.

Election	Conservative	Labour	Liberal
1938	51	20	13
1945	32	44	8
1946	28	48	7
1947	32	47	4

The period was not one of total disaster for municipal Liberalism. In 1945 the Bath Liberals rejected an alliance with the Conservatives, who had adopted the label Progressive, and contested twelve seats in that year's municipal elections. In the event the party only lost two seats, and it retained a base in local politics with eight elected councillors. Indeed, the Liberals actually won all three seats in the Walcot South ward, despite

Labour and Progressive opposition, and they even regained a seat lost to the Conservatives in 1938. In 1947 the Bath Liberals captured a seat from Labour, and the defeated Socialist candidate said that he did not have a 'chance against an organization of D-Day efficiency'.[29] Similarly, by 1947 the Liberals had made a number of gains in Exeter, and this enabled them to become the second-largest party on the council.[30] In 1949 the Poole Liberals captured the Newtown ward from Labour, and were only 133 votes short of winning Branksome.[31] It is significant, however, that these gains were usually obtained in straight fights with Labour. The Conservatives were willing to allow some Liberals to have a clear run against Labour, and this enabled both parties, but mainly the Conservatives, to benefit from the anti-Socialist mood of the electorate in the late 1940s. Moreover, the party failed to capitalize on its limited successes. Municipal Liberalism in Bath was in decline after 1947, with the party concentrating on its remaining strongholds in order to retain a presence on the council, while the Exeter Liberals failed to exploit their position as the second party and by 1950 their number of councillors was also falling.[32] In both municipal and parliamentary politics, then, the reality in the late 1940s was of a party that was now struggling to survive.

Change in the Countryside

An additional problem for the regional party was that its electoral position was being undermined in its rural heartland. During the inter-war period the Liberals had benefited from Labour's weakness in the countryside, but the swing to Labour throughout the four counties in 1945 was an obvious threat to the party. Social factors, such as the late development of rural trade unionism and the relative decline of the old family voting tradition, meant that Labour was still expanding, and had 'yet to reach its peak' in the far South-West.[33] Furthermore, the Liberals were unable to make a unique contribution to the debate over regional problems. Both Labour and the Conservatives claimed that they would be able to provide better amenities and employment opportunities for the countryside. Although some Liberal candidates showed an interest in local issues, there was no organized attempt by the party to develop a regional programme.

Labour's parliamentary representation in the South-West fell from six to three in 1950, but the party succeeded in increasing its electoral support in rural areas. The party's progress in country areas was recognised by its opponents, and these gains were mainly at the expense of the Liberals. In Yeovil and Taunton there were reports that the rural vote was finally 'turning towards' Labour which helped to compensate for the loss of thousands of wartime workers and evacuees who had voted for them in 1945.[34] Even in Torrington, the most rural seat in Devon, Labour was building up its support in agricultural polling districts. By 1950 Labour had become the main alternative to the Conservatives in the majority of agricultural seats, and only in North Dorset and North Cornwall was the party still a minor force. This progress was assisted by the growth of the National Union of Agricultural Workers. The union was most successful in Dorset, which had become the third-best organized district in Britain by the late forties. The county organizer reported that 81 per cent of Dorset farm workers had joined the NUAW, and in some villages the entire work force was now unionized. A membership drive in the immediate post-war years had been combined with a political campaign by Labour. For example, when the county organizer established a union branch at Charminster, Labour officials, who formed a party branch, accompanied him. The secretary for West Dorset Divisional Labour Party emphasized that the 'utmost co-operation must exist between local parties and trade union branches'.[35] Although becoming a union member did not guarantee that an agricultural labourer would become a Labour voter, this development did make it more likely. The NUAW also made some progress in the other counties. Bodmin Divisional Labour Party was said to have benefited from the fact that the constituency's farmworkers 'now speak with a collective voice of a thousand strong'.[36]

During the inter-war period the region's farming community had feared that a majority Labour government would introduce land nationalization. Yet Labour's Agriculture Act in 1947 was to provide the framework for the industry in subsequent years. The majority of farmers still identified themselves with the Conservative or Liberal cause, but the agricultural community in general was reasonably content with the main lines of the government's agricultural policy.[37] In 1950 Labour candidates like John Kane, a local dairy farmer who contested West Dorset, claimed that 'farmers and farm workers have never before enjoyed such prosperity in peace time'. Farmers could have 'confidence in the future of the industry', while their workers could rely on good wages and decent working conditions'.[38] In addition, the party's candidates for at least six rural constituencies in the region were either farmers or market gardeners, which proved a useful asset. A good example of this occurred in Tavistock where Labour pushed the Liberals into third place. The party's candidate, Frank Harcourt-Manning, was a popular Devon farmer who symbolized Labour's attempt to replace the Liberals as the party of rural radicalism:

> The thorn in their flesh is an ex-Liberal Mr F.W. Harcourt-Munning, a farmer near Holsworthy, a life-long Methodist, inveterate talker and chain smoker. There is no denying the fervour of this impressive man of 19 stone, nor is there much doubt that he will overshadow his opponents on the platform.[39]

Another obstacle to Labour in the past had been the strength of family voting. In rural districts there was a tendency for the younger generation to vote in the same way as their parents and grandparents, and it was only in urban centres that the Labour party really benefited from these new voters. By 1950, however, this influence was said to be 'largely on the wane'.[40] Family voting had been closely connected to the power of the local gentry, and the growth of rural trade unionism represented a direct assault on the 'feudal grip' of the landowner, especially in Dorset and east Devon. In addition, those men who had been called up for National Service had been subjected to new social and political influences. Martin commented that those ex-servicemen who returned to Devon after the Second World War believed that they now had 'a stake in the country', and were determined to improve working conditions in rural areas. In addition, it was said that 'war brides' from industrial centres in the North of England were changing family voting patterns, and thereby undermining the old Liberal–Conservative alignment.[41]

Yet the significance of social change should not be exaggerated. The greater concentration of small farms in Cornwall and north Devon still remained a problem for the Socialists. For example, St Ives was described as a 'division of small farms and market gardeners'. While the NUAW had been active since the war, the 'few workers [were] by no means the decisive element they [were] likely to prove' in the eastern counties of Somerset and Dorset.[42] Indeed, the trade union movement was still quite weak in the most rural constituencies in the far west. Martin concluded that in the west Devon area only railwaymen and quarry workers were likely to be trade unionists. Key groups like farm workers, forestry employees and council workers tended to remain outside the trade union movement.[43] It would also be a mistake to assume that the family voting tradition was no longer relevant. According to Liberal activists it remained a key factor in the political alignment of the countryside until at least the 1960s. While National Service probably encouraged a new political outlook for those individuals that returned to the countryside, its main effect was to contribute to depopulation in rural areas and this factor limited the electoral benefits for Labour. Thus, it was reported that National Servicemen were reluctant to return to the countryside, and those with a more 'venturesome spirit' tended to either move to urban centres like Plymouth or left the region entirely.[44] The Labour party also claimed that the 'feudal grip' of the squire was still a serious problem in rural seats of the region like Tiverton. This particular constituency had always been represented by local landowners, and the family firm of Derick Heathcoat Amory, the Conservative MP (1945–60), was the largest employer in the Tiverton area.[45]

Above all, the Liberal tradition in the Cornwall–Devon borderland was still sustained by religious nonconformity. Even in the 1960s, the majority of rural Methodists in the Okehampton area had a 'view of life very like that of older Bible Christians', and Perry has remarked that Methodist preachers in the more isolated parts of Cornwall still 'denounced cinemas, dance halls and public houses in the town, even whist drives in the village hall, as ... the Devil's snares for idle hands'.[46] This dislike of modern life ensured that many nonconformists retained their traditional family loyalties to the Liberal party. It was said that John Foot's meetings in Bodmin were 'attended by a religious fervour that could have been plucked from a page of Victorian history', while the network of nonconformist chapels in Torrington provided the basis for the local Liberal organization in 1950.[47] It is interesting that this situation was quite similar to rural Scandinavia where Rokkan commented that the Old Left were seen as defending the traditions of 'orthodox evangelism against the onslaught of urban secularism and the evils of modern life'.[48] The significance of social change, than, should be kept in perspective. While Labour's advance in rural areas contributed to the

Liberal *decline,* conditions also ensured that the latter party was able to *survive* because it still had a hard core of committed supporters.

Consideration should now be given to the peninsula's relationship with Westminster. Regional issues have traditionally played an important part in national politics, and this was certainly the case during the inter-war period when the Liberals had been helped by the general consensus that so many local industries depended on free trade. By 1950, however, local opinion was less certain over the benefits of free trade. The Liberal party's opposition to protection for the fishing industry and market gardening was said to have done 'irreparable harm' to candidates like John Foot. The Conservatives claimed that the 'intention' of the Liberals to 'allow the free flow into our markets' of foreign agricultural produce would seriously undermine the prosperity of agriculture and related industries. Conservative policy, in contrast, would benefit the main local industries like tourism, construction, and agriculture, which would maintain rural prosperity in the future.[49] The Liberals, moreover, made little attempt to appeal specifically to local interests. There were a few exceptions. Whitmarsh in Truro championed the interests of the fishing industry and he advocated higher subsidies, a separate government department and the establishment of Cornish pilchard factories, while Rashleigh felt strongly that rural communities should be provided with more amenities and 'one of the things she would fight for would be to see that the villages were not neglected'.[50] Yet many Liberals concerned themselves purely with national issues. Indeed, John Foot criticized Douglas Marshall, his Conservative opponent in Bodmin, for concentrating too much on the interests of his constituency:

> There were too many MPs already who were more concerned with the welfare of their own constituencies than with the wider and more important national and international issues. They were 'Little Jack Horners' who treated the House of Commons as if it were a huge pie. They would put in their thumbs, pull out a plum and go back to their constituencies with a nice report in the paper to tell their constituents 'What a good boy am I'.[51]

But the Liberal party's opponents rejected Foot's call for a greater emphasis on national and international issues. Labour's success in 1945 had represented a serious challenge to Conservative supremacy, and a number of sitting MPs were now vulnerable to a small swing of votes. It was customary for MPs to stress their parliamentary record, but in 1950 it was of even greater importance with constituency service a major plank in the election campaigns of sitting MPs. Victor Collins (Labour), who won Taunton in 1945 with a majority of only 2,000, knew the 'value of constant publicity', and a great deal of emphasis was placed on his parliamentary achievements. He claimed that since his election he had dealt with 10,000 personal cases, written 80,000 letters and asked over 400 questions in Parliament.[52] Another example was Marshall who had 'proved himself the servant of South-East Cornwall':

> There is not a village that he has not visited more than once and there is hardly an MP at Westminster who has not been made aware of the fertility of the Tamar Valley and the nutritional value of the pilchard. This passionate zeal led Mr Marshall to take up well over 20,000 cases in the last Parliament and earned for him a personal prestige which it is impossible to assess.[53]

During the immediate post-war period there was renewed interest in regional issues. In 1947 the University College of the South-West (later the University of Exeter) published a survey of the economic conditions in Cornwall and Devon. The survey committee found that mid Cornwall and south-east Devon were relatively prosperous and increasing in population, but the rest of the region suffered from limited vocational opportunities, relatively high unemployment and out-migration. The committee pointed to a 'dead area' of the region which had suffered most severely in the past. This area was essentially the Cornwall–Devon borderland, extending from north and mid Devon into east Cornwall and covered the North Devon, Torrington, Tavistock, North Cornwall and Bodmin constituencies. The committee concluded that a more balanced industrial structure was required in order to 'counteract' the tendency for younger members of the community to leave the region in search of better employment opportunities. It was further proposed that there should be an improvement in housing conditions and rural amenities.[54] The Conservatives claimed that they would be more successful than their opponents in dealing with these issues. In 1947 a group of Conservative and National Liberal MPs from the South-West had tabled a motion in the House of Commons which called on the government to give agricultural workers the same rations and consumer goods as coal miners.[55] The Conservative candidate for Falmouth & Camborne argued during the 1950 election campaign that one of the 'glaring omissions' of the Labour government had been its failure to provide more rural amenities, in particular piped water supplies, housing and electricity. He added that 'these matters would be given priority by a Conservative Government'.[56]

Finally, the staple industries of Cornwall and Devon were of national significance in the immediate post-war years. Agriculture and fishing were naturally vital at a time of food rationing, while the china clay industry was a major exporter to the United States and an essential 'dollar earner'. In 1946 the *Cornish Guardian* had reported that the national importance of problems in the fishing and clay industries had enabled the Cornish members, the majority of whom were Conservatives, 'always to command attention when bringing them before the House or Ministry officials'. Labour and the Conservatives disagreed in 1950 over who should claim the credit for any benefits. For example, Marshall claimed that it was his personal efforts in Parliament which had helped the fishing industry in south-east Cornwall, while his Labour opponent said that the credit should go to the government.[57] John Foot was naturally excluded from this debate and from the electoral benefits. After Horabin's defection in 1947 the Liberals no longer had any MPs in the west of the region, and the failure of candidates like Foot to raise local issues did not help. The Labour government and active Conservative MPs were therefore the beneficiaries of any economic improvements.

Pacts and Strategies

The 1950 debacle might have been avoided if the Liberals had fought the election on their own terms. Four years earlier the party had accepted the conventional wisdom of contesting the next election with the aim of forming a government, but there were a number of other possibilities. Many Liberals during the Sinclair years had recognised that the only way in which the party could obtain a share of power was by working with other parties. One possible route that the party could have pursued after 1945 was to have exploited the divisions within the Conservative opposition. Many progressive Conservatives in the Tory Reform Group believed that the party needed a 'thorough reformulation' of policy, and they were concerned by Churchill's cautious approach. While the Industrial Charter received overwhelming endorsement at the 1947 conference, there was still 'evidence of a potential split' in the party. Edelman has concluded that 'at least half the conference was emotionally more in harmony with its wide-ranging extremists than with the paternal Conservatism of Macmillan'. The progressive wing was actually weaker than it had been before the 1945 election since the sheer scale of the Conservative defeat meant that the parliamentary party was 'left with a high proportion of safe-seat candidates'. Hoffman has claimed that this meant that the 1945 survivors were 'even less representative' of British society than before, and the failure rate of members of the Tory Reform Group in 1945 was actually 'higher than for Conservative MPs-candidates as a whole'.[58]

Moreover, a number of younger Conservative MPs favoured the formation of a Centre party consisting of all parties and individuals opposed to state Socialism. After July 1945 these individuals were trying to devise a new liberal agenda which would appeal across the political spectrum and in February 1947 representatives of the Conservative, Liberal and Liberal National parties signed a joint manifesto, entitled *Design for Freedom*.[59] It must be emphasized that the *Design for Freedom* movement differed from later attempts to form an anti-Socialist front in the sense that it was seen very much as a threat to Conservative unity. Peter Thorneycroft, the leader of the Conservative signatories, already had a reputation as a rebel because of his public disagreement with the party leadership at the 1946 Blackpool conference and his subsequent resignation from the shadow cabinet. In these circumstances Thorneycroft and five of his parliamentary colleagues, including Simon Wingfield Digby (West Dorset) and Derick Heathcoat Amory (Tiverton), were threatened with expulsion.[60]

Evidence of a potential split in the party can be seen in events in Plymouth. John Astor, the son of Lady Nancy Astor and prospective Conservative candidate for Sutton, was a supporter of *Design for Freedom*, and in March 1947 he invited Thorneycroft to address a public meeting in the constituency. Thorneycroft's rhetoric was clearly provocative. He claimed that the respective headquarters of the Conservative and Liberal parties were putting the interests of party before their country, and added that if a pact in Plymouth could not be formed by 'old people then take action with the young Liberals and young Tories'.[61] Some Liberals recognized the benefits of exploiting this situation. Hubert Young, one of the Liberal signatories and the prospective candidate for Bath, told Sir Archibald Sinclair, the party's former leader, that 'there is no fear whatever of any of us joining the … Conservative Party. … What we are trying to do is to detach the Young Tories from it.' Sinclair believed that Thorneycroft was genuine 'in his wish to create a new combination of Liberals and Tory Reformers', and he believed that circumstances might arise in which Thorneycroft and his colleagues would 'take the same path that Winston and Jack Seely took in 1905' by defecting to the Liberals. In the event the Liberal leadership adopted a hostile attitude to the *Design for Freedom* movement. Douglas concluded that this lack of official encouragement prevented any further development.[62]

The basic obstacle to the formation of a Centre party was the constant dilemma of the Left/Right political divide. The Radical wing of the Liberal party had no wish to be identified with the Conservatives, and they were naturally concerned, especially in the South-West, that they would have to stand down in favour of 'Tories or Simonites'. In 1947 Thorneycroft had confidential discussions with Dingle Foot on the possibility of an agreement. Foot emphasized that his party would not favour an 'arrangement whereby we had to withdraw our candidates in, say, Bodmin and Barnstaple in return for a clear run' in Labour seats. Even if such a pact proved possible there was 'not the slightest likelihood that Liberal voters in the country seats would meekly go to the polls in support of the hereditary enemy'.[63] Furthermore, many Liberals were suspicious of Davies because he had been a Liberal National in the 1930s, and he was therefore in no position to adopt a more flexible stance, even if he wanted to. Sinclair argued that the situation had been 'handled with extraordinary clumsiness' by all sides. He added that the Liberals were not 'a mighty army … Surely we are a band of guerrillas and we cannot afford positional warfare—we must manoeuvre.'[64]

One possible line that the Liberal leadership could have pursued was to have called for a Centre party or alliance that included members of *all* of the three main parties. The advantage of such a strategy was that the presence of discontented Labour MPs would have been more acceptable to the Radicals within the Liberal party. While Dingle Foot was opposed to a 'Tory–Liberal line-up to oust the Socialists', he told Thorneycroft that he was more willing to support a 'new all-party coalition'.[65] Newspapers in the South-West, both Liberal and Conservative, were also advocating an all-party alliance. In September 1945 the *Cornish Guardian* called for 'a new grouping in politics' consisting of the Liberals, the Tory Reformers and the right wing of the Labour party, while by 1947 the *Western Morning News* was claiming that the economic crisis was so serious that no single party was 'big enough to steer the nation through the next few years; the need for unity was as urgent as during the war'.[66]

While the chances of a National Coalition may have been remote, it would have provided, as in the late 1930s, an attractive campaign platform. An anti-Socialist pact was not in the interests of the Liberals in the South-West, but defections to the party would have been beneficial. In the first place the two Liberal National MPs, Alan Beechman (St Ives) and George Lambert (South Molton), were likely to favour a new Centre group. After the 1945 election the Liberal National MPs wanted to 'distance themselves' from the Conservatives in order to improve their relations with their former colleagues, while local Conservative activists, who had never liked the idea of supporting another party, started to select their own candidates in seats like South Molton.[67] Moreover, the defection of some of the younger Conservative MPs would have undermined the new progressive image of that party. In 1950 the Conservatives depended on individuals like Heathcoat Amory, a member of the committee which produced the Industrial Charter and a cabinet minister in the 1950s, in order to attract the 'floating vote'.[68] Defections to the Liberal party could well have had the effect of dividing the anti-Socialist vote, and in these circumstances Whitmarsh's claim that the Conservatives would never recover from 1945 may possibly have turned into a reality.

Another course of action was to have moved in the opposite direction by concentrating on the formation of local electoral pacts with Labour. That party's decision to fight every seat in the region in 1950 effectively undermined the position of the Liberals. Since 1931 the Liberals had only won seats where there was no Labour candidate, and the slender victories of Horabin and Byers in 1945, majorities of only 2,665 and 1,965 respectively, were really due to the fact that they had won their seats in straight fights with the Conservatives. In 1950 the Conservative victors in North Dorset and North Cornwall were both returned on a minority vote, and the view of local observers was that the defeat of Byers and Dingle Foot was essentially due to Labour intervention.[69] Although the Liberals had apparently moved to the right at the national level since 1945, the survival of the radical tradition of the regional party, symbolized by progressive candidates like the Foot brothers, meant that local pacts with Labour still provided a logical road to survival.

Furthermore, at the start of the election campaign it was far from certain that Labour would contest all of the region's constituencies. In Bridgwater, where Stephen King-Hall had succeeded Vernon Bartlett as the Independent Progressive candidate, there was speculation of a straight fight with the Conservatives, but in the event the Co-operative movement decided to put forward a candidate 'without the full support of its Labour allies'.[70] The possibility of an electoral agreement was even more likely in the west of the region. In January 1950 the Labour party had not selected its candidates for North Cornwall, Honiton, Bodmin, St Ives and Tavistock. The Conservatives were returned on a minority vote in all but one of these seats (Honiton), and the Liberals would probably have been the eventual victors had there been no Labour candidate. In November 1948 the Conservative agent for Bodmin had warned of the possibility of Labour standing aside in favour of John Foot, while there were discussions in St Ives between the Liberal candidate and local Labour supporters concerning an anti-Conservative front. Even in 1950 Labour supporters in Bodmin recognized that they were fighting 'a hopeless cause', while in Honiton many 'leading Socialists had no great wish to contest the seat' and the decision to adopt a candidate actually led to a number of resignations.[71] A determined bid by the Liberals to secure local agreements might well have been successful.

Both of these strategies depended upon developments within the other parties, but there was another route that the Liberals could have pursued themselves: a narrow front. In retrospect it seems clear that the party's decision to contest the election on a broad front was a mistake. The Liberals failed to appreciate that they no longer had the credibility to pose as an alternative party of government, and even in the South-West the Liberals had been relegated to third place in 1945 in the majority of constituencies. In marginal seats like Taunton and

Devonport the electorate was unwilling to waste their votes on Liberal candidates, and this was repeated across the country with the party losing some 319 deposits in 1950.[72] This scenario should have been obvious to the party before the election. In February 1946 the *Liberal Magazine* concluded that 'one of the party's first tasks' had to be the consolidation of the 'existing Liberal vote', while poor results in parliamentary by-elections, local government contests and opinion polls all indicated that the Liberals had not improved their position since 1945.[73]

The obvious problem with a broad front was that it prevented the party from maximizing its potential vote in its best seats. The Liberals should have ensured that good candidates had been selected at least two years before the election, but, apart from the Foot brothers, the situation in the South-West was characterized by frequent changes in candidates who rarely had any association with the area. A good example was North Devon where the Liberals selected Guy Naylor in January 1950 after their two previous candidates had resigned. Naylor was a London barrister who had no connection with the area, and he made his first public appearance after the campaign had started. Overall, only 25.0 per cent of Liberal candidates had fought seats in the region in 1945 compared to 42.3 and 69.2 per cent of Labour and Conservative candidates.[74] The broad front also forced the Liberals to spread their financial resources too thinly. Lack of finance does not necessarily mean that organization was equally weak, but it certainly indicates the flawed nature of the campaign. In Somerset, where the Liberals had little chance of winning even one seat, the party spent £682 per candidate. In Cornwall the Liberals had a reasonable chance of winning at least three seats, but expenditure still amounted to only £697 per candidate. Individual constituencies are even more revealing. North Devon should have been one of the party's main target seats in the region, but the Liberal candidate only spent £664, compared with £774 for the Conservatives and £741 for Labour. Taunton had not been contested since 1929, and the Liberals only polled 10.2 per cent of the vote in 1950. However, Labour and the Conservatives spent £899 and £903 respectively, and in order to compete effectively with their opponents the Liberals had to spend £811.[75]

Although party members tended to support a broad front, there was a minority view which questioned the wisdom of such tactics. For example, in 1945 four officers of the Oxford University Liberal Club, including Alan Gibson who was to contest Falmouth & Camborne in 1959, expressed their opposition to the idea of a broad front. Their view was that instead of posing as an alternative government, Liberalism should become an 'energetic though small force in the political life of the nation'.[76] Sinclair also believed that the party had to operate as a 'band of guerrillas'. A few victories in 1950 would, he thought, provide the basis for a more substantial recovery in the future, and in a letter to Dingle Foot in 1947 his views were in direct contrast to the idealistic attitude of the new party leadership:

> What with Frank Byers raking in the shekels, reported successes in debates in several universities and the new found unity of the Liberal Party, our guerrilla warfare is going well. I am beginning to feel that we are almost strong enough for a battle provided that we are very selective in our choice of ground. North Cornwall would be an ideal place for it! Nothing could so quickly transform the outlook for the Liberal Party as your victory there.[77]

Admittedly, there were problems associated with a narrow front. It was a view that appealed especially to the libertarians within the party on the grounds that a large number of candidates would divide the opposition vote. Lord Reading and Lord Rennell, two of the leading anti-Socialist Liberals in the House of Lords, called for the party to 'select and support a few well-chosen candidates whose local or national repute would command wide respect, and in other constituencies to seek to persuade Liberals to vote anti-Socialist'.[78] This merely served to aggravate the basic divisions within the party, and in turn frustrated the attempts of those individuals who genuinely wanted a change in strategy to restore the party's fortunes. Moreover, timing was essential. One of the main advantages of a broad front was that the idea of a Liberal government appealed to the basic instincts of party stalwarts, and this was responsible for the revivalist atmosphere within the party after 1945. Once the leadership had committed the party to such a course it was very difficult to change direction because of the effect it would have on morale. In 1949 Edward Martell, personal assistant to Davies and formerly the main advocate of a broad front, apparently suggested that the party should 'concentrate its efforts where it was strong and leave the remaining constituencies to fend as best as they could'. However, pressure from the grassroots prevented a change in direction.[79] In January 1950 Lord Samuel, the former Liberal leader, told Reading that a last-minute decision to fight on a limited front would be disastrous for the party:

> Tens of thousands of new recruits [are] flocking in ... There is indeed more vigour and enthusiasm in the ranks of the Liberal Party now than I have known at any time since the election of 1929 ... All this would be struck dead if hundreds of constituencies were told that they were to have no candidates.[80]

Nevertheless, if the party had adopted Martell's suggestion at an earlier date, it would probably have been in a stronger position by 1950. A narrow front would have enabled the Liberals to meet their opponents on equal terms in a selected number of target seats. In future elections the Liberals would deliberately concentrate on local issues and select a number of distinctive and charismatic candidates. Even in 1950 the Liberals were able to capture the Scottish seats of Orkney & Shetland and Roxburgh & Selkirk from the Conservatives in three-cornered contests, and by concentrating on similar peripheral seats the party could well have increased its parliamentary representation. If such a policy had been pursued the South-West would have been a key region. In 1945 the party had polled over 30 per cent in five of the region's constituencies, and there were two further seats contested in 1950, Truro and Torrington, which had a strong Liberal tradition. Yet by embarking on an idealistic crusade, the Liberals were paradoxically undermining their own position in the region and at Westminster.

Conclusion

Developments during the immediate post-war period ensured the continuation of the Liberal decline. The progress of the Labour movement in rural areas like the South-West had the effect of weakening the Liberal party's electoral base in those few constituencies where it had survived as a significant force, while other voters defected to the Conservatives on the grounds that it was the only party which could prevent another Socialist victory. The third party was therefore in no position to mount a broad-front challenge to its opponents. After the

Second World War the Liberals could either have supported a realignment of the anti-Socialist opposition or attempted to secure local electoral pacts with Labour. Finally, the party could have abandoned the idealistic goal of a Liberal government and concentrated instead on building up a small but more secure parliamentary base based on a selected number of target seats. Such an approach would have meant that the South-West would have become a key area in the party's campaign because there were quite a number of seats in the region where it still had a good chance of victory. Instead, the Liberals found themselves on the defensive once again, and the disastrous result of the election created the circumstances that led to the near extinction of independent Liberalism in the early 1950s.

6

Towards the Promised Land: 1950–1955

Introduction

By 1951 the Liberal party, with just six MPs in the House of Commons and 2.6 per cent of the popular vote, appeared on the verge of complete extinction. The next electoral contest could quite conceivably have seen the demise of organized Liberalism. In the event the Liberals were able to survive the 1955 general election, while activists could take some satisfaction from the fact that the party was able to stem its constant decline in parliamentary representation for the first time since 1931. Moreover, the period also witnessed the early recovery of the party in some of its traditional rural strongholds like Cornwall and Devon. This chapter will analyse the dynamics of this regional recovery, ranging from organizational improvements associated with the local implementation of 'Operation Basic' to the emergence of a regionalist agenda based on rural discontent. On a wider level this investigation will also consider how many of the ideas associated with Jo Grimond's leadership of the party from 1956 to1967 began to be raised in the early 1950s by a new generation of Liberals. In that sense developments at the community level paved the way for Grimond and the party's national recovery from the late 1950s onwards.

'The darkest days'

The early 1950s represented the nadir of the fortunes of both British and South-West Liberalism. As Rasmussen remarked, the party needed time to recover from the shock of the 1950 disaster, but with only a narrow majority the Labour government decided to hold an election in

October 1951. With the party 'low on morale, funds, and potential candidates', it was in no position to contest another election.[1] The South-West could not escape from these problems. At a meeting of the executive committee of the Western Counties Liberal Federation in July 1950 there was a gloomy report on the availability of full-time agents and prospective candidates, while in September 1951 the number of seats that the party intended to contest 'varied from day to day'.[2] The situation was just as serious in the western counties. Following the announcement of the date of the 1951 election, the pro-Liberal *Cornish Guardian* claimed that the regional party was 'less ready to enter a contest than it has ever been'. Even in Cornwall the Liberals had only one candidate, Dingle Foot in North Cornwall, at the start of the campaign. A good example of the confusion within the party can be seen in Bodmin. The Liberals lacked a candidate after the resignation of John Foot in October 1950, and there were rumours that the party would not contest the election. Stuart Roseveare, a vice-president of the constituency association and a local farmer, was invited to become the party's candidate in February 1951, but it was not until a few days after the start of the election campaign that he finally accepted the offer in order to prevent an agreement with the Conservatives.[3]

This mood of despair that beset the Liberal party after its humiliation in 1950 led to an increase in resignations and defections. In September 1949 the Western Counties Federation claimed 10,037 members, but by June 1952 this number had fallen to only 2,660.[4] While the decline in membership could have been deliberately exaggerated in order to meet future targets, it does suggest a significant fall in the number of party loyalists. Several of the party's leading figures in the region even defected to the Conservatives on the grounds that it was now the only force that could defeat Socialism. For example, Anthony Marreco, the Liberal candidate for Wells in 1950 and a recent recruit from Labour, contested Goole in Yorkshire as a Conservative & Liberal in 1951, while Elizabeth Rashleigh, prospective candidate for Torrington, rejoined the National Liberals on the grounds that the Liberals had to be either 'for or against this Government and I am against it'.[5]

This situation was complicated by press rumours of an imminent Conservative–Liberal pact. Prominent Liberals like Lady Violet Bonham Carter and Sir Archibald Sinclair believed that the party would only survive if it could obtain electoral reform, and they were willing to support an anti-Socialist pact in exchange for the alternative vote or proportional representation. On the Conservative side individuals like Sir Winston Churchill and Harold Macmillan favoured an alliance in order to defeat the Labour government. In May 1950 R.A. Butler and Bonham Carter even held a meeting to devise a manifesto for an anti-Socialist coalition. Opposition from Conservative activists eventually prevented a national agreement, but many radical Liberals, especially in the rural South-West, were worried by the formation of local pacts in seats like Colne Valley and West Dundee. Dingle Foot and Megan Lloyd George presented an anti-pact memorandum to the national leadership in May 1950. In their view an alliance with the Conservatives would 'drive over to the Labour Party a considerable body of Liberal voters, especially in the Radical areas such as North Wales and the West Country'. Foot and Lloyd George added that in these circumstances the alternative vote 'would be little value', and they emphasized that the Liberals had to be seen as an 'alternative Labour Party' and not an 'alternative Conservative Party'.[6] Once again Liberalism was being considered in terms of the conventional political spectrum: Left versus Right.

It was therefore not surprising that the Liberals were unable to develop a coherent plan to contest the election. The idea of a broad front rapidly lost favour following the debacle of 1950, but it was clear that this approach was not replaced by a planned concentration on key regions and constituencies. Although the 1951 manifesto claimed that there was a definite policy of contesting selected seats, the reality was that the situation at the grassroots was one of total confusion as the number of candidates dropped from 174 at the beginning of the campaign to 109 by nomination day. This was reflected in the South-West, with candidates standing in hopeless seats like Camborne and Poole while some of the best prospects for the party (Torrington, Truro, Tavistock and Wells) went uncontested. In a number of seats, such as Taunton and West Dorset, the party announced its intention of contesting the election, but found that a lack of finance and a weakness in organization meant that it was impractical to do so. In the event the number of Liberal candidates across the four counties fell from 24 to 13.[7] Edward Martell, deputy chairman of the Liberal Central Association, concluded that this chaos at the local level was exacerbated by a total lack of leadership, which ensured that the party 'could not have gone into a general election in a more haphazard or rudderless way'.[8]

Once again there was a failure to present a clear image to the electorate. A typical example occurred at an election meeting in West Dorset when the local Liberals asked the Labour and Conservative candidates for their views on typical Liberal policies (proportional representation, profit sharing, home rule for Scotland and Wales, free trade and Europe). Although some of the responses appeared vague, the Labour candidate came out in favour of profit sharing, free trade, devolution for Scotland and Wales and a United States of Europe. Simon Digby, the local Conservative MP, advocated an inquiry into electoral reform, favoured the introduction of profit sharing and a lowering of tariff barriers, was concerned at the 'increasing centralisation of administration in London' and believed that Britain should 'sponsor ... the movement towards European unity'.[9] This demonstrated the problems that the Liberals had in convincing voters that they represented a distinctive alternative.

As expected, then, the election proved to be the low point of regional Liberalism. Once again the party failed to win a single seat, while only four candidates took second place. The Liberals generally fared worse in the two eastern counties. In North Dorset Frank Byers narrowly increased his vote at the expense of Labour, but the Conservative candidate still increased his majority. Elsewhere in Dorset and Somerset the Liberals failed to save a single deposit. Even in rural Devon the party lost ground to Labour and the Conservatives. The only seat in the county in which the Liberals could win even a fifth of the vote was Honiton, while in the party's target seat of North Devon its share of the vote plunged from 30.4 to 19.4 per cent. By comparison the Cornish Liberals came second in two of the four seats that they contested. Although the party lost its deposit in Camborne, Dingle Foot in North Cornwall was still the main challenger to the Conservatives with 34.8 per cent and Roseveare held onto second place with 25.6 per cent.

In retrospect there were some indications that Liberalism still had a hard core of support in the region on which it could build. It is significant that, despite an almost continual decline since the First World War, the party could still poll an average vote of nearly a fifth of the vote in the thirteen constituencies that it contested. In one part of the region, the east Devon seat of Honiton, the Liberals were already regaining lost ground. At the previous general election the party, which was contesting

Honiton for the first time since 1931, had come third. In 1951, however, the new Liberal candidate, John Halse, was able to push Labour to the bottom of the poll at a time when his party was losing ground across the region. The Halse surname was synonymous with local Liberalism since John's father had been the party's candidate for Honiton back in the 1920s. The 39-year-old John Halse proved to be a capable and popular candidate in his own right, while the fact that he was a Congregational lay preacher enabled him to appeal to the nonconformist tradition.[10] Nevertheless, the election was on the whole an unprecedented disaster for the regional Liberals, Allen concluded that the logic of Britain's electoral system meant that as political opinion 'crystallises round two distinct poles, [the] party in between is invariably squeezed out at the bottom'.[11] In 1951 it seemed as if the long decline of Liberalism had reached this final stage. Apart from North Dorset and North Cornwall the Liberals had little chance of increasing their representation, since even in former strongholds like North Devon and St Ives they were now in third place. It seemed that regional politics was now finally polarized between Labour and the Conservatives with the two-party share of the vote reaching its highest level ever at over 90 per cent.

Table 6.1: The 1950 and 1951 election results in the South-West.

	1950			1951		
	Seats	% Vote	Ave. vote	Seats	% Vote	Ave. vote
Conservative	23	47.9	47.9	24	54.1	54.4
Labour	3	34.1	33.2	2	37.2	36.3
Liberal	—	17.3	19.8	—	8.6	18.5

The Wider Background: 1952–1955

Although the Liberals were clearly struggling to survive in 1951, it is more difficult to establish the actual turning point in their fortunes. The conventional view is that it was only with Grimond's succession to the leadership in 1956 that the party took its first steps on the long road to recovery. Cook has claimed that while 1955 was the first election since 1929 'in which the party had made any improvement on its previous election performance, the ground for optimism was hardly very great'.[12] Watkins concluded that it was a period 'characterized by poor by-election results, desertions from the ranks and growing dissatisfaction with the leadership of Clement Davies'. The results of the 1955 election showed that there was 'in short no sign of the promised land. The small band were still in the desert, some of them plodding in one direction, some in another. But the green fields and cooling streams were as far away as ever.'[13] Admittedly, there is a great deal of evidence to support this interpretation. In 1955 fewer than 300 local associations were affiliated to the national party, while financial rock bottom for the Liberals was not reached until February 1957. The party still had difficulties in securing candidates. Just over a year before the general election of 1955, when the Liberals contested 110 constituencies, the party had only about thirty-five candidates ready to stand. In addition, the Gallup Poll's monthly survey of voting intentions found that Liberal support was consistently in single figures from March 1953 until September 1956. The annual average of these surveys suggests that the party's potential vote continued to decline gradually until 1955.

Table 6.2: Annual average of Liberal support according to Gallup, 1950–1955.[14]

1950	10.0 %	1951	8.8 %	1952	8.8 %
1953	7.9 %	1954	6.7 %	1955	7.2 %

The Liberal party certainly remained deeply divided. During the early part of the decade the libertarian wing was in the ascendancy, and resolutions were passed at the 1953 Assembly calling for unilateral free trade and the abandonment of assured markets for agriculture. Some extreme libertarians were even hostile to the Welfare State. They were supported by the *Economist* which called on the Liberals to move to the right of the Conservatives. By becoming the 'avowed champions of the middle classes' the Liberals could appeal to a 'considerable body of frustrated Tory voters' who felt that their own party had moved too far to the left.[15] This horrified the collectivists, and in 1953 they formed the Radical Reform Group with the object of promoting the 'policy of social reform without Socialism'. In 1954 the RRG even temporarily dissociated itself from the Liberals, although individual members of the group still remained active in the party. In the general election of the following year Dingle Foot, a vice-president of the RRG, supported Labour candidates in seats not contested by the Liberals, while Lord Samuel and Violet Bonham Carter advocated an anti-Socialist platform.[16]

Nevertheless, the Liberals began to make some progress at the national level. In December 1951 the party decided to appoint a paid Director General who would be in charge of organization, while in the following month Frank Byers, now chairman of the national executive, launched 'Operation Basic'. The aims of the 'Operation' were to increase membership, arrange the appointment of suitable candidates, reorganize finance, and generally create a more efficient organization at the regional and constituency level. Teams from party headquarters would work with constituency officials to establish local needs and set a target for an increase in membership. Although problems remained at the local level, Herbert Harris, the party's Director General, was able to announce in 1955 that membership had increased by nearly 50 per cent within a year.[17] In addition, the Liberals were finally moving in the direction of a co-ordinated narrow front. In November 1951 the Liberal Party Organisation privately concluded that the party's main priority had to be its survival. The LPO recommended three essential objectives: to retain the party's six seats; win the eleven seats where the Liberals had come second in 1951; and secure electoral reform. Party headquarters would therefore ensure that target seats would have priority allocation in regard to candidates, agents and available finance.[18] At the 1953 Assembly party members were still in favour of a broad front, but they decided to leave electoral policy for 'further discussion by the Executive'. By 1954 the party was talking of a 'realistic front' with constituencies classified into 'those which must be fought; those in which a good Liberal vote must be maintained; those in which the "average" Liberal vote (about 4,000) must not be allowed to fall; and others in which it might be disheartening to fight'.[19]

There were a number of other positive developments after 1951. In the first place the party began to give greater attention to its depressing performance in municipal elections. A Local Government Section was set up in January 1953 for the purpose of providing information and advice to associations and candidates, and the party began to recover gradually in local elections from 1952 onwards, making its first net gains in 1955. The most significant Liberal advance at the local level took place in Blackpool where the party increased its representation on the borough council from six in 1949 to twenty by 1954. The party also won control of Mossley UDC in 1952, and became the largest group at Bacup in 1955.[20] Growing support amongst university students suggested that post-war Liberalism was also starting to appeal to the younger generation. A survey of party activists in 1953 found that the Union of University Liberal Societies had an active membership of only 400, but by 1956 membership had increased to over 2,000. By 1957 membership had risen to over 3,200 following a successful campaign for the suspension of H-bomb testing, and enabled the UULS to claim that it was larger than the equivalent Labour organization. This undoubtedly helped the cause of the Radicals within the party, with the *Economist* concluding in May 1954 that the RRG had 'gathered strength' from the Liberal revival in the universities.[21]

Yet this still left the public perception that Liberalism was still in terminal decline. It was increasingly recognized during the 1950s that achieving good results in parliamentary by-elections was the way to remove the party's negative image and provide the necessary momentum for success in the subsequent general election. However, in the first ten years after the Second World War mid-term contests rarely occurred in seats that still had a relatively strong Liberal tradition. Indeed, Torquay in December 1955 was the first contested by-election in the South-West since North Cornwall in July 1939. This meant that the Liberals always appeared on the defensive, and during the lifetime of the 1951–5 parliament they only contested eight out of a total of forty-eight by-elections, with lost deposits in seven of these contests. The one exception was Inverness in December 1954. In this by-election the party's candidate, John Bannerman, fought a charismatic campaign in an area with strong Liberal traditions. He centred his appeal on the 'popular local issue of Scottish nationalism', and surprisingly came quite close to winning the seat from the Conservatives.[22]

The significance of this result has been underestimated. Watkins believed that 'nothing very much could be deduced from an election in a constituency as far-flung as Inverness'. The *Western Morning* News similarly concluded that 'nobody [would] attempt to draw any sweeping conclusions from this result' and added that 'it is the centre of Britain that must be captured by any party aiming at power'.[23] Yet this

Table 6.3: The Inverness by-election, 21 December 1954.

	1950 %	1951 %	1954 %	% Change since 1950
Conservative	45.5	64.5	41.4	−4.1
Labour	31.8	35.5	22.6	−9.2
Liberal	22.7	—	36.0	+13.3

interpretation fails to appreciate the real significance of Inverness. In the first place the propaganda value of the result was immense. Party activists had been demoralized by poor results for many years, and they naturally exploited the psychological significance of a good second place. In areas like the South-West it was claimed that the result 'proved conclusively that the Liberal vote was not a wasted vote', while in 1955 the confident boast of candidates in seats like North Devon was that they could stage 'another Inverness'.[24] Furthermore, the peripheral 'Celtic Fringe' contained virtually all of the seats which the Liberals had a reasonable chance of winning. Electoral gains in the rural areas of Scotland, Wales and the far South-West would enhance the party's credibility, and provide the momentum to expand into other regions. Inverness suggested that the party's long-term decline had finally been arrested, and it was now in the position to move forward.

Reconstruction in the Region

Furthermore, historical research on the period has tended to concentrate almost exclusively on national developments. While the Liberal recovery did not appear obvious until the late 1950s, the party had already begun to revive in some of its old strongholds during the first half of the decade. This section will concentrate on regional improvements in the area of organization and the party's general sense of direction. The situation in the South-West certainly demonstrates the danger in making a sweeping generalization on the state of the party at this time. By 1955 the Liberals had made little progress in the two eastern counties. In the key seat of North Dorset the Conservative majority over the Liberals actually increased from 747 to 7,159, while the other candidates lost their deposits and failed to significantly increase their share of the vote. The Devon and Cornwall Liberals were more successful. The party's average vote per candidate in the two counties rose from 18.0 to 24.2 per cent, while its share of the vote increased 4.1 per cent. Unlike in the east of the region, the party's vote increased in every seat that it had contested in the previous general election.

Table 6.4: A comparison of the percentage change in the Liberal vote in the seats contested in 1951 and 1955.

Area federation	Seat	1951	1955	% Change
Devon and Cornwall	North Devon	19.4	32.5	+13.1
"	North Cornwall	34.8	42.9	+8.1
"	Totnes	15.0	18.7	+3.7
"	St Ives	14.9	18.3	+3.4
"	Honiton	21.3	24.7	+3.4
"	Bodmin	25.6	28.0	+2.4
Western Counties	Poole	10.0	11.6	+1.6
Devon and Cornwall	Torquay	13.0	14.2	+1.2
Western Counties	Yeovil	12.1	12.2	+0.1
"	South Dorset	11.1	11.0	–0.1
"	North Dorset	45.0	32.4	–12.6

The Liberal revival was most evident in the rural seats of North Devon and North Cornwall. New candidates Jeremy Thorpe and Edwin Malindine were now in a far more secure position to seriously challenge the Conservatives, partly because of their success in regaining votes lost to Labour after 1945. Patterns of voting are developed over the long term, and this ensured that many former Liberals, still influenced by the survival of the Old Left cause after 1918, were not really committed to the two main parties, especially Labour. This factor was reinforced by the strength of the rural *petite bourgeoisie,* groups like small farmers, village shopkeepers and even pensioners, who were still neglected by the collectivist nature of British politics. Admittedly, the relative strength of collectivism elsewhere in the South-West limited the scale of the Liberal revival. In Somerset the mixed industrial/agricultural base of the local economy meant that the Labour vote remained more solid, while the mid-Cornwall Liberals were unable to overcome the strength of trade unionism in the St Austell china clay area and a tradition of Labour voting that had been established back in the 1930s. The party still had a credibility problem in many seats in the region, and, despite Inverness, many candidates had to spend the election reassuring potential supporters that a Liberal vote was not wasted.[25] Nevertheless, the significant aspect of the general election was that the regional Liberals had clearly strengthened their position for the first time since 1929.

Only a few years earlier, however, party activists were far more pessimistic about the future. Geoffrey Taylor, who was to contest Yeovil in 1955, concluded in 1953 that there were only 'four possibilities facing the party—1. We could peter out. 2. We could commit suicide. 3. We could hope for better days. 4. We could try and use what strength we have to negotiate with the other parties.' He felt that the party should 'negotiate with anyone', but suggested that Labour should withdraw in North Dorset and Yeovil. This was unacceptable to a member from Bath who thought that if the Liberals had an 'arrangement' with another party 'they may as well give up' in his division.[26] This sense of despair was not just restricted to those seats in which the party polled badly in 1951. Honiton was one of the few places in Britain where the Liberal vote had increased. In the following year, however, some of the officers of the Exmouth town branch resigned on the grounds that the party had no future, and the branch only survived because of assistance from the local Women's Liberal Association.[27] The Liberals had particular problems in the eastern counties of Somerset and Dorset. The Western Counties Federation was consistently faced with financial difficulties, and in September 1952 had only enough money to 'cover the next few weeks'. The treasurer declared that the situation had reached the stage when members had to ask: 'Is the Federation to go on, or is it to fold up?' Indeed, it was only financial support from the national party that enabled the federation to survive. Although some constituency associations increased their membership quite significantly, the party found it difficult to stage a significant recovery. In 1953 only four divisions had adopted prospective candidates (Poole, South Dorset, Wells and Yeovil), and little progress had been made by the time of the election, with only six candidates eventually standing. This was probably due to problems at the federation level, since at a national meeting in

October 1955 it was stated bluntly that 'organization in the Western Counties was rotten'.[28] .

There was also no real sign of a grassroots improvement in municipal politics. Although the Liberals first began recording net gains at the national level in 1955, it was not until two years later that the party started to increase its number of councillors in the South-West. By 1951 Labour had once more replaced the Liberals as the second-largest party on Exeter City Council, and the party's representation fell from fourteen to eight between 1949 and 1951. In Bath the Liberals continued their slow decline with their number of city councillors falling to five by 1951 and in order to survive the party concentrated on its remaining strongholds and rarely contested any other seats. For example, in 1951 the Liberals only fought one seat (Walcot North) which they retained in a straight fight with the Conservatives. The situation was even worse in Poole. In 1950 the party came third in the only two seats that it contested in the borough council elections, while a year later it lost a seat that it was defending because of Conservative intervention. The *Poole and Dorset Herald* concluded that it was 'absurd' for the Liberals even to contest local elections since they lacked a distinctive identity.[29] Municipal Liberalism in the South-West, then, was still characterized by a slow but consistent loss of seats to their opponents. The one exception was Yeovil. In 1953 the local Liberals put forward a candidate in the borough council elections 'for the first time for many years', and in the following year won the same seat in a straight fight with Labour. Even in Yeovil progress was limited. Considering that 1955 was a general election year it would have been an advantage to the party if it had continued the momentum by winning more seats on the council. In the event the Yeovil Liberals did not even bother to contest the local elections that year![30]

However, in terms of parliamentary politics the party had greater success in the rural seats of the far west of the peninsula. When Jeremy Thorpe was selected as candidate for North Devon in 1952 it proved to be the catalyst for the revival of the local Liberal organization. In February 1953 it was reported that the constituency party had recruited 600 new members within six months, while a month later the women's branch at Barnstaple held its first AGM since 1948.[32] Progress was also made in St Ives where John Kellock, the prospective parliamentary candidate, opened a new divisional headquarters in December 1951 after

Table 6.5: Net changes in representation on borough councils in the South-West.[31]

Election	Conservative	Labour	Liberal	Independent
1949	+26	−24	−1	−1
1950	+4	+3	−2	−5
1951	+9	−3	−2	−5
1952	−17	+33	−2	−14
1953	−12	+14	0	−2
1954	−11	+10	−1	+2
1955	+4	−3	0	−1

a lapse of twenty years. Kellock also announced that the party intended to create a comprehensive network of local branches throughout the constituency, form a local council of the Association of Liberal Trade Unionists and provide more activities for younger Liberals.[33] The launch of 'Operation Basic' strengthened these local initiatives. In April 1953 the Devon and Cornwall Liberal Federation was 'well ahead' of the rest of the country by already having prospective candidates selected for twelve constituencies. The early adoption of new candidates, as in the late 1930s, generated greater enthusiasm, and the number of members in the area had 'more than doubled' since 1951. A good example was in Truro where the adoption of a female candidate, Nancy Seear, encouraged the growth of the local Women's Liberal Association. From 1952 to 1954 membership increased from 35 to 350, and Truro was awarded the Wintringham Shield in two consecutive years for the highest increase of new members in Britain.[34] Not all constituencies were so successful. In 1955 it was said that 'not much effort had been made' to revive the Falmouth and Camborne Liberal Association, and a low turnout at that year's AGM suggested that local Liberalism was 'at a low ebb'.[35] Nevertheless, 'Operation Basic' produced a general and significant rise in membership throughout the two counties. This was confirmed in 1955 when the Devon and Cornwall Federation achieved the highest annual increase in membership in Britain.[36]

'Operation Basic' also brought a new generation to the fore. In a number of constituencies older officers, whose 'enthusiasm and long records of loyal service were no longer matched by their ability', were replaced by younger activists. A good example of this occurred in North Cornwall. In 1955 the local Liberals were quite successful in winning the support of younger voters because Edwin Malindine, the party's candidate, and his 'band of workers were all young men—and—young "women"'. Malindine was 43 years old and younger than his Labour and Conservative opponents (aged 49 and 64 respectively), while the officers of the association were mainly in their twenties and thirties. Thus, William Hosking, the chairman and a future parliamentary candidate himself, was only 31, the constituency agent was in his early thirties, and the party's treasurer was in his twenties. Younger activists generated new campaign ideas. Hosking explained the Liberal revival in North Cornwall on the grounds that Malindine had 'gone to the people' in the more rural parts of the constituency. This was in contrast to previous candidates who had appeared more aloof by restricting their public appearances to addressing the party faithful at indoor Liberal meetings.[37]

The North Cornwall example was repeated across the South-West with several younger candidates being adopted during the early1950s. This was of long-term significance since these new candidates tended to be in the Radical mould with a university education and sympathetic to the RRG, and therefore highly receptive to the policies that were to be pursued under Grimond's leadership. Two of the leading individuals associated with the RRG contested South-Western seats in 1955. These were Richard Moore, aged 23 and chairman of the UULS, who fought Tavistock in 1955, and 37-year-old Desmond Banks, chairman of the RRG, who was candidate for St Ives. Similarly, Maxwell Goode, who contested South Dorset in 1955, was 28 and educated at the University College of Wales, Aberystwyth, while 26-year-old Barbara Burwell, educated at Bristol University and vice-chairman of the National League of Young Liberals, fought Bath.[38] Peter Bessell and Jeremy Thorpe, the key personalities associated with the regional Liberal revival in the 1950s and 1960s, both fought their first election in 1955. At the beginning of the 1955 election campaign the Torquay Liberals were without a candidate, but the executive committee made a last-minute decision to put forward the 34-year-old Peter Bessell.[39] When Thorpe was selected for North Devon in 1952 he was only 23 and had been president of the Oxford Union. The *Western Morning News* reported in 1955 that he had been 'proclaiming the gospel of his Radical Reform Group' with the energetic support of university students from Exeter and Bristol, and he played a key role in finding like-minded candidates for other seats in the region. Thorpe proved to be a skilful and charismatic candidate. By 1955 he had visited every town and village in the division, while even Labour and Conservative activists admitted that on 'sheer personality and swift answering of questions he was streets ahead' of their own candidates.[40]

Policies, Relevance and Identity

Charismatic candidates and a larger membership assisted the party's revival, but it was essential for Liberalism to project a distinctive image to the electorate. The immediate concern of the Liberal party was to retain the allegiance of its existing supporters. Methodism, which remained central to the concerns of the Old Left, played an important part in this consolidation process. This was especially the case in the Cornish seats of North Cornwall and Bodmin where the party's survival as a major force in 1951 was due to the continuing existence of a 'hard core of Radical Nonconformity'.[41] Malindine believed that the strength of Methodism in North Cornwall would be one of the 'seeds of a resounding Liberal victory in the near future'. He claimed that Liberalism was based on 'moral principles and spiritual values', and at party meetings he was assisted by a Methodist minister.[42] The Foot family had dominated Liberal politics in Bodmin for over forty years, and this consolidated the links with religious nonconformity. In addition, Roseveare was well known in the area as a Methodist lay preacher, while the Foot family continued to campaign in Bodmin on his behalf. It was therefore not surprising that in 1954 the Rev. R.J. Day, a local Methodist minister, supported the Liberal cause when he opened a garden fete organized by a local branch of the party. Apart from expressing his personal support for Roseveare, the minister added that Liberalism and Christianity needed to be motivated by the same evangelical fervour:

> I am not only a convinced Christian, but also a convicted one. There is a difference ... because if you are a convicted Christian you feel you must spread your message abroad. You workers should not only be convinced Liberals but also convicted ones and you must therefore let others know about the goodness of your cause.[43]

155

Such comments reflected the fact that there was still considerable agreement between the Liberal party and the Free Churches. Although temperance was not mentioned in national Liberal manifestos after 1935, the issue was still raised in the far South-West, at least by older activists. Isaac Foot, now in his seventies, claimed in 1952 that 'people now distrusted the Conservatives who had spent a great deal of time in passing as their first measure a Bill promised to the brewers while the pledges they gave to the people were put to one side'. He added that once again the Conservatives had been revealed as the 'brewers' party'.[44] The post-war period had also produced a range of issues, such as the Cold War, racism and colonial discontent, which deeply concerned the Free Churches. One of the key themes of Roseveare's election address in 1955 was that the party stood for a 'better kind of world', while policy statements on issues like racism and tax reform had a distinctly religious flavour.[45] When Lord Rea, Liberal Chief Whip in the House of Lords, addressed a party meeting in Cornwall in 1952 he began by saying that Liberalism was a 'great cause because like religion it aimed at the good of all. That was why both were out of fashion in a world of hysterical self-interest.'[46]

The nonconformist influence was especially evident in the Liberal party's attitude towards nuclear weapons. Rasmussen has emphasized that Grimond was mainly responsible in 1957 for the party's decision to oppose Britain's manufacture and use of nuclear weapons.[47] However, Liberal opinion in the South-West was already moving in this direction as the nonconformists announced their opposition to the H-bomb. During the early part of the decade Methodist Synods in the region were passing resolutions against the use of nuclear weapons, and by 1955 the national Assembly of the Free Churches had condemned the use of the bomb. A leading critic was Dr Donald Soper, president of the Methodist Conference in 1952, who was well known in nonconformist circles as a passionate critic of the government's defence policy, and on his regional tours of Britain, including the South-West, he called on Christians to express their opposition. By April 1954 he was claiming that if the 'Churches said "No" to the H-bomb, no politician would say "Yes" to it'.[48] A growing number of Liberals echoed these views. For example, Guy Barrington, the party's prospective parliamentary candidate for Taunton, claimed that opposition to the bomb was a 'moral view and must prevail if we as a Christian country are to prevail', while Roseveare declared that nuclear warfare was from 'the Devil and must be outlawed'.[49] In that sense the old Liberal–nonconformist tradition was partly responsible for what was one of the party's most distinctive policies during the Grimond years.

Another advantage for the Liberals was that their Labour opponents were increasingly beset by internal problems. Aneurin Bevan and his supporters argued that Labour should move further towards Socialism, and this led to public disagreement with the party leadership, particularly over the defence issue. Evidence from the South-West suggests that discontented Labour supporters were now looking towards the Liberals, with local newspaper reports suggesting that in seats like Bath and Taunton the majority of Liberal supporters in 1955 had voted Labour in 1951.[50] This was confirmed by a detailed study of voting behaviour in the neighbouring seat of Bristol North-East. Milne and Mackenzie found that the composition of the Liberal vote in 1955 had changed since 1950. The Liberals had not contested the seat in 1951, and on that occasion over two-thirds of their supporters had voted Conservative. In 1955 many ex-Liberals remained with the Conservatives, but the Liberals attracted significant support from those lower middle-class voters that had previously supported the Labour party. Milne and Mackenzie concluded that Labour's 'old party images … had faded without any new images having taken their place'. While some Labour voters either abstained or voted Conservative, the 'comparatively large Labour loss to the Liberals in 1955 was yet another symptom of the general movement of opinion away from the party'. This was significant since the Liberals under Grimond were to portray Labour 'as a spent force, whose policies were irrelevant to the needs of the 1950s'.[51] The evidence suggests that many Labour voters were already becoming disenchanted for this very reason.

The Liberals could also argue by 1955 that the two major parties had failed to implement Liberal policies. In 1951 the Conservatives had appeared sympathetic to ideas like control of cartels and wider share ownership, and this limited the distinctive appeal of independent Liberalism. However, the failure of the new Conservative administration to give adequate attention to these issues enabled the Liberals to present an alternative political spectrum based on radicalism versus conservatism. In 1952 John Foot declared that the 'Conservative–Socialist battle was a sham. They are going out of their way to find things at which they are at issue'.[52] Thorpe emphasized this view in 1955 when he claimed that the two main parties were united on a whole range of issues like monopolies and opposition to co-ownership:

> The two other parties are as alike as two peas ... We can rely on both to pour out a torment against the other for crimes which their parties themselves committed while in office. The cost of living has gone up—and its deadly toil has been taken in terms of old age pensioners ... and others unable to strike for higher wages ... Who represents the ... consumer today? Certainly not the Tory party, who are the watch dog of big business and the other Conservatives, the Labour Party, who are the ineffective protagonists of the TUC.[53]

By concentrating on consumer issues the party was able to appeal across the political spectrum. The Bristol North-East survey found that Labour voters believed that the cost of living was the main issue in 1955, while the Conservative 'rank and file' were also concerned by rising prices.[54] Inflation was a particular problem in the far South-West because of the greater concentration of groups like non-unionized workers and old-age pensioners. The *Western Morning News* concluded in 1955 that it was the 'major issue' of the election at the local level. Tourism was the only growth industry in places like Torquay, Newquay and Ilfracombe, but it was associated with low wages and unemployment. While the 'rest of the country' believed that Cornwall and Devon was the 'land of the idle rich', the reality was that low and fixed income groups formed the main section of the population.[55] This view was echoed by Liberal candidates like John Halse (Honiton) who argued that many voters in his constituency were dependent on pensions, savings and low wages, and they were therefore 'doing very badly' because of the rise in prices. In 'pleading their cause' the Liberals were establishing themselves as the champions of a neglected interest group that ranged from pensioners to small businessmen.[56]

This concern for the local interests of the *petite bourgeoisie* complemented the party's emphasis on regional concerns. In 1964 Grimond was to portray regionalism as the 'great issue of this decade', but it was an idea which became associated with Liberalism in the early 1950s.[57] At previous post-war elections the South-Western Liberals had mainly concentrated on national issues, particularly in 1950 when it had campaigned as an alternative government. After 1951, however, the party was fighting for its very survival, and many Liberals saw their only role, at least in the short term, as being that of a parliamentary pressure group. By campaigning on those issues which voters felt strongly about, but which were ignored by the other parties, the Liberals could find a new role. The socio-economic problems confronting the peripheral regions of Britain fitted into this new approach, while the fact that these areas had a Liberal tradition provided a foundation for the party's expansion. At the regional Liberal rally at Pencrebar in 1952 the prospective Liberal candidate for Tavistock, Gerald Whitmarsh, combined the need for a narrow front with a proposal that the party should become the voice of the countryside. Whitmarsh believed that in previous elections the party had 'made the mistake of trying to do too much with too few resources'. An alternative way was to concentrate on rural areas, and he even suggested that the party should adopt a new title to demonstrate its commitment to the countryside:

> For the future they had to concentrate on the seats most likely to be won … This meant leaving the industrial centres and attacking in the country areas, such as Wales and Cornwall … We must get down to looking after the countryside [and] design a country policy to give long-term security. It might be that we should change our title to the Liberal and Country Party.[58]

Roseveare was the other guest speaker at the Pencrebar rally, and it is significant that he also concentrated on the same issue. In his view the Churchill administration was already neglecting the agricultural interest, and he concluded that the 'Tories were more interested in big business and high finance'. With his farming connections he was in an ideal position to exploit the grievances of the rural community, and in 1955 it was reported that over the previous three years he had been wooing the agricultural vote. For example, at the annual dinner of St Antony Farmers Union in January 1953 Roseveare had proposed that agriculture should be recognized as the 'No. 1 industry in the country with a minister of cabinet rank'.[59] Whitmarsh and Roseveare were not alone in recognizing the importance of the farming vote. At the 1953 Assembly Seear emphasized the need for a new Liberal policy on agriculture. She claimed that neither of the two main parties had the 'guts to face the problems of agriculture. We have a real opportunity if we have the courage to say we are not satisfied with the present position.'[60] The agricultural vote eventually proved to be the key factor in the party's regional revival. During the early 1950s the farming community, particularly smallholders, were concerned by the government's failure to provide a permanent solution to agricultural problems like production and prices. A price review in February 1955 provided a 'temporary fillip', but the farmers were still 'worried'. In 1955 the political correspondent for the *Western Morning News* reported that in Cornwall and 'some parts of the Devon countryside' many farmers were 'thinking this time of voting Liberal'. He added that polling day would show whether 'these thoughts would be converted into actions', but he concluded after the election that the swing against the Conservatives in seats like North Cornwall, Bodmin and North Devon was due to the fact that a number of farmers either abstained or voted Liberal.[61]

The future of farming, however, was a controversial subject for the Liberal party as a whole. In 1953 the national executive proposed a resolution opposing guaranteed prices and assured markets for agriculture, and in a somewhat modified form it was passed by that year's Assembly. This was totally unacceptable to the Devon and Cornwall Liberals who believed that it would be 'quite useless' to fight a rural constituency on official policy. Immediately after the resolution had been carried Thorpe rushed to a microphone on the platform and appeared to suggest that all twelve candidates in Devon and Cornwall were resigning.[62] In the event the regional Liberals decided to put pressure on the executive in order to reverse the decision, and the 1955 Assembly produced a more acceptable compromise. Nevertheless, the election addresses of South-Western Liberals in 1955 revealed that they were still going further than the party's manifesto. They supported free trade when it came to abolishing tariffs on fertilizers and feeding stuffs as it was in the interests of both farmers and consumers. Yet the regional Liberals stressed their support for assured prices and markets, and called for extra financial help for the 'small farmers, the farmers on the poorer land, the farmers remote from the market'.[63]

Rural discontent formed part of the wider centre–periphery cleavage. Differences in the electoral performance of Liberal candidates in 1955 actually reflected the varying economic conditions that existed across the South-West. The two eastern counties had a more balanced economic base, and the growth of industries like engineering, especially in Yeovil, South Dorset and Poole, prevented problems like depopulation, unemployment and low wages. Between 1931 and 1951 Somerset's population increased by 17 per cent, and a considerable number of the new residents had come from neighbouring counties in search of work. The *Poole and Dorset Herald* in June 1954 used the headline 'Boom Town', and rejoiced that the problem in east Dorset was to 'find enough workers to fill the vacancies which came up'.[64] In total contrast there was growing concern that the so-called 'dead area' of Cornwall and Devon was still in decline. The number of agricultural workers in the west fell by nearly 900 from 1952 to 1953, while those individuals who were anxious to better themselves were forced to leave the area in search of higher pay. Depopulation was a serious problem in a number of rural constituencies, especially Bodmin, St Ives, North Devon and Torrington. The 1947 survey by the University College of the South-West had concluded that the region needed improvements in essential services like water and electricity. Similarly, the 1951 census found that whilst 17 per cent of houses in England and Wales were without piped water, the figure for rural North Devon was 50 per cent.[65]

This evidence of regional stagnation, particularly at a time of growing national affluence, complemented the new Liberal agenda. In 1955 the North Cornwall Liberals vigorously exploited the fact that only one third of farms in the area had access to electricity.[66] Whitmarsh also criticized the government's claim that the average wage was £10 a week. While this 'might have been true of industrial areas, it was certainly not true' for a constituency like Tavistock. He added that the real standard of living in some parts of the region had actually declined since 1945.[67] Regionalism offered the Liberals a purpose since it reinforced their argument that the House of Commons needed a number of MPs who were independent of the 'Tory and Socialist machines'. The party could now claim that the west of the region was still in decline, despite the regional policies of the 1945–51 Labour governments and the interest shown by local Conservatives when they had been in opposition. As Malindine put it, seats like North Cornwall would be 'far better served by a man [who] represents the people of his constituency, not a party headquarters in London'.[68]

Finally, mention should be made of the wider implications of regionalism. One of the Liberal party's most distinctive policies in the early 1950s was that of domestic self-government for Scotland and Wales. Political developments, such as public support for the Scottish Covenant in 1948 and local government successes by both Plaid Cymru and the Scottish National Party, suggested a renewed interest in the issue after the Second World War. These events encouraged a younger generation of Celtic revivalists in Cornwall to move in a political direction.[69] While the Cornish movement had emerged in the early years of the twentieth century with an essentially cultural and antiquarian image, the creation of Mebyon Kernow (Sons of Cornwall) in January 1951 symbolized a new approach since it was committed to the goal of domestic self-government within the United Kingdom. Its initial line was to operate as a pressure group, working with other organizations to protect the interests of the region and producing policy documents on a broad range of subjects. Although Mebyon Kernow did not make a real impact on public opinion until the 1960s, the mere existence of this new group reinforced the position of the Liberals who were already attempting to establish themselves as the principal anti-metropolitan party in Cornwall. Malindine and Seear portrayed Liberalism as the traditional ideology of the Cornish people, while Roseveare's campaign slogan in 1955 was 'a Cornishman for a Cornish seat'.[70] Some Liberals accepted the constitutional objectives of the Cornish movement. In May 1952 John Foot and Roseveare expressed their support for some form of Home Rule on the grounds that the 'Cornish people were a separate nation'. A representative from party headquarters in London even hinted that Cornwall could have total control over its own domestic affairs with just defence and foreign policy remaining with Westminster.[71] Once again this demonstrates how regionalism was effectively restricting the momentum for a Liberal revival to the far west.

Conclusion

Although the early 1950s represented the final stage of the Liberal decline, these years also witnessed the first phase of recovery. This was certainly the case in the South-West. In 1955 the Liberal party made little progress in the eastern counties but its early revival in number of rural seats in the hinterland of Cornwall and Devon served as a beacon of hope for demoralized activists, while improvements in organization, new candidates and the abandonment of the broad-front approach contributed to later successes. Moreover, the party was able to present a distinctive alternative to perceived central government indifference by combining policies like regional development with measures to tackle the cost of living. By presenting themselves as the free and independent champions of regional interests, at least in Cornwall and some parts of Devon, the Liberals now had a new image which was a crucial factor in future election success. In order to translate these advantages into parliamentary victories, however, the party needed the decisive leadership and greater credibility associated with the Grimond era.

7

The Dawn of Victory: 1955–1959

Introduction

The progress of the mid-1950s was consolidated by events during the latter part of the decade. When Jo Grimond became Liberal leader in 1956 he set out to provide the party with a clear sense of direction. By 1958 the Liberals enjoyed rising support in parliamentary by-elections, municipal elections and opinion polls. This progress at the state level provided a more secure environment for expansion in the localities since greater credibility enabled the party to really exploit its dormant strength in areas like the far South-West. In addition, it was good by-election results at Torquay and Torrington that heralded the advance of the third force at a wider level. Consideration is also given to the underlying reasons for rebirth, ranging from contemporary ideas of social change at a time of growing national affluence to regionalist discontent in rural areas. Finally, the areas of strategy and organization are explored, with particular emphasis placed on the growing recognition of the benefits of a narrow front.

The Liberal Advance

During the late 1950s the party's fortunes began to change with a number of impressive by-election results. Although this recovery was in the first place due to dissatisfaction with government policy, the subsequent combination of good results created its own momentum. The Torquay by-election on 15 December 1955 provided the first indication of progress. This contest followed the death of Charles Williams, a Conservative, who had represented the constituency since

Figure 7.1: Faces of the revival: Jo Grimond, Eric Lubbock (MP for Orpington 1962–70) and candidates from the four counties, 1962.

1924. Peter Bessell, the managing director of a local dry-cleaning firm, was already established as the prospective Liberal candidate, and he was able to increase his share of the vote by 9.6 per cent. The significance of the result for the South-West was that it showed the party was now expanding from its 'Tamarside' heartland into the east of the region. Yet the by-election also had wider implications. Steed remarked that Torquay was the first 'really good performance in urban Britain and began the first period of Liberal runs of mid-term by-election support which have subsequently become a regular feature of periods of Conservative government'.[1]

Over the following two and a half years the party appeared to be on the verge of a major electoral breakthrough. On 14 February 1956 the Liberals polled over a fifth of the vote at Gainsborough (Lincolnshire), and on the same day there was another good result in Hereford when the party increased its share of the vote from 24.8 to 36.4 per cent. This early revival had lost momentum by the end of the year and in February 1957 the Liberals even lost Carmarthen to Labour. By the summer of

Table 7.1: Parliamentary by-elections in the South-West, 1955–1959 (percentages).

| | 1955 general election | | | By-elections 1955–9 | | |
	Liberal	Conservative	Labour	Liberal	Conservative	Labour
Torquay	14.2	60.4	25.4	23.8	51.0	25.2
Taunton	8.4	52.1	39.5	—	50.8	49.2
North Dorset	32.4	52.1	15.5	36.1	45.1	18.3
Torrington	—	65.1	34.9	38.0	37.4	24.6
Weston-super-Mare	—	62.7	37.3	24.5	49.3	26.2

1957, however, there were signs that a bandwagon effect was being created with the party polling respectable votes at Edinburgh South, Gloucester and Ipswich. The North Dorset by-election in June presented the possibility of an actual victory in a traditional stronghold. At the start of the campaign local Conservatives had expressed doubts as to whether they would hold the seat, but in the event the Liberals had to be content with reducing the Conservative majority from 7,159 to 3,102.[2] The party's credibility was further enhanced by its success at Rochdale in February 1958. In the previous election the Conservatives had narrowly won the seat in a straight fight with Labour, but in the by-election the Liberals forced the Conservatives into third place and came a close second to Labour with 35.5 per cent of the vote.

The emergence from dormancy culminated in the party's victory at Torrington on 27 March 1958. This by-election followed the resignation of George Lambert, a Conservative and National Liberal MP, who moved to the House of Lords as Viscount Lambert after the death of his father. In 1955 Lambert had held Torrington with a comfortable lead over Labour of 30.2 per cent. Yet this figure was deceptive. A significant number of voters had abstained in 1951 and 1955 because of the absence of a Liberal candidate, and the by-election revived the traditional Conservative–Liberal antagonism in the constituency. In the event Mark Bonham Carter, a grandson of Herbert Asquith and Liberal candidate for Barnstaple in 1945, defeated the government nominee by 219 votes. Torrington was the first Liberal gain at a by-election since Holland-with-

Boston (Lincolnshire) in March 1929, and the psychological benefits of Bonham Carter's victory were considerable. *The Times* concluded that Torrington was of particular significance for the South-West since candidates in adjacent constituencies would now 'look much more like potential members of Parliament'.[3] Indeed, Bonham Carter 'laid down a target of not fewer than eight seats' in the region, while Grimond predicted the election of forty Liberal MPs, who would hold the balance of power after the next general election.[4]

Although Torrington proved to be the last by-election defeat that the government suffered during this period, the Liberals continued to achieve some respectable results. The party concentrated on residential and agricultural seats, and its candidates polled between 24.2 and 27.5 per cent at Weston-super-Mare, Argyll, Aberdeenshire East, Southend West and Galloway. The Weston-super-Mare by-election on 12 June 1958 was a good example of this final phase of the Liberal advance. In the previous election the Conservative majority was actually lower than it had been at Torrington, and in theory this meant that the party's

Figure 7.2: Peter Bessell, MP for Bodmin (1964–70), and Paul Tyler, MP for Bodmin (1974) and North Cornwall (1992–present), crossing the Tamar Bridge in 1970.

position was now vulnerable. However, while the Liberal candidate, Edward Taylor, came a good third, the government retained the seat with a comfortable majority. In previous by-elections the Liberal advance had mainly been at the expense of the Conservatives, but significantly Taylor attracted votes from the two main parties in fairly equal proportions.[5] This provided the background to the 1959 general election when extra Liberal votes in the east of the region came primarily from Labour.

The Liberals had not enjoyed such a consistent record of good by-election results since the late 1920s, and this naturally had an impact on public opinion. As one party activist remarked in 1958, 'whereas a year or two ago hardly anyone bothered to express their opinion about Liberalism, it is an interesting reflection that nowadays people of all creeds are devoting their time to it, some for, others against'.[6] Bessell, who became prospective candidate for Bodmin in 1956, claimed that the significance of Torrington was that the 'wasted vote argument was dead for ever ... for here in the South-West we shall not put in Labour candidates instead of Conservatives: we shall put in Liberals'.[7] By the time of the 1959 general election the party's advance had started to lose momentum, but remarkable results in seats like Torrington and Rochdale meant that the Liberal image was no longer that of a party in decline. L.K. Way, political correspondent for the *Western Morning News*, observed that even in Somerset and Dorset the Liberals were 'being treated with solemn respect by Tories and Socialists alike'.[8]

This advance was reflected in local elections. At the national level the decline of municipal Liberalism had ended in 1955 when the party had emerged with more gains than losses. Over the following four years there was a fairly steady increase in the number of net gains (seven in 1956, twenty-seven in 1957, seventy-six in 1958 and thirty-three in 1959), which provided the base for the more spectacular municipal victories of the early 1960s. But this grassroots revival was limited in the South-West. The party only began making net electoral gains in 1957, and even in 1959 it held a mere twenty-one of the 958 borough seats in the region. Indeed, by the end of the decade the Liberals still only had official representation on eight (Yeovil, Poole, Bath, Torquay, Exeter, Bridport, Weymouth and Taunton) of the forty borough councils.[9] It was not until 1962 that the party began to make more significant gains, which is perhaps surprising considering the fact that the South-West, particularly Cornwall and Devon, was a key area in the party's revival in national politics.

There was a combination of factors that limited the regional advance of municipal Liberalism. One problem was that the party failed to build on initial successes. For example, in 1957 the Liberals won their first seat on Bridport Town Council (West Dorset) for fifty years, and their position was further strengthened by a by-election victory later that year. Yet the local party's failure to contest a single seat in 1958 led to a loss of momentum, and in the following year the party actually lost a seat to Labour. The Bridport example further demonstrates the failings of the area federations. In 1955 the Western Counties Federation had expressed its concern over the lack of progress made in West Dorset, but no mention was made of the possible benefits of contesting local elections. Indeed, in the late 1950s the subject of municipal politics was not even raised.[10] The Independent tradition remained another obstacle. Although in 1959 Labour and the Conservatives held considerably more council seats than the Liberals, 192 and 206 respectively, the Independents still dominated the smaller councils with 539 seats A similar situation applied to the four county councils which were controlled by the Independents, and in 1958 only two county council seats, both in Dorset, were held by the Liberals. Finally, the Liberals found it difficult to reverse their decline on councils where they were already established. Liberal representation on Bath City Council fell from five in 1953 to just two in 1958, and it was not until the following

Table 7.2: Net changes in representation on borough councils in the region.

	Labour	Conservative	Liberal	Independent
1956	+3	+1	−1	−3
1957	+7	−2	+2	−7
1958	−2	−3	+7	−2
1959	−4	+3	+3	−2
1960	−9	+6	+5	−2
1961	−10	+2	+12	0
1962	−2	−20	+27	−5

year that the party began to make progress when it increased its number of councillors to four.[11] The revival was even later in Exeter. In 1956 the party held six seats, but three years later it was struggling to survive with a mere two councillors. The main problem was that the local association lacked any real purpose or direction. This was to change following the victory of David Morrish in 1961, since under his leadership the Exeter Liberals were able to stage a dramatic recovery, with the party gaining five seats in 1962 and a further six in 1963.[12]

There were three councils (Torquay, Yeovil and Poole) where the party had some success at this time. During this period the Torquay Liberals, building on their parliamentary by-election success, began to contest local elections for the first time since the war. In 1958 they won a seat from the ruling Independents, and after the 1959 elections they emerged with three seats on the council.[13] The Yeovil Liberals had first won a seat on the local council in 1954, and during the latter part of the decade they gradually built up their representation to five out of twenty-four seats. By 1959 the Liberals were in an influential position since they held the balance of power between Labour and the Conservative-dominated Independent group. Geoffrey Taylor, Liberal parliamentary candidate for Yeovil, emphasised his party's achievements in local government, and he claimed that Britain would also benefit if the Liberals held the balance of power at the national level.[14] Poole was different from Torquay and Yeovil in the sense that the Liberals had regularly contested local elections in the past in Poole. During the early 1950s, however, the party had lost its remaining elected councillors, and by 1956 it had only one representative, an alderman, on the borough council. This began to change in 1957 when a Labour councillor defected to the Liberals. He was narrowly defeated in the May elections, but a few months later the party won a seat from Labour in a by-election. By 1959 the Liberals had made three net gains at the expense of Labour, and by 1962 they had become the main opposition to the Conservatives with thirteen seats.[15]

When the general election was finally held in October 1959 the Liberals enjoyed somewhat mixed fortunes. Although there was a failure to increase the party's representation in the House of Commons, the number of seats where it polled over a fifth of the vote increased from 18 to 46 and its overall vote rose from 2.7 to 5.9 per cent. In the South-West the Liberals, polling 18.7 per cent, emerged as a significant regional force, but this figure disguised a wide variation between the west and east. There was certainly a rise in the party's vote in Somerset and Dorset, especially in Poole and Yeovil, but North Dorset was the only constituency where the party was able to poll over 30 per cent of the vote and even then its performance was worse than in 1951. In the far west, however, the Liberals were in a stronger position to actually win seats. Although Bonham Carter lost Torrington by 2,265 votes, Thorpe was returned with a majority of 362 in North Devon. In the adjacent Cornish seats of Bodmin and North Cornwall the party was again close to victory, with Bessell reducing the Conservative majority from 7,659 to 2,801 and Malindine only 989 votes behind. Taking Cornwall as a whole, the Liberals moved into second place with 28.7 per cent of the total vote.

Another feature of the election was the relative success of the Liberals in winning votes at the expense of Labour. In the east of the region observers saw the election in terms of a 'battle of the minorities', with the Liberals mainly gaining votes from Labour and the Conservatives maintaining their share of the vote.[16] Tactical voting contributed to this process in the west. The party was seen as the main alternative to Conservatism in the Cornwall–Devon border area, and the apathy of Labour voters made it easier for the Liberals to exploit the wasted vote argument. Labour's share of the vote in Bodmin and North Devon fell by 7.1 and 5.3 per cent, while in Torrington the party lost 9.8 per cent of the vote in comparison with the by-election in the previous year. The North Devon Liberals predicted that the Labour candidate would lose his deposit, while Bessell declared that 'if you want to get rid of Tory rule in Bodmin, there is only one way of doing it, and that is by voting Liberal'. In the latter seat the Liberals were actually helped by the Conservative campaign. The local Conservatives had initially used posters entitled 'If you want a Socialist Government, vote Liberal', but by the beginning of October they were 'fast disappearing from the hoardings' because they had had the effect of encouraging Labour voters to support Bessell.[17] This Liberal advance ensured that the swing against Labour was greater at the regional level. At the state level the Socialist vote declined by 2.6 per cent in comparison with 1955, but in the South-West it fell by 5.2 per cent. In real terms this regional decline was even greater because Labour's national vote in 1955 (46.4 per cent) was higher than in the South-West (34.9 per cent).

New Man or Little Man?

The underlying reason for the Liberal party's revival in the late 1950s and early 1960s has been the subject of quite considerable debate. One contemporary argument was that the party was attracting the support of the so-called 'New Man'. Political observers claimed that social change was undermining the Labour vote, and that this created an environment which was more favourable to Liberalism. Labour's success in the 1960s, however, cast doubt on these conclusions. The explanation for the Liberal revival was actually more complicated, particularly since Grimond's policy was to form an alliance of those groups that were discontented with the major parties. Apart from influencing the actual timing of the revival throughout Britain, this approach ensured that markedly different regions were attracted to the third party. As Driver put it in 1962, the post-war Liberals were 'not one party but two … people from dying rural communities and people from brisk modern suburbs'.[18] Indeed, it was not 'New Man' but rather the 'Little Man' and Woman, such as the small farmers, shopkeepers and pensioners, who were probably responsible for the party's advance in the South-West. By 1959 a variety of factors, including regional discontent, tactical voting and even the old nonconformist vote, ensured that the region became the party's main growth area in Britain.

In the first place Grimond certainly created a more favourable environment for a Liberal advance. The party's new leader supported the ideas that had been raised by the Radical Reformers in the early 1950s, with regionalism and opposition to an independent British nuclear deterrent becoming official policy. Policy statements, such as *New Orbit* and *New Directions,* projected a fresh image for the party, and Grimond played a key role with books and pamphlets like *The New Liberalism* (1957) and *The Liberal Future* (1959). This move, to be repeated by Tony Blair and New Labour in the 1990s, was a conscious decision on the part of the leadership. In 1957 Grimond created a Political Research Unit which had the task of monitoring public opinion. The PRU concluded that Liberal propaganda had to emphasize that the party was 'forward-looking' in order to 'obtain a fashionable image' in the minds of younger voters:

It will be … no use adopting a 'take a step forward—Vote Liberal' attitude if our publicity dwells too much upon what the Liberals have done in the past. If we do so, we will be associated with the past and people may doubt if we have emerged from it. As a forward-looking Party we must stress our policies for the future above everything else.[19]

This modern stance, according to Cyr, provided the foundation for the Liberal revival because the 'popular spirit in many quarters of Britain was one of disillusion and despair in the face of … conservatism and stagnation'. Discontent covered a whole range of issues including economic problems, foreign and colonial policy, particularly at the time of the Suez crisis, and the need for reform of the political system. Cyr claimed that Grimond's emphasis on the need to accept change and reform was an attractive alternative to the two major parties who gave the impression that they were 'frozen into an unchanging *status quo*'.[20] This New Liberalism was also designed to appeal to a specific social group: the middle-class professionals. The party's by-election victory at Orpington in 1962 led a number of political observers, such as Abrams, to study these 'new men', and it was concluded that they were reacting against the class orientation of the two major parties.[21] There is some evidence to suggest that the Liberals were already starting to benefit from these voters in the late 1950s. Based on information collected in the last three months of 1958 the PRU identified the 'average Liberal [as] a young technician, farmer or executive, with a wife and young family'. The PRU added that the party's potential supporters were 'roughly the same as those groups appealed to in *The Midland Bank* personal cheques campaign'.[22]

Investigations into the new social base of the party were influenced by the wider theory of *embourgeoisement*. During the 1950s social observers claimed that rising prosperity was encouraging the upper working-class to adopt 'middle-class virtues and pursuits'. Social change was therefore undermining working-class solidarity, and this created an unfavourable climate for Labour. Butler and Rose's study of the 1959 election was influenced by this thesis. They claimed that the Conservative party had deliberately encouraged the 'spread of middle-class attitudes', particularly in the housing estates of urban Britain. Only a 'narrow majority of those in the New Towns voted Labour; Conservative *and* Liberal candidates drew support in surprising numbers'. Butler and Rose accepted that 'any verdict on the political implications' of social change had to be tentative, but they believed that Labour's position was likely to be further undermined as working-class voters were now being 'exposed to conflicting political pressures'.[23]

This interpretation was subsequently challenged. In 1962 Goldthorpe et al. tested the thesis by means of a sample of affluent manual workers in Luton in Bedfordshire, and concluded that 'no process of *embourgeoisement* [was] evident'. Affluent workers still believed that a Labour government would provide a greater 'pay-off [in] the way of higher living standards and better social services'. Their support, however, was probably more 'instrumental' than traditional working-class voters who gave 'almost unconditional allegiance'.[24] Tiratsoo, in a study of Coventry in the period from 1945 to 1960, claimed that what had actually happened was that Labour lost contact with 'those groups who were at the centre of change—young people and new home-owners'. In 1945 Labour had been able to address the electorate 'as if it was a homogeneous whole', but the 'old working-class "sameness" was rapidly becoming a thing of the past'.[25] Moreover, it is debatable whether voters were attracted to the new Liberal image. In March 1959 a Gallup poll suggested that nearly 60 per cent of the electorate did not know what the party stood for, and this included nearly half of those who intended to vote Liberal. While Grimond was stressing the need for 'change', the mean reason given for voting Liberal was that the party stood for 'moderation'. Curtice has concluded that the party's electoral support was based on a 'volatile protest vote'. The majority of Liberal voters were a 'constantly shifting group' who saw the party as a convenient but 'temporary refuge from their normal Conservative or Labour home'.[26] In that sense the Liberal revival in the late 1950s was simply an illusion based upon negative protest votes.

Another explanation, however, can be put forward for the Liberal advance. Any study of the subject must take into account the fact that the Liberals were still in no position to campaign effectively against the two main parties at the national level. Butler and Rose concluded that the party fought the election as a 'federation of independently operating candidates, rather than as a broad national movement'. The party was able to turn this into an advantage by raising issues which were ignored by Labour and the Conservatives. Trade unionism was too controversial to be raised by the two major parties, and this enabled the Liberals to claim that they were the only party to advocate trade union reform. Questions like the government's road programme and farm subsidies also received little attention at the national level, but the Liberals ensured that they became key election issues in the South-West.[27] During the late 1950s the Liberals had attempted to give some coherence to this approach. The protest vote thesis is based on the idea that the party was attracting temporary votes, but what was significant during this period was the way in which the Liberals actually attempted to channel electoral protest into the creation of a new force. In *People Count*, the party's election manifesto, Grimond declared that a Liberal vote was a 'protest against the British political system being divided up between two powerful party machines'.[28] Peripheral socio-economic groups would provide this basis of this 'protest' alliance. Thus, Philip Watkins, the Liberal candidate for Bridgwater, claimed that the two main parties were 'ignoring the legitimate needs of the "Little Man"—whether small trader, old-age pensioner or owner occupier'.[29] Grimond himself was well aware of the potential benefits of appealing to specific interest groups:

> There are ... millions of young people and uncommitted voters who simply do not see themselves mirrored in the image of Tory bigwigs or Labour bosses. They are all the consumers, small business owners, professional men and technicians, craftsmen and farmers, fishermen, shopkeepers, and pensioners who have no interest in the Capital v. Labour struggle and are greatly harmed by it.[30]

The Liberals were even accused of moving in a neo-Fascist direction because of their efforts to attract the support of the *petite bourgeoisie*. Dominic le Foe, the party's publicity consultant and a former professional magician, encouraged an intensely psychological and effervescent approach to party meetings. He even arranged a torchlight procession through the town of Bideford following Bonham Carter's victory at Torrington which had obvious similarities with the processions of Nazi Germany. Indeed, Morgan Philips, secretary of the Labour party, claimed that the Bideford celebrations showed that there was an 'unhealthy tinge in this new "Liberalism" with its victory torch parades and irresponsible appeal to the self-interest of the lower middle classes'.[31] Some Liberals even believed that their immediate role was to provide a positive alternative to the other parties on the grounds that frustration with the political system would otherwise lead to the formation of an extremist party. In March 1956 Desmond Banks, chairman of the Radical Reform Group and candidate for St Ives, claimed that if it were not for the existence of the Liberals 'we might well be witnessing today the growth of some dangerous movement akin to that of M. Poujade in France'.[32]

This frustration was due to a belief that government policy was especially detrimental to the interests of the *petite bourgeoisie*. The economic situation had worsened soon after the Conservative victory in May 1955, and in October of that year the government had introduced an anti-inflationary budget which it was claimed had 'hit small men the hardest'. For example, fishermen in Cornwall and Devon were furious that their subsidy had been withdrawn. The government had introduced an alternative scheme, but the only beneficiaries were 'big fishermen' in other parts of Britain. The small farmers also believed that the government was undermining their position. There was a 'very strong wave of discontent' amongst farmers and market gardeners after a reduction of farm subsidies in the 1956 Price Review. This was particularly the case in Cornwall which it was claimed was 'hit worse than any other county in the country'.[33] In February 1956 *The Times* reported that the government's 'credit squeeze was resented by small farmers and traders', while Thomas Lynch, President of the National Union of Small Shopkeepers, complained that his members were also faced with rate revaluation, which had increased rates by 'up to four times':

> The small shopkeeper is at the end of his tether. He has been hit by … the effect of Purchase Tax and the credit squeeze. Revaluation comes as the last straw. The small shopkeeper cannot stand any further increase in either direct or indirect taxation.[34]

These groups needed an alternative party in order to express their discontent. They were unlikely to support Labour because of their fear of Socialism, and this had been demonstrated in 1950 and 1951 when 'big and small alike' had united behind the Conservatives. The Liberals were therefore the only alternative. Stevenson's observation that the

Figure 7.3: Jeremy Thorpe and his supporters celebrating the Liberal victory at North Devon in 1959 with a torchlight procession through the streets of Barnstaple.

Figure 7.4: Preparing for the Tiverton by election in 1960. Jeremy Thorpe, James Collier (candidate for Tiverton), Meddon Bruton (candidate for Taunton) and Lilian Prowse (agent for North Devon).

electoral system has been an advantage to the party in enabling it to remain as the third force in British politics certainly applied in the 1950s.[35] In other European countries proportional representation had led to the formation of parties which could defend minority interests. Thus, Agrarian parties could represent the countryside in Scandinavia, while the Poujadists had emerged as a force in French politics in the mid-1950s by championing the cause of the small traders. The electoral system was obviously an obstacle to the formation of similar parties in Britain, but the *petite bourgeoisie* still wanted a party that could represent their interests. In arable areas like East Anglia the farming community had received 'careful tending by successive protectionist and subsidy-minded Conservative and Labour administrations'.[36] Small farmers in pastoral regions like the South-West were effectively neglected by this policy. Similarly, Lynch claimed that Britain was 'ripe for a Poujadist movement' on the grounds that neither of the two main parties could adequately represent the interests of the small traders. The Conservatives had given 'ample evidence that they were helping big business and the multiple store', while Labour was 'tied to nationalisation and the Co-operative movement'.[37]

Furthermore, the Little Man and Woman had traditionally provided the backbone of the Liberal party's support in areas like the South-West. In 1957 Dingle Foot said that there was a tendency to 'equate the Liberal vote with the middle-class', but in his view it was 'more correct to say that the Liberal votes [were] mainly drawn' from self-employed groups like shopkeepers and small farmers. He added that it was significant that the 'main Liberal strength' was centred in regions where there was a 'great number of family farms and one-man enterprises'.[38] Considering that many of the existing Liberal voters already came from the *petite bourgeoisie,* it made it easier and more natural for the party to regain the support of similar voters who had defected to the Conservatives in the early 1950s.

The main obstacle to constructing an alliance of these groups was the fact that they were divided over the extent of their opposition to the collectivist system. This was not really a problem in remote regions like the South-West because the future prospects of the traders depended on the prosperity of the farming community. When groups like the farmers, shopkeepers and traders were combined, they formed the overwhelming majority of rural voters. A good example can be seen in

Northlew (Torrington) where the 'way of life of its people' in 1958 was based 'fundamentally on the land'. Farming families accounted for 47 per cent of the population, while a further 34 per cent consisted of labourers and tradesmen who provided services for local farmers.[39] However, at the national level the extreme libertarians within the party, especially from the Home Counties, were frequently in conflict with the more pragmatic activists in the marginal agricultural areas of Britain. The overwhelming concern of the former group was to challenge a political and economic system which threatened the small trader, and many of these activists were themselves minor entrepreneurs. The libertarians were totally opposed to ideas like guaranteed prices and assured markets, and a Cheap Food League was formed by Oliver Smedley, the prospective Liberal candidate for Saffron Walden (Essex), which campaigned for the removal of restrictions on the dumping of cheap food from abroad. In 1956 Smedley and his supporters had obtained a victory when that year's Assembly had committed the party to 'unilateral free trade'. At the 1958 Assembly there was a fierce debate over the agricultural issue, and a compromise resolution failed to satisfy the extreme wings of the party.[40]

Nevertheless, there was a growing recognition of the benefits of a balanced policy. Howard Fry, the candidate for Aylesbury (Buckinghamshire), claimed that the libertarians had prevented the party's revival 'from being as rapid as it might have been. The reason the West Country candidates are making such good progress is that they are talented, hard-working candidates who are in favour of a sane, balanced liberalism.'[41] Grimond was also opposed to the pure free trade argument on the grounds that it failed to take into account the 'lives of people living on the land'. He naturally encouraged those individuals who held similar views, and in 1958 Bonham Carter, his brother-in-law, was appointed as chairman of the Liberal agricultural committee.[42] Although events were moving in their favour, the Devon and Cornwall Liberals wanted to go even further. In March 1959 the federation took the initiative by publishing its own policy statement, entitled *Thought for Food*. This document, written on the basis of 'practical experience' of agriculture, recommended greater financial assistance for small farmers, and not surprisingly it proved popular with the agricultural community. *Thought for Food* was then accepted for debate at the national level, and a public argument was avoided only because of the cancellation of that year's

Assembly. Nevertheless, during the election campaign candidates like Bessell and Alan Gibson (Falmouth & Camborne) campaigned on the basis of *Thought for Food* rather than the party's official policy.[43]

Assessing the Regional Evidence

Having considered the theories behind the appeal of the Grimond Liberals, this debate needs to be applied to the grassroots. It has already been pointed out that the four counties of the South-West cannot be regarded as a single entity. Whilst the remote communities of Cornwall and north Devon were more likely to respond on regionalist grounds of rural discontent, some voters, particularly in urban and affluent areas, were also attracted to the 'New Man' image developed by Grimond. Not surprisingly, this was certainly the case with the younger generation. In 1959 the Labour candidate for Plymouth Sutton, in line with Tiratsoo's observations, concluded that his defeat 'could be attributed to the younger people' with their 'more materialistic outlook' on life. This factor was emphasised by a delegate of Exeter Divisional Labour Party when he addressed that year's party conference:

> Back in the thirties when we were young and fighting to get a job … we had something to fight for. Today they get it easy: good wages, regular hours … They have never had it so good [and] it is not a damn bit of good going out and telling them what we had to do …: they will either not believe it or tell you it is a dead duck.[44]

It could also be argued that Labour's 'spent force' image had alienated younger voters. There was a growing belief that the party had lost the radical fervour of 1945, and this view was reinforced at the grassroots by its conservative attitude towards local government. A classic example of this occurred in the 1958 county council elections when the spokesman for the Somerset Labour Federation declared that the party's candidates would 'serve the county in the maintenance of services, and where reasonably possible to extend them. "Orderly development" might be taken as the key-word.'[45] Such statements enabled Bessell to claim that the 'Labour party to-day is a smooth political machine, but it has no fire, no depth of belief and no sense of urgency'.[46] Assuming that younger voters were more likely to be attracted by a radical image, it was understandable why Labour had problems in attracting their support. In contrast, the new Liberal image was likely to appeal to these voters. Indeed, it was reported that a number of younger Labour supporters in Falmouth & Camborne voted for Gibson because of his well-publicized involvement with the Aldermaston march and the Campaign for Nuclear Disarmament. This was apparently reflected across the region since political observers claimed that the Liberals were quite successful in attracting the support of first-time voters.[47]

The situation in Poole provides an interesting case study of how Labour was failing to communicate with many of its potential supporters. Labour's problems had started in July 1954 when the Conservative-controlled borough council had introduced a rent surcharge scheme in which more affluent workers would pay higher rents. The scheme was bitterly attacked by council tenants who claimed that it offered 'no incentive to work harder', and in the Hamworthy ward 89.4 per cent of those tenants that were canvassed signed a petition against the surcharge. Local tenants, moreover, were infuriated by the failure of the Labour group to object to the changes. They believed that this was the main reason why the scheme had secured such a 'smooth passage through the Council Chambers'.[48]

In the mid-1950s the Poole Liberals rarely contested local elections, and they therefore failed to exploit this particular issue. However, after 1957 the party attempted to represent the interests of the council tenants. Liberal candidates claimed that the housing committee had unfairly evicted some families to 'serve as an example to others', and they called for council tenants to have the same protection as private tenants. The Liberals also argued that several of the Labour representatives were 'put on the council more as a reward for party service than for an ability to contribute anything of value'.[49] By 1959 this strategy was starting to succeed, with the party winning seats from Labour in the Newtown and Hamworthy wards. Once again it appears that the younger voters were the main group to defect from Labour. In 1959 the leader of the Liberal group on the borough council claimed that his party was attracting the support of voters under the age of 40. 'People in their fifties, he said, were confirmed in their ways, but it was the young married couples who were looking to the Liberal Party for a fresh deal.' This view was echoed in the following year by the victorious Liberal candidate for the Newtown ward who claimed that his party's vote would continue to increase in the future as 'more and more young people came on the register'.[50]

The significance of the Poole result was the way in which the Liberals were able to exploit the more 'instrumental' nature of Labour support. By offering a 'fresh deal' on housing the party was effectively usurping Labour's traditional role as the champion of the council tenants. Yet Poole was an exception. Wallace has claimed that one of the mistakes of the Grimond era was the failure to appeal to working-class voters in industrial and urban areas. Many in the party assumed that the working class would 'disappear with universal education, television, cars and a middle-class wage'.[51] In retrospect the party's failure to target Labour areas was a serious mistake. Labour's conservative approach to local government in Somerset and Poole was surprising considering that the party was not the ruling group on either council. There were possibly even greater opportunities that the Liberals could have exploited in industrial areas where Labour councils had become complacent after many years in office.

In the South-West, however, the principal factor for recovery was the regionalist discontent of the *petite bourgeoisie*. Revaluation and the 1955 budget were the main issues at the Torquay by-election, and the Conservative candidate admitted that even loyal party supporters were critical of government policy. Bessell focused his campaign on revaluation which he claimed would 'bring ruin to the Torbay towns', and many protest voters preferred to vote for him as an 'alternative candidate' rather than express their criticism by 'simple abstention'.[52] *The Times* concluded that the two main groups that defected to the Liberals at Hereford and Gainsborough on 14 February 1956 were the small farmers and the traders. The third by-election to be held that day was at Taunton, but a lack of finance prevented the Liberals from putting forward a candidate. If the party had contested the seat it may well have benefited from protest votes. Voters were again concerned with inflation and the Price Review, with the latter issue being particularly significant for small farmers on Exmoor. Although Labour was able to reduce the Conservative majority, many of the small farmers expressed their dissatisfaction by abstaining rather than voting Labour.[53]

The issues at Torrington in 1958 also favoured the Liberals. Two of the subjects that were raised, pensions and the cost of living, had been of particular importance to the *petite bourgeoisie* in the early 1950s. In addition, the Conservative and National Liberal candidate, A.H.F. Royle, had been on the defensive on the agricultural issue before the by-election. When the government had announced its 1956 Price Review the local branch of the National Farmers' Union had ominously concluded that 'we can tell the Government what we think at the next election', while Royle's selection had been received 'unfavourably' by the agricultural community since he was a 'city candidate'.[54] At the start of the campaign the government had announced a further reduction in subsidies for the small farmer. Royle's speeches were interrupted by cries of 'You let the farmers down', and Barnstaple NFU called on voters to show their 'disgust with the Government's "anti-farming policy"'. Bonham Carter argued that the Price Review would especially affect 'this part of the world' because 80 per cent of local farms consisted of only 90 acres or less, and it was widely believed that the farming issue was the main reason for the narrow Liberal victory.[55]

The basic problem for the Liberals was how to sustain this momentum. While discontented voters were willing to support the party in a by-election, political conditions were naturally different in a general election when a division in the non-Socialist vote could lead to the return of a Labour government. Although many discontented voters remained with the Liberals, a reduction in income tax, purchase tax and beer duties in the pre-election budget of 1959 helped the Conservatives to win back vital support in that year's election. Yet in the more rural areas of the region the small farmers were still dissatisfied. The shock of its defeat at Torrington forced the government into providing special financial assistance for farmers in the more marginal agricultural areas, and early in 1959 these proposals formed the basis of the Agriculture (Small Farmers) Act. This assistance probably won back the support of some farmers, but Way found that in pastoral seats the farming community was still critical of government policy. Cornwall especially was described by Way as a 'land of disgruntled small farmers'.[56] The 'narrow boundaries' of the Act meant that many in the industry failed to qualify for any further assistance, while local farmers were faced with the prospect of 'more acute foreign competition' because of an Anglo-Danish trade agreement in 1959. Bonham Carter's victory at Torrington had established the Liberals as the main alternative to the government in rural Cornwall and Devon, and they were therefore the obvious beneficiaries of this discontent.

The Liberals connected the discontent of the small farmers with the wider need for a regional agenda. Grimond had been an early advocate of such an approach in his own remote constituency of Orkney & Shetland, and when he became leader in November 1956 he ensured that individual initiatives were integrated into official policy. In *People Count* he declared that it was 'essential to revitalize the countryside'. Improvements in essential services like water and electricity would help the entire community, while Britain had to double its existing expenditure on roads to strengthen the rural economy. The Liberals also proposed a land bank which would provide cheap credit for farmers and rural industries.[57] Although candidates from the other parties were also now starting to look at local issues, what distinguished the Liberal approach, at least in the far west, was the party's co-ordinated plan for regional development. In 1958 Bonham Carter had commissioned the *Economist* Intelligence Unit to carry out a survey of the economic and social conditions in the north Devon area. The inquiry recommended a ten-year development plan to improve the local infrastructure, and the professional nature of the report was emphasized by both Bonham Carter and Thorpe.[58] In Cornwall the party's candidates did not restrict the discussion of local issues to their own constituencies, but instead used slogans like 'Open up the West' and 'A Fair Deal for Cornwall' to show that they were defending the cause of the 'forgotten county'. This concern for the economic problems of the Duchy even led to calls for a decentralization of political power by the Cornish Liberals. While Labour and the Conservatives were opposed to the idea of a regional assembly, the Liberal candidates were all in favour of 'real devolution', with Gerald Whitmarsh (St Ives) and Bessell especially claiming that Cornwall was 'in a similar category to Wales'.[59]

Growing concern over the high level of local unemployment was another factor in this tide of regionalist discontent. This was demonstrated at Torrington in 1958 where it was the most important issue in the by-election campaign after the plight of agriculture. *The Times* reported that 6 per cent of the workforce in the Bideford and Torrington area, three times the regional average, were unemployed, and the fact that this was a long-term problem made it 'all the more serious'. By 1959 all three parties recognized that local unemployment could be a deciding factor in a number of contests in the west of the region.[60] Table 7.3 shows that while the percentage level of unemployment in Somerset was actually below the national average, it was much higher in Cornwall and parts of Devon. Furthermore, unemployment tended to be concentrated in certain areas, and this meant it was even greater in places like Penzance (6.8 per cent) in the west and Gunnislake in south-east Cornwall (14.4 per cent).

Table 7.3: Unemployment in Great Britain and the South-West in October 1959.[61]

Cornwall	Devon	Somerset	Dorset	Great Britain
4.9 %	3.1 %	1.5 %	1.9 %	1.9 %

In 1959 the Conservatives tended to fare worse in those regions such as Scotland and Lancashire where unemployment was relatively high.[62] The peripheral areas of Cornwall and north Devon were no exception. An example was the success of Harold Hayman, Labour MP for Falmouth & Camborne, in going against the national trend by increasing his majority from 1,047 to 4,197. Hayman benefited from a strong personal vote, but local unemployment was a major factor. In September 1959, usually a 'favourable month' for employment, about 5 per cent of the workforce were out of work, and this 'nurtured' memories of the 1930s when Falmouth & Camborne had been 'one of the grimmest depressed areas in Britain'. The Conservatives admitted that it was difficult to increase their vote when 'Government promises had brought no new jobs'.[63] In the event the Conservative vote fell to its lowest-ever level in the post-war period at 36.2 per cent, while the Liberals increased their share of the vote from 9.6 to 18.0 per cent in comparison with 1951. Falmouth & Camborne forms part of a wider picture. While Somerset, Dorset and many of the Devon seats saw a 'swing to the Right', the opposition parties, particularly the Liberals, fared much better in the less affluent area of Cornwall, North Devon and Torrington.[64] The Conservatives won all of the seats in the former group, and they were able to increase their majorities by an average of 2.8 per cent. Conservative majorities in the far west, however, were reduced by an average of 8.3 per cent, while Thorpe overturned a lead of 14.7 per cent to become the first Liberal to gain a seat in a general election in the region since Frank Byers in 1945. Thorpe's comments after the declaration of the results point to the importance of regional discontent:

> I look upon this as a declaration of independence by the people of North Devon; I look upon it as a declaration of war on unemployment in this area and I look upon it as a cry from the countryside to see that we bring services to those in our rural areas.[65]

Finally, it would be a mistake to ignore the party's traditional nonconformist supporters. Butler and Rose found in a case study of Tiverton in 1959 that the party had polled especially well in parishes where 'nonconformity was held to be a strong influence', while Way concluded that in the Cornish countryside Liberalism still 'walked hand in hand with Methodism'.[66] Williams' study of the village of Northlew in 1958, under the pseudonym of 'Ashworthy', provides further evidence that political alignment was still based on religious denomination. Thus, eleven of the twelve committee members of the local branch of the Torrington LA were Methodists, while fifteen of the sixteen Conservative branch officers were Anglicans. This division was 'characteristic and well-established over a great part of the rural West Country'. Above all, Williams presented an image of a society that had hardly changed since the 1920s. He concluded that

> the people are either Church of England or Methodist, in roughly equal proportions. It is no accident that ... the officers of the Liberal Club are nearly all Methodists, while those of the Conservative Association are Anglicans. In Ashworthy this is regarded as part of the natural order of things.[67]

The Liberal view was to consolidate the party's vote by appealing to the survival of Free Church sentiment. In the far west the nonconformists were still a significant force at this time. Indeed, Winter has pointed out that Cornwall was one of only six English counties where the Methodists increased their membership during the period from 1951 to 1961. They had less success in Devon, but some circuits like Okehampton and Northlew had 'not fared badly so far as numbers go'.[68] It was not surprising that Liberal candidates still emphasized their nonconformist connections. Bessell was a Congregationalist preacher, and he stated in his election address that he had preached in many of the Methodist chapels in the Bodmin area. Similarly, newspaper reports stressed that Gibson was a lay preacher, and that his father had been the minister of Falmouth Baptist Church.[69]

Many Liberals still believed that politics and religion were connected. Thus, Emlyn Jones, the party's candidate for North Dorset, declared that politics should be a 'practical outlet for your religious beliefs', while Bessell also concluded that the 'very nature of the religious man indicated he should have political views and express them'.[70] Moreover, political developments at this time probably strengthened this nexus. Radical nonconformist ministers regarded the Suez crisis as the 'last fling of a dying Westernism'.[71] Even some prominent activists in the Conservative party defected to the Liberals on moral grounds over this issue, and a good example was James Collier who contested Tiverton for his new party in 1959 and the 1960 by-election. Furthermore, the materialistic image of Macmillan's Conservative government conflicted with the puritan beliefs of rural nonconformists. A notable feature of the regional Liberal campaign in 1959 was the way in which party spokesmen concentrated on such words as 'morality' and 'materialism'. Bessell, influenced by his links with American religious organizations, called for a new 'theological–democratic order' in which spiritual values would provide the 'driving force' in society. Similarly, Gerald Whitmarsh in St Ives campaigned for morality and honesty in politics. He added that Britain had enjoyed 'material progress but not moral progress', while behind the 'apparent prosperity of our people today was the great social evil of people over-committing themselves on hire purchase agreements'.[72] This was yet another indication of how regional factors, rather than 'New Liberalism', provided the real catalyst for the Liberal breakthrough in the rural west.

Strategy and Organization

The Liberal advance was assisted by a more professional approach to electioneering. Political developments after 1955 ensured that the national party continued to pursue a narrow-front line, which provided a more conducive framework for the regional advance of the Liberals. To start with, Bessell's relative success at Torquay in December 1955 led the party to formulate a specific by-election strategy. Constituency associations had previously contested by-elections on their own resources, but Bessell enjoyed considerable assistance from outside the region. Visits by personalities like John Arlott, the well-known BBC broadcaster, ensured that the party's meetings had a good attendance rate, while 'large teams' of university students assisted the Liberal campaign. Thereafter, headquarters decided to provide outside assistance at selected by-elections on a regular basis, and this enabled the Liberals to 'meet their opponents on almost equal terms in a limited local context'.[73] Such an approach was obviously influenced by the narrow-front argument and impressive results like Rochdale and Torrington suggest that it was a success.

Paradoxically, the initial effect of the party's by-election revival was to encourage demands for a broad front. Many Liberals still assumed that their supreme goal was to form a government, and they believed that Bonham Carter's victory at Torrington presented the party with its 'greatest opportunity since 1906'. Even Herbert Harris, director general of the Liberal Party Organisation and an advocate of a more realistic approach in the early 1950s, claimed that 'if we go about our business properly, we may well be the Opposition, and we could be the Government, so swift is the tide of disillusionment with the other parties'.[74] The party's failure to sustain the momentum of its revival after Torrington subsequently reduced the pressure for a broad front. On 12 June 1958 the Liberals contested three by-elections (Ealing South, Weston-super-Mare and Argyll) on a single day. Although the party polled between 17.2 and 27.5 per cent, the results were disappointing when compared with Rochdale and Torrington. *The Times* claimed that there could be 'no doubt about one of the factors that contributed to the Liberal failure ... They simply had not resources of troops and treasure to deploy for keeping up the pressure' in all three seats.[75]

In these circumstances the Liberals decided that their organization was 'too weak' at the local level to contest a majority of the seats in the House of Commons. While the final decision to put forward a candidate was still made at the local level, the national party would only give its support if Harris 'satisfied himself' that the local association had sufficient finance and organization and had already adopted a candidate.[76] Grimond was able to retain the loyalty of local activists because he presented the narrow-front idea as the first stage towards the ultimate aim of becoming a party of government. In 1957 the Liberal leader declared that his aim was to form a government within ten years, but in order to achieve this objective the party had to concentrate on building up a strong bloc of Liberal MPs. This would be the catalyst for a political realignment in which the Liberals would replace Labour as the 'progressive wing' in British politics.[77] In other words Grimond had not abandoned the aim of a Liberal government, which reassured activists at the grassroots, but in the short term the party would concentrate on a narrow front.

The South-West became a key area for the party with the national leadership finally recognizing the importance of targeting key seats. *The Times* reported that Cornwall and Devon especially was regarded as the 'site of the [party's] most cherished prizes', which was confirmed by Bonham Carter who said that the party 'expected a great deal from the West Country—which at heart was Liberal—and there was not a single seat there which could not be won'.[78] Nationally, a lack of finance meant that the Liberals were only able to 'make a token effort' in most divisions. Only four seats held by the Conservatives (North Devon, North Dorset, North Cornwall and Hereford) received financial assistance from headquarters, but it is worth noting that three of these constituencies were in the South-West.[79] This new approach was most evident in the way in which target seats were finally receiving regular visits from leading figures. A good example was North Devon where outside support had the effect of reinforcing the 'revivalist' atmosphere that Thorpe and his supporters had created in the constituency. Grimond first spoke at a Liberal meeting in the constituency in July 1956 and once he became party leader he made at least one visit every year, while well-known by-election candidates like Ludovic Kennedy (Rochdale) and Manuela Sykes (Ipswich) were guest speakers at local rallies. In 1959 virtually all of the party's well-known figures, such as Lord Beveridge, Frank Byers and Lady Violet Bonham Carter, toured the area, while Grimond spoke at Barnstaple during his helicopter tour of target seats.[80]

It could be argued, however, that the leadership should have been even more vigorous in this area. Admittedly, the party still had financial problems during this period, but Grimond has been criticized for adopting a relatively low profile in 1959. The Liberal leader launched his party's campaign by addressing a rally in London on 15 September, but he spent most of the election campaign in Orkney & Shetland and was 'hardly heard from for the next fortnight'. It was not until 5 October, three days before the election, that he briefly went on a tour of the country with his one-day helicopter tour of the party's target seats. In the South-West he spoke in just two constituencies, North Cornwall and North Devon. Butler and Rose remarked that with 'no other well-known leaders available to tour the country … the Liberals could not mount anything like a full-scale national campaign'.[81] Watkins was even more critical. He argued that Grimond was 'hardly likely to lose' Orkney & Shetland, which he had held in 1955 with a massive majority in a three-cornered contest, and if the Liberal leader had 'stomped the countryside the picture might have been different'. Watkins added that Macmillan, in a 'sixteen-day tour, made seventy-four speeches; Gaitskell, in thirteen days, made fifty-three. Compared to these, Mr Grimond's effort was insignificant indeed.'[82]

A more positive feature of the election was a general improvement in organization and membership. Bonham Carter claimed that the regional Liberals were 'fighting [with] more experienced candidates and stronger organization than at any time since the war'.[83] There is evidence to support this statement. For example, the organization of the North Devon Liberals was at least the equal of their Conservative opponents. Thorpe and his new agent, Lillian Prowse, had concluded after the 1955 election that the Conservatives would only be defeated by 'perfect organization'. The local Liberals therefore made an 'all out effort' to increase their membership, which by 1960 apparently numbered nearly 4,000, by using such ideas as a three-month publicity campaign and extensive 'Membership Drives'. By May 1959 the Liberals had thirty-seven branch associations in North Devon which compared with only six in 1955, while the *Western Morning News* reported that the Liberals were the only party which had every polling station covered on Election Day.[84] The Bodmin Liberals made similar progress during this period. When Bessell became prospective parliamentary candidate in December 1956 he introduced a new approach to campaigning and organization based on American election techniques which he had studied on visits to the United States. In 1959 he deployed this new style of electioneering with a greater use of open-air meetings, while divisional headquarters was organized on a professional basis with 'carefully timed schedules, progress reports [and] memos galore'.[85] Evidence of the effectiveness of the Liberal campaign can be seen in the reaction of the local Conservatives. An inquiry concluded that the party's organization, in

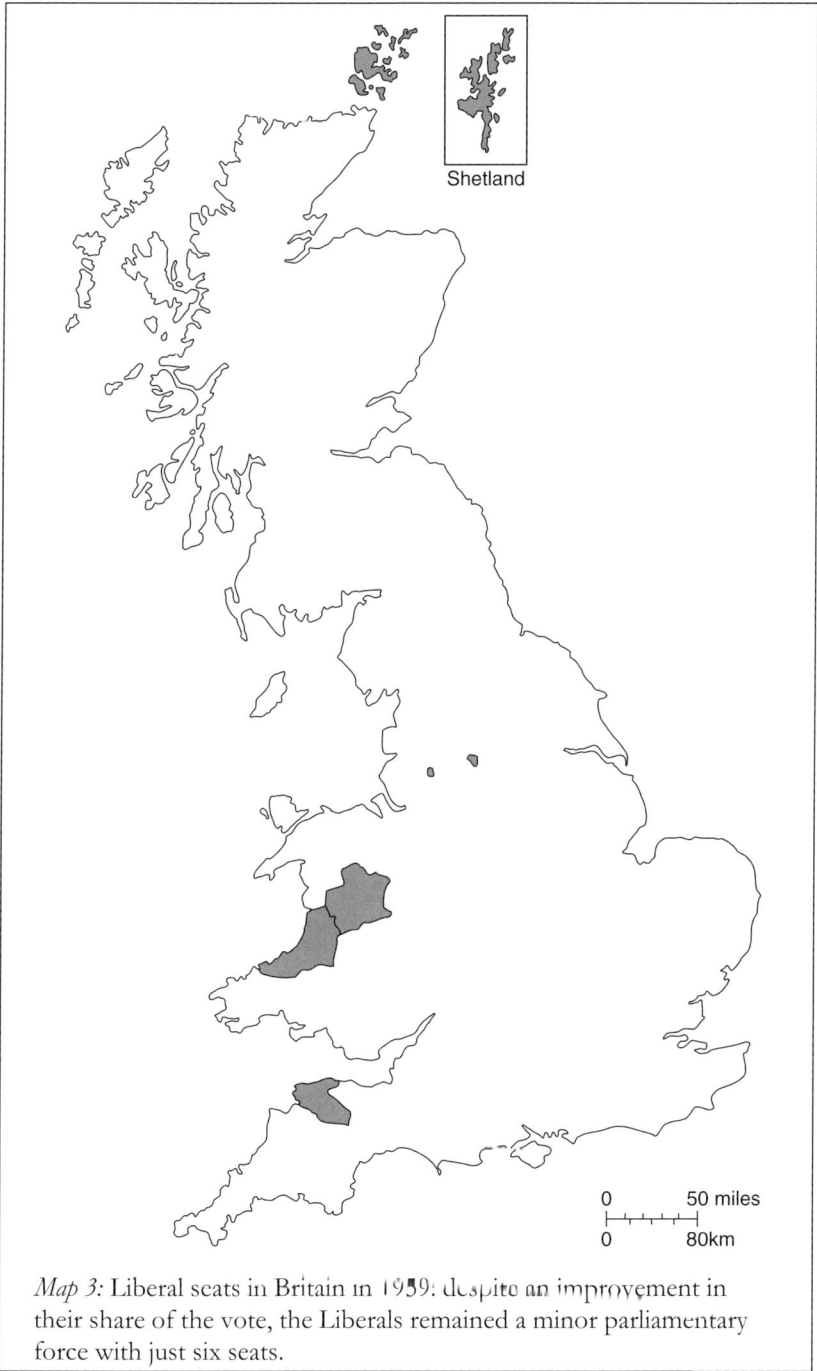

Shetland

0   50 miles

0   80km

Map 3: Liberal seats in Britain in 1959: despite an improvement in their share of the vote, the Liberals remained a minor parliamentary force with just six seats.

contrast to that of its main opponents, had suffered from 'apathy between elections', while senior officers of the association also pointed out that the Liberals had 'somehow spent twice as much as we had on Publicity'.[86]

This situation did not exist in all constituencies. In Bridgwater the party had not contested the seat since 1935 and its local organization was virtually moribund, while the Tiverton Liberals did not appoint a professional agent until after the start of the campaign.[87] A more surprising example was North Dorset, which was one of the party's target seats. The 1957 by-election revealed that some parts of the division had received 'no contact with Liberals for some time', and party members from other seats in the area were highly critical of the failure of the North Dorset Liberals to consolidate their position.[88] Nevertheless, the Liberals had even made progress in some of the seats where their organization had been virtually non-existent. For example, after the 1955 election the Torquay Liberals had attempted to 'remedy the defects shown in that campaign'. By December local membership had increased by more than a thousand, and a full-time agent and secretary had been appointed before the by-election campaign.[89] When Meddon Bruton became prospective candidate for Taunton in 1957 the local Liberals were in a demoralized condition. The party had been in no position to contest the 1956 by-election, and a year later there were only fifty 'paid-up members, three Liberal associations and £30 in the kitty'. Bruton, as Way put it, 'transformed the scene with his burning faith in the party's revival', and within two years the constituency had 1,200 members, 23 branches and 'enough money to fight the campaign at full strength'.[90]

The Taunton example clearly points to the vital role of the candidate. Indeed, Liberal activists have suggested that the crucial factor in the party's regional success was the presence of 'a few strong Liberal candidates' like Thorpe, Bessell and Halse. Although there was a general trend back towards Liberalism, the party was only able to translate this advantage into a significant revival in those seats where it had an energetic and popular standard bearer.[91] This is demonstrated by a comparison of North Devon, Bodmin and North Dorset. Thorpe and Bessell were able to make a considerable impression in the two former constituencies, but the North Dorset Liberals never recovered from the resignation of Frank Byers as prospective candidate in 1953.

Table 7.4: A comparison of the Liberal percentage vote in North Devon, Bodmin and North Dorset in 1951 and 1959.

	North Devon	Bodmin	North Dorset
1951	19.4	25.6	45.0
1959	42.9	38.3	30.2
% Change	+23.5	+12.7	−14.8

Liberal constituency campaigns in the region were often based on the personal qualities of their candidate. Way reported that two of the advantages in Bonham Carter's favour in 1959 was an 'impressive catalogue of constituency service' and the 'psychological factor' of winning the 1958 by-election. Torrington Liberal Association made 'continual use of the Christian name [Mark] to project Mr Bonham Carter as one of them, their member, their triumph'.[92] In the adjacent constituency of North Devon 'Jeremy Thorpe' was a household name by this time. In 1959 the *Economist* reported that the Liberals were 'deliberately conducting an American-style campaign' based on the slogan 'This Time Jeremy'.[93] Another interesting example was Bessell whose campaign concentrated on his growing international reputation. In the late 1950s he had made a number of well-publicized visits to the United States where he met leading figures from American politics, business and religion. His election address in 1959 contained personal tributes from Mrs Eleanor Roosevelt and the former Rajah of Sarawak, while *Truth Magazine* described him as the 'outstanding politician of the year'.[94] When this was combined with his reputation as a successful businessman, Bessell could claim that he was in an ideal position to attract new industries to Cornwall. He even formed Cornish Development Ltd, a non-profit making organization, to assist new business enterprises in the county. Such a personal commitment reflected the traditional belief in the region that a MP should be the active leader of the community, and it helped candidates like Bessell to appeal to the floating vote.

Conclusion

The Grimond years cover the period when dormancy finally turned to rebirth. Whilst a recovery had started in the remote corners of Britain a few years earlier, it was only at Torrington, later confirmed by Orpington in 1962, that the dominant parties had to recognize the challenge from the third force. The strength and weakness of this New Liberalism was its ability to appeal to different audiences. A more fashionable approach was to win over the young and affluent voters in suburban Britain, discontented first with the Labour opposition and then, by the early sixties, with Macmillan's Conservative government. Arguably, the real opportunity lay in exploiting the concerns of rural groups, particularly the *petite bourgeoisie,* since this would have represented a natural extension of the party's surviving base in the countryside. It was only to be expected that the latter option provided the road to recovery in the South-West. Along with the commitment to a narrow front and the vital factor of credibility after Torrington, this ensured that in 1959 the far South-West was the party's main growth area in Britain.

8

Past to Present: 1997 in Context

Introduction

Jeremy Thorpe's victory at North Devon in 1959 confirmed the return of the Liberals as a credible force. This chapter traces the party's story through to 1997 when its successor, the Liberal Democrats, obtained the best performance by the heirs of Gladstone for nearly seventy years. Although the intervening period since the late 1950s deserves special treatment in its own right, this study is an attempt to examine more recent developments within the context of the party's historical evolution after the First World War. Against a background of rural politics, a society still influenced by religious nonconformity and a growing tide of anti-metropolitan discontent, the Liberals moved on into the 1960s and 1970s searching for ways in which to expand their small parliamentary base. Even the years of promise in the 1980s, when the Liberal/SDP Alliance threatened to replace Labour as the national opposition to the Conservatives, resulted in just a modest regional presence at Westminster. The final section briefly examines the Ashdown years when local government victories, in combination with the emergence of a professional approach to electioneering, paved the way for success.

Building on the Foundations

Our understanding of the political history of the South-West can only benefit by first approaching the subject from a comparative perspective. Chapter 1 considered the Scandinavian model where there could be significant regional variation with class-based politics competing for supremacy with more traditional forms of cleavage. An example of this occurred in Norway after the early 1900s. In urban and industrial areas the electorate was polarized between Socialism and Conservatism at an early stage. A similar process, as noted earlier, took place in the hierarchical fishing and forestry districts in the north and east. Yet in the more egalitarian communities of the south and west the traditional forms of political alignment were more strongly entrenched. The Old Left had developed in the nineteenth century in these regions as a reaction to the religious and political power of the centre. Even in the late 1950s religious and territorial issues were still more important than class politics. As Rokkan pointed out, the 'decisive criterion' of this form of alignment was *'commitment to the locality and its dominant culture*: you vote with your community and its leaders irrespective of your economic position'. Such an approach was in total contrast to the usual twentieth-century view of *'commitment to a class and its collective interests*: you vote with others in the same position as yourself whatever their localities'.[1] This created a complex political system in Norway with the Middle parties (Liberals, Agrarians and the Christian People's party) dominating the south and west, while the Conservatives became the main opposition to Labour in the other regions.[2] Similar developments occurred in both Sweden and Denmark where the Liberals succeeded in keeping the Conservatives in third place.[3] Significantly, the electoral performance of the Old Left throughout Scandinavia was considerably better than the British Liberal party which was struggling to survive by the early 1950s.

It could be argued that there are fundamental differences between the political systems of Britain and Scandinavia that prevent any meaningful comparisons. An obvious contrast was that whilst the Conservatives were the main force in British politics after the First World War, in Sweden, Norway and Denmark it was the Socialists who were the dominant party of government. There is also the fact that the size of the British population far exceeds that of the combined total of the five

Table 8.1: The average percentage vote polled by the parties of the Old Left in Britain and Scandinavia, 1944–1959.[4]

Sweden	Denmark	Finland	Norway	Iceland	Britain
32.2	31.7	29.0	28.3	23.0	5.8

Scandinavian countries. This factor could have a significant impact on the nature of party politics since, according to Rokkan, 'smaller polities' are less encumbered by problems of administration.[5] Support for a fairer electoral system was also more evident in smaller democracies. All of the Scandinavian countries had adopted some form of proportional representation by 1920, and this was obviously a crucial factor in the subsequent development of party politics. Electoral reform 'helped to stabilize' those cleavage structures existing in the 1920s, which contributed to the survival of the traditional forms of political alignment. Finally, there was a long tradition of conflict between landed and urban interests in Scandinavia, which ensured that rural-based parties like the Swedish Agrarians were not prepared to unite with the urban Conservatives against the Social Democrats. This was partly due to the fact that proportional representation removed the need for a single anti-Socialist party. Nevertheless, many of these rural parties preferred to co-operate with the Socialists, and bourgeois coalitions only really started to be formed in the late 1960s. Although this cleavage had also affected political alignment in Britain, its form and durability appeared to be fundamentally different. The English landed interest had tended to identify with the Conservatives, and even before the rise of Labour the conflict of rural and urban interests was less intense than in Scandinavia. This enabled the Conservatives to construct an anti-Socialist alliance of the rural and urban elites, especially from 1931 onwards.[6]

Yet on the other hand the British Liberals had more in common with their counterparts in Scandinavia than anywhere else in Europe. According to Henig and Pinder, the majority of the continental Liberal parties had 'developed as a riposte' to the secular influence of the Roman Catholic Church and during the twentieth century they have tended to adopt a strict libertarian approach. Only in the United Kingdom and Scandinavia have Liberal parties campaigned on a progressive agenda 'whilst differing from [Labour or] the Social Democrats in being less tied to the aspirations of Trade Unions'. For example, in Sweden the Liberals attempted to establish themselves as the 'progressive alternative' to the dominant Social Democrats and, like their British counterparts, they have received support in rural areas from temperance and Free Church movements.[7] The Agrarian parties were also quite similar in ideological terms to the British and Scandinavian parties.

Indeed, the Danish Liberals were originally founded as an Agrarian party, and the Radicals found a relevant role after 1905 as the champion of the small farmers. In Iceland the Progressives were sometimes labelled as Liberals, while the Swedish Liberals co-operated with the Agrarians on many issues. These similarities were strengthened by developments towards the end of the period. The Agrarians had originally regarded the articulation of the grievances of the farming community as their main priority. After the Second World War the farmers began to decrease in number, and this meant that the Agrarians had to broaden their electoral base in the countryside. They achieved this aim by appealing to those sections of society that had similar interests to those of the farmers, such as other rural groups, artisans and small entrepreneurs. By the late 1950s the Swedish and Norwegian Agrarians even adopted the title of 'Centre Party' in order to distinguish their ideological position on the political spectrum.[8]

There is evidence to suggest that the British Liberals might even have survived as a major force if they had concentrated on devising a new role for themselves as an Agrarian party. After all, the Conservatives were actually losing ground by the 1920s in rural areas, especially in the South of England. Agricultural depression at this time, combined with concern felt by small farmers and land labourers over the threat from tariffs in 1923, led to a revival of rural Liberalism. In the peak year of 1923 the Liberals captured half of the parliamentary seats where the agricultural interest represented more than 30 per cent of the working male population.[9] Indeed, it is intriguing that while many of the party's traditional strongholds in industrial areas were falling to Labour, some rural seats like Tiverton and Basingstoke elected Liberals for the first and last time. These victories reflected the hidden importance of the rural–urban issue in British politics. Although the Conservatives tended to be regarded as the defenders of the agricultural interest, the potential for realignment went further than just a simple process of Labour replacing the Liberals as the principal centre-left party. Kinnear, basing his work on the 1921 census, concluded that the Conservatives fared worse throughout the inter-war period in those seats that had a higher proportion of the working population engaged in agriculture. As Kinnear recognized, this decline was not based on any noticeable 'regional differences' at this time. While the other core cleavages of religion and territory added to the Liberal strength in the remote regions of Britain, rural discontent could be found in counties like Kent and Essex. Since there were 141 divisions in Britain where the farming vote was 'politically significant', an attractive role for the Old Left still theoretically existed after the war.[10]

However, the Liberals were unable to turn their rural victories into a permanent electoral base. The agricultural system in much of England, despite major changes in land ownership, was still based on large farms, which made it difficult to form an alliance of farmers and labourers, while in the long term the free trade beliefs of the Liberals were unlikely to appeal to arable areas, such as East Anglia, which felt threatened by cheap imports from abroad.[11] Furthermore, the dramatic turnover of seats in 1924, when the Liberals lost all of their agricultural seats in England to the Conservatives, demonstrated how fear of Socialism took precedence over the rural cleavage. Significantly, the few rural seats to remain Liberal on that occasion were in the remote regions of North Wales and the Scottish Highlands where the party was more securely entrenched. The only consolation for the party was that it remained the main alternative to rural Conservatism. Dawson concluded that after 1924 it was the agricultural constituencies that offered the 'last ditch for a Liberal party whose best, perhaps even its only, hope lay in a deadlock between the two larger parties'. If the agricultural labourers, who unlike their urban counterparts had not embraced the Labour party, could be combined with those farmers that still remained loyal to Liberalism it would lay the foundations for a revival. Lloyd George, in particular, believed that rural Britain would provide the cornerstone of a new realignment:

> Whatever happens we must strengthen our grasp on the rural districts and the capture of a few towns where Liberalism is still a force. My aim would be a minimum of 100 Liberals in the next parliament and if Toryism breaks down then the not altogether remote possibility of the non-Socialist Elector turning to Liberalism as he did towards Toryism at the last election.[12]

This would have represented an interesting variation on Rokkan's cleavage model. If the Conservative defeat had been greater in 1929, particularly in the agricultural seats where the Liberals hoped to make major inroads, Lloyd George would have been in a position to resurrect his old idea of a 'Centre Party'. The rural interest, along with the other traditional cleavages, could have been fused with anti-Socialism to provide an attractive platform for the Liberals to compete against the Socialist *and* urban Labour party. Yet Lloyd George's challenge to the two-party system was not translated into a significant increase in representation in the House of Commons. The Liberals did well in Cornwall and some parts of East Anglia, even making a few freak gains like Ashford in Kent which they had never won before, but in general the Conservatives retained their supremacy over the rural divisions of southern England. A critical factor in the survival of rural Conservatism was that party's ability to retain a broad swathe of territory from Berkshire to the River Tamar. In 1923 the county constituencies in this area, roughly equivalent to the old kingdom of Wessex, had elected over twenty Liberals, but six years later the party regained only one seat, the border division of South Molton in Devon.[13] The loss of Wessex symbolized the failure to find a new role as the party of the countryside. Although the Liberals were to win some rural seats outside the Celtic fringe after 1929, such as North Dorset and Buckrose in 1945, the opportunity for a major breakthrough was lost.

The Liberals themselves were partly to blame for this failure. Admittedly, the party was not helped by a rise in the number of Labour candidates, from 427 in 1923 to 569 by 1929, which had the effect of allowing many Conservatives to be returned on a minority vote. Yet the Liberals can be criticized for not pursuing their original intention of focusing on the countryside. Despite Lloyd George's earlier declaration that the 'real ground of attack is the *Land*', the party's campaign in 1929 did not adequately reflect that view. Internal divisions meant that the radical programme of land reform contained in the Green Book, the rural version of the so-called Yellow Book (*Britain's Industrial Future*), was, in Dawson's words, 'nothing but a mill-stone for Liberals'.[14] Since even the party's modified rural programme was generally ignored by 1929, the national focus switched to Lloyd George's 'We Can Conquer Unemployment' slogan. This was hardly an ideal platform on which to fight an election in rural Britain. It was clearly targeted at the party's former industrial strongholds in areas like the North of England and South Wales, but this contradicts Lloyd George's earlier statements which had appeared to discount the idea of a major advance outside of the country areas. Indeed, events were to prove that progressive ideas on Britain's industrial problems would not win back the support of working-class voters in urban and industrial areas. Labour actually consolidated its grip on such seats, with two-thirds of the borough seats in England falling to Labour and further gains in Derbyshire and Lancashire.[15]

After all, the group of voters that the Liberal Party's manifesto concentrated on in 1929 was too small to actually secure parliamentary victories. As Searle remarks, the Yellow Book was targeted at the 'growing class of white-collar workers and professional people', essentially the grey area in between the owner and the blue-collar worker.[16] This move was to be repeated thirty years later by Jo Grimond when the Liberals attempted to attract the support of younger middle-class voters, the so-called 'New Man' of the 'Age of Affluence'. But just as the promise of the Orpington by-election in 1962 proved to be an illusion, so was the idea that managerial and technical voters could pave the way for a Liberal future. This group might have been attracted to Liberalism, but those seats where the broader 'middle class' represented a substantial section of the electorate, which tended to be in urban areas like London, were loyal to the Conservatives.[17] Only the marginal rural areas, therefore, held out any hope for a third party. With hindsight it appears that the shift in focus in the Liberal campaign strategy in the late 1920s, from rural to urban/industrial Britain, probably cost the party vital votes. A programme that focused more on the needs of rural voters, rather than the problem of unemployment in Labour strongholds, might well have resulted in a Liberal breakthrough.

Thereafter, the party was increasingly forced back to those rural peripheries where socio-economic conditions were more suitable for its survival. No longer in a strong enough position to fight back against the consolidation of a new two-party system in England, the question now was whether the Liberals could survive in their last bastions in the remote backwaters of Britain. The political ecology of these western and northern areas was promising. Just like the remote communes of South and West Norway the agricultural system in pastoral areas tended to be based upon small family farms, while the political significance of religious nonconformity was likely to survive longer in such peripheral regions. This was demonstrated in 1950. In the election of that year the Liberals fielded 475 candidates in a brave attempt to challenge their opponents, but they polled just 9.1 per cent of the total vote and forfeited some 319 deposits. Only in three regions, Cornwall and Devon, North Wales and North-eastern Scotland, did the party poll over a fifth of the vote. There were a few urban seats where Liberalism was still strong, such as Bolton West and Huddersfield West, but in general the party was now even more restricted to remote areas, particularly the rural Celtic fringe.[18]

It was these regions which also saw the first signs of rebirth only a few years later. A good second place for the Liberals at the Inverness by-election in December 1954 was echoed a few months later in the 1955 general election when it was remote constituencies like Orkney & Shetland, North Cornwall and North Devon which saw a significant increase in the Liberal vote. More surprising, however, was the failure of the Welsh Liberals to participate in this success. In the early and mid-1950s the northern constituencies of the principality still provided the mainstay of the Liberal parliamentary group in the House of Commons, with five out of nine seats in 1950 and three out of six in 1951 and 1955. Yet the loss of Carmarthen to Labour in 1957 was a clear sign of the party's decline in Wales. By 1959 the party found itself very much on the defensive, with a stagnant performance in most seats and its share of the vote in Anglesey and Conway falling well below the results achieved nine years earlier. Part of the problem was that both Labour and the Conservatives were still expanding in the remote parts of the region, which was in stark contrast to the far South-West of Britain. Another crucial factor, however, was that Plaid Cymru was now attracting a respectable vote in rural and Welsh-speaking constituencies. While anti-metropolitanism provided the momentum for a Liberal advance in other remote areas, the Welsh Nationalists were already consolidating their position in preparation for their breakthrough in North Wales in the 1960s. Once again this is a reminder of the way in which regional diversity in the British Isles provides the basic framework for political change.

These developments provide the essential context for exploring the electoral dynamics of South-West Liberalism after the First World War. The isolated nature of the peninsula, particularly in the far west, ensured that the Liberals had a more secure electoral base in the region than in Britain as a whole. Older voters saw no reason to change their political allegiance to a new party like Labour, while the strength of family voting meant that there was a tendency for the younger generation to vote in the same way as their parents and grandparents. Indeed, one activist, who was to become chairman of a Liberal constituency association in the region in the 1980s, explained his decision to join the party at the age of fifteen in 1935 on the grounds that his family had supported the progressive cause since the Civil War period.[19] This emotional loyalty to Liberalism found a focus in nostalgia for the days of Gladstone. Even in the mid-1960s it was still common in remote areas to find pictures of the old Liberal leader in the homes of those voters who were born at the turn of the century.[20] In practical terms this veneration was evident from the way in which traditional cleavages were still important for many voters after the First World War. The Liberal–Free Church alliance, in particular, was still a powerful force in many rural constituencies, and the emergence of new issues, such as the debate over the Prayer Book in 1929 and concern over a new age of materialism in the late 1950s, had had the effect of consolidating the party's appeal to nonconformists. Some Liberals were able to exploit the wider significance of this tradition by presenting Liberalism as the 'high ground of politics'. The classic example was Isaac Foot, the doyen of Liberal nonconformity, who enjoyed enormous respect throughout the South-West by presenting modern issues in the context of the Radical tradition established by the Civil War period. His public support for Bessell and Thorpe in the 1950s symbolized the feeling of continuity with the past.[21]

In addition, the economic structure of the region had more in common with the Gladstonian rather than the Collectivist Age. Before 1914 the *petite bourgeoisie* had provided the backbone of support for the Old Left, but it was an interest group which was in long-term decline.[22] In the South-West component groups like the small farmers, fishermen and shopkeepers were also confronted with serious problems after 1918, but the isolated conditions of the region ensured that they remained a significant section of the electorate. This meant that there were always a considerable number of voters for whom the owner–worker cleavage had little relevance. Admittedly, the nature of Britain's electoral system encouraged many of these voters to support the Conservatives on the grounds that they were the only non-Socialist party which could realistically form a government after the 1920s. Yet the *petite bourgeoisie* still had their own priorities, and the evidence suggests that voters from this group were prepared to defect to the Liberals if they believed that Conservative policies were not in their interests. Thus, in 1924 many shopkeepers and small businessmen voted Conservative because of their fear of Socialism, but they returned to the Liberals in 1929 because of their opposition to the government's rating reforms. This was repeated in the 1950s when the 'Little People' voted Conservative in 1950 and 1951 to remove Atlee's Labour government, but were moving to the Liberals by the end of the decade in order to protest at tax and rate increases. The small farmers are perhaps the most obvious economic group from which the local Liberals continued to attract substantial support. To some extent this was no doubt due to the fact that pastoral areas, in particular the border sub-region between Cornwall and Devon, were also the heartland of the Free Churches. An additional reason was that many small farmers after 1918 did not believe that the introduction of tariffs would be in their interests. Even in the thirties the Liberals continued to attract the support of those farmers and land labourers who were disenchanted with the government's agricultural policy. Tenant farmers also regarded the Conservatives as the party of the 'Anglican Landlord', and this factor still assisted the Liberal cause in the 1960s.[23]

While this traditional type of Liberal voter was an essential factor in the survival of the party, it seemed necessary to attract other sources of support, particularly younger voters, in order to expand. By 1950 there were indications that even in the South-West the tradition of family voting, though still important, was being eroded, while the proportion of the electorate engaged in agriculture was declining. In Cornwall and some parts of Devon, at least, the anti-metropolitan mantle provided the party with a role that could attract new voters while retaining its existing supporters. There was a growing belief that this area was being neglected by central government, with farmers and fishermen claiming that they were not receiving a fair share of financial assistance compared to other regions and low wages, combined with rural unemployment, creating problems for the younger generation. The Liberals had a relevant message in their claim that local interests would be better served by MPs who were independent of the 'big party' machines in London. Popular candidates, in particular Thorpe, Bessell and Pardoe, also benefited from the traditional view that a Member of Parliament should be an active and charismatic leader of the local community. It is interesting that this paralleled the developments taking place in Scandinavia. The Agrarians had originally concentrated on articulating the grievances of the farming community, but after the Second World War they started to exploit the wider significance of the urban–rural divide by becoming the voice of the countryside.[24]

By the early 1960s, then, the local Liberals were optimistic about their chances of a political rebirth. James Collier's progress at the Tiverton by-election in November 1960, when he increased his share of the vote from 19.2 to 36.7 per cent and pushed Labour into third place, was a sign that the party was consolidating its rural base in the west. This seat was hardly natural Liberal territory since it had moved away from the party after Sir Francis Acland's defeat back in 1924, but it now became one of the party's target seats in the region since the Conservative percentage majority was only 9 per cent. A series of local government victories, particularly in Bath, Exeter and Poole, suggested that a breakthrough was even possible in the eastern constituencies, while the enhanced position of the national party in the immediate aftermath of its famous by-election victory at Orpington in March 1962 provided further encouragement.[25] When the general election was finally held in October 1964 this revival had lost momentum as voters drifted back to the other parties, a fact that was demonstrated quite early on in the South-West when the Liberals made only modest progress in the South Dorset by-election in November 1962. In the event the party emerged at the national level with nine MPs and its highest share of the vote since 1929, 11.2 per cent. The South-West was once again in the forefront of this advance, with Peter Bessell winning Bodmin by 3,136 votes and the party polling an impressive 24.8 per cent of the vote across the four counties.

A more detailed analysis of the 1964 result suggests that the basic features of the revival of the previous decade were still present. The core area remained the cluster of seats around the River Tamar, with Jeremy Thorpe retaining North Devon with an increased majority and good results in North Cornwall, Torrington and Tavistock. There were some signs of an enlargement of the potential Liberal territory. Both Collier and Gerald Whitmarsh (St Ives) took second place, while William Hosking, whose slogan 'A Cornishman for a Cornish Seat' symbolized the nature of his election campaign, came a good third in Truro on 27.9 per cent and pointed the way to David Penhaligon's successful challenge in 1974.[26] In the eastern counties the Liberals were, with the solitary exception of North Dorset, still in third place. The only consolation was that in Wells, Yeovil, Poole and Weston-super-Mare the party won a more respectable vote of between a fifth to a quarter of the vote. The extent of variation across the four counties can be seen in Table 8.2. While differences were less marked than in the early 1950s, the share of the vote obtained in the weakest county, Somerset, was less than half that polled in the five constituencies in the Tamar area.

But the past also exerted a negative influence on the rebirth of

Table 8.2: The average percentage vote for Liberal candidates in 1964.

Tamar Zone	Cornwall	Devon	Dorset	Somerset
43.4 %	33.5 %	30.8 %	24.1 %	20.3 %

Liberalism. The gradual nature of the revival reflected the party's long-term failure to pursue a consistent and effective strategy after 1918. Socio-economic factors may have been somewhat more conducive to recovery in seats like Bodmin and North Devon, but there were a number of other fairly similar constituencies, such as North Dorset and Truro, where the party had done well as late as 1950 yet had failed to make a breakthrough later in that decade. The mere fact that the Liberals appeared to be gaining ground in a particular seat ensured that they enjoyed local credibility, but constituency campaigns lacked momentum in those places where the party had perhaps lost ground in 1955, had not put forward a candidate or had come third. Voting patterns are developed over the long term and failure to maintain its position in one particular contest ensured that the party was at a disadvantage in subsequent elections. Table 8.3 demonstrates that the party's position was steadily undermined in the region after 1929. The elections of 1931 and 1945 were major stages in a process that culminated in 1951, when the regional Liberals were a credible force in just four constituencies. As a result the party had only a narrow base, essentially the Cornwall–Devon border zone, from which to expand in the 1960s. Indeed, even in 1964, the high point of the Grimond revival in terms of votes, the number of seats where the Conservative majority over the Liberals was less than 10 per cent of the vote was actually less than in 1945. Two years later the party's total list of potential seats had fallen back below the level of 1959.

Could the party have pursued an alternative strategy during the critical

Table 8.3: Actual and potential Liberal seats in the four counties, 1924–1966.

Election	Liberal MPs	Liberal within 10% of victor	Other Liberals in second place	Total
1924	1	9	11	21
1929	8	8	7	23
1931	2	3	10	15
1935	2	2	11	15
1945	2	3	1	6
1950	—	2	3	5
1951	—	1	3	4
1955	—	1	4	5
1959	1	3	3	7
1964	2	2	6	10
1966	3	1	2	6

period of the mid-twentieth century? It can be argued that after the 1920s the Liberal party no longer had the credibility to present itself as an alternative government, while it lacked sufficient resources and organization to campaign effectively at the national level. This study of the South-West suggests that the Liberals should have paid more attention to retaining their existing seats rather than attempting to compete with the two main parties on unequal terms. In practice such a policy would have meant abandoning the idea of contesting a majority of constituencies in favour of a narrow front, and this approach could then have been combined with a greater emphasis on local issues. The task of party headquarters would then have been to ensure that actual and potential seats had all the requirements for victory—good candidates, effective organization, adequate finance and regular visits from prominent Liberal personalities.

There were a number of factors that prevented the adoption of such an approach. In the first place the party's stalwarts found it difficult to abandon the goal of forming a government. It has already been mentioned that nostalgia for the old days of Gladstone helped to ensure the party's survival. Many older supporters looked forward to the 'next

Liberal government', and a decision to abandon this objective would have been a severe blow to the party's morale. Connected with this view was the fear that the concept of a narrow front would threaten the national character of the party. A rational approach would have been for those Liberal associations which were not contesting parliamentary elections to have strengthened their position by concentrating on local elections, but it was really only in the 1950s and 1960s that the party leadership began to give serious attention to municipal politics. Another problem was the belief that a broad front enabled the party to demonstrate its independence from the two main parties. By claiming that they could form a government it was hoped that the party would not have to make difficult decisions over pacts with other parties but, as the 1950 election had demonstrated, this approach merely aggravated tensions within the party. It was only the shock of their defeats in the early fifties that forced the Liberals into taking drastic action. Operation Basic symbolized the acceptance of the need to ensure that target seats enjoyed essential requirements like good organization, while Grimond was able to retain the loyalty of the grassroots because it was presented as the first stage on the road to government

However, the failure to adopt this line earlier in the period meant that it only enjoyed limited benefits. By 1959 there were few seats in Britain where the Liberals were still a realistic option for voters and this meant that the party's base was too small to exploit subsequent opportunities. This had already become apparent by 1966. Liberal representation in the House of Commons returned to the level of 1945, with twelve MPs elected, but the party's share of the overall vote fell to 8.6 per cent. At the local level John Pardoe, fighting his first election in the region, captured North Cornwall from the Conservatives, while Thorpe and Bessell were returned with reduced majorities. More depressing was the fact that the party's wider base outside these three seats was now far weaker. Apart from a lower regional vote, down to 20 per cent, the Liberals came second in just six constituencies, with a general swing to Labour pushing the party down into bottom place in St Ives, Tiverton, Torbay and Honiton. Ironically, the Liberals had been remarkably successful in making the most of their narrow base, winning three out of the six seats where they still represented a serious challenge to the Conservatives. This provided little comfort for a party that only a few years earlier had been anticipating a more substantial advance.

The subsequent frustration at the grassroots also reflected a growing realization that Liberalism had now lost its basic sense of direction. When Grimond had taken over the leadership in 1956, his ultimate aim of a realignment of the centre-left of British politics seemed possible given the divisions within the Labour opposition. Eric Lubbock's decisive win at Orpington in 1962 further strengthened the prospect of 'new' voters in the affluent Home Counties deserting both Labour and the Conservatives for the dynamic and class-less New Liberals. Harold Wilson's narrow victory in 1964, however, destroyed the rationale behind Grimond's strategy. Critics claimed that the approach of the leadership was a mistake from the start. In 1967 John Vincent declared that the party's 'obsession' with representing the suburban interests of the 'new' middle class was 'market research gone mad'. While in 'social theory there was an obvious opening' in the commuter belt, the real 'opportunity was in the Highlands and in the west of England'.[27] Orpington was the only suburban seat in southern England to go Liberal, and that was a victory due more to local circumstances rather than any process of *embourgeoisement*. Grimond's *Charter for New Men* in 1964, like Lloyd George's pledge to conquer unemployment some thirty five years before, was hardly the ideal rallying cry for a party whose best prospects for victory lay in the provinces. A more coherent policy by the national leadership in the mid-1960s, which, as Vincent suggested, 'spotlighted place' instead of a 'particular social group', might well have led to even greater successes in other similar regions.[28] As it was, the small bloc of Liberals elected in 1966 faced an uncertain future, with a reaction to the Wilson government likely to lead to a consolidation of the anti-Socialist vote around the Conservatives.

Thorpe to Thatcher

Grimond's decision to stand down from the leadership in 1967 was another indication that the dream of realignment had ended. His successor, Jeremy Thorpe, was the first leader of the party to represent a constituency in the South-West. At the age of 38, he was very much in the Grimond mould, and keen to continue with the idea that Liberalism was the radical but non-Socialist alternative to the Conserv-atives. Not surprisingly, perhaps, the early years of his leadership were hardly a honeymoon. In December 1967 the Liberal executive

Figure 8.1: Leader of the party: Jeremy Thorpe addressing the Liberal Assembly at Eastbourne in 1970.

committee noted its 'serious concern' that they were failing to make an impact on the electorate as 'an alternative to the two discredited main parties'. Thorpe's leadership was criticized by implication and one MP even called for the creation of a new party under the leadership of Grimond.[29] The left-wing stance of the Young Liberals, the so-called Red Guards, created internal friction, while the possibility of boundary changes threatened to undermine the party's slender presence at Westminster.[30]

At the state level the party's by-election performance was disappointing as the protest vote went to the Conservatives in England and the Nationalists in the Celtic fringe. Only Wallace Lawlor's personal triumph over Labour at Birmingham Ladywood in June 1969 provided some consolation. The Honiton and Weston-super-Mare by-elections in 1967 and 1969 reflected the wider pattern. In both cases the Liberals narrowly moved into second place, but there was only a small swing in their favour because the loss of support by Labour had to be shared with the Conservatives.[31] Bridgwater in the spring of 1970 was even worse because in this case both Labour and the Liberals lost ground to Tom King, the new Conservative candidate. The Bridgwater result was repeated on a greater scale in the general election of that year. Only six Liberal MPs retained their seats, while the large number of deposits lost, 184 in total, marked a return to the level of 1950. In some ways the situation was not quite so disastrous in the South-West. Admittedly, Bodmin was lost following Bessell's resignation and his subsequent move to the United States, but both North Devon and North Cornwall were retained, albeit with slender majorities, while the total number of seats where the party came first or second increased to seven. Nonetheless, a further reduction in the regional vote, at 17.4 per cent only fractionally higher than in 1950, was obviously not an encouraging start for the Devon-based leader of the Liberals.

Thorpe's greatest moment on the national political stage was yet to come. Cyril Smith's victory at Rochdale in October 1972 paved the way for a series of dramatic by-election successes over the following year at Sutton & Cheam, Isle of Ely, Ripon and Berwick-upon-Tweed. Against a background of serious economic difficulties and increasing bitterness between the two main parties, voters responded positively to the 'Centre Party' image of the Liberals. When Edward Heath called a snap election in February 1974, Thorpe's party emerged with fourteen seats and nearly a fifth of the national vote. The *Economist* concluded that this remarkable rise in support for the third force could only be explained in a European context. Rising prices and political uncertainty in a number of continental countries had led to the sudden emergence of Poujadist-style parties in the previous two years, such as those led by Mogens Glistrup in Denmark and Veikko Vennamo in Finland. Their popularity, particularly with groups like the *petite bourgeoisie,* had led a sizeable number of voters to withdraw their allegiance from the established parties. Although the *Economist* accepted that the British Liberals were more 'responsible' than the maverick parties of Scandinavia, in its view more akin to the increasingly successful Centre party of Sweden, they nonetheless served the same constituency of discontented voters:

> Mr Thorpe's Liberals ... lack the coherence of objective both at the top, and in the rank and file of voters below. The popular vote they carry with them into the new Parliament is largely the voice of the baffled and the uncertain in a declining country bemused by its problems. Like those related parties in other bemused countries, they are chiefly in the business of avoidance.[32]

The *Economist* certainly had a point. Despite a much larger share of the vote, the vague image of Liberalism ensured that the party's electoral position was still vulnerable. At the October 1974 election it was estimated that about one-third of Liberal support had been attracted during the actual campaign; in contrast, the party had lost a third of its support since the summer of that year.[33] The party itself seemed to lack a coherent approach on how to use its new strength, which was demonstrated by the furore within the party over the prospect of supporting a minority Conservative administration. One could also conclude that the Liberals were still unable to formulate a rational electoral strategy. By-election victories, with the exception of Rochdale, had been achieved in seats where the party was not a serious alternative in 1970. Many activists, led by Pardoe at the party's 1973 Assembly, were convinced that the best way to maintain this momentum was by fighting on a broad front, but this prevented a focus on those seats which in the following year remained with the Conservatives. For Vincent the answer still lay in winning seats in rural Britain, since the gains of 1974 had been obtained 'as a country (rather than Liberal) party'.[34]

Set against this national framework the Liberals succeeded in bringing their number of seats in the South-West back to the level of 1966. Thorpe and Pardoe were returned with substantial majorities, 11,072 and 8,729 respectively, and Paul Tyler, who snatched Bodmin from the Conservatives by the narrow margin of just nine votes, now joined them in the Commons. Whilst Bodmin was lost in the October election, David Penhaligon won the adjacent seat of Truro, a victory that showed the Cornish Liberals were now expanding out of the northern and eastern parts of the county. It is worth noting that this advance in Cornwall was not really repeated in other parts of Celtic Britain. Nationalist by-election victories in Wales and Scotland during the Wilson years had led the way to success in 1974. With Plaid Cymru and the SNP emerging as the main challengers to Labour and the Conservatives, the Liberals were now restricted to a limited number of seats held by popular MPs like David Steel. Although Mebyon Kernow had entered the electoral arena by the 1970s, it was not until the end of the decade that the party mounted a major challenge in Westminster elections. This left the field clear for the Cornish Liberals. In the late 1960s Bessell and Pardoe had proved their anti-metropolitan credentials by declaring that the 'Cornish people have the same right to control their country, its economy and its political future, as the other Celtic peoples of Scotland and Wales'.[35] Penhaligon's populist articulation of a distinctly Cornish agenda, leading to claims that he 'spoke for Cornwall with the same Celtic spirit that the young Lloyd George spoke for Wales', further strengthened his party's ability to tap into regional discontent.[36]

Perhaps the real significance of this period for the South-West as a whole lay in an expansion from the old Tamar zone base. Apart from confirming the position of the Liberals as the main alternative to the Conservatives in the rural areas of Cornwall and Devon, their candidates came second in a majority of the seats in the eastern counties for the first time since 1929. Only the mixed industrial–rural seats of South Dorset, Taunton, Bridgwater and North Somerset placed Labour in second place. This performance was to be repeated in the October of that year, with only the Yeovil Liberals narrowly dropping from second to third. A more disappointing feature was that the rise in popular support did not lead to an increased number of MPs. Although the local Liberals had been quite successful in 1966 in exploiting the full potential of their relatively small number of target seats, the tendency by 1974 was for the party to gain disproportionately in those areas where it stood little chance of winning. Boundary changes helped to ensure that Peter Mills enjoyed a larger Conservative majority in West Devon than in the old constituency of Torrington, 5.6 per cent in 1964 and 11.3 by February 1974, while Bodmin was less reliable because of the personal vote given to Robert Hicks. With the exception of Truro all other possible seats now required a fairly significant swing of at least 5 per cent to change hands. Taking the region as a whole the Liberals, on 32.0 per cent of the vote, needed a swing of 6.5 per cent from the Conservatives before they could undermine that party's supremacy. Even assuming that the Liberals could have reached that figure it would still have left them with just over a third of the region's parliamentary representation. Tactical voting by Labour supporters was not really a realistic option. In the October election there was little variation in the swing to Labour, with just three constituencies, significantly one of which was Truro, seeing a small fall in support.[37]

Unfortunately for the Liberals the narrow win of Labour at the state level in October 1974 was to put an end to the revival of the Thorpe years. Margaret Thatcher's election as the new Conservative leader placed that party in a strong position to exploit the growing unpopularity of the government. Public concern about Britain's stagnant economic performance, combined with industrial militancy on the part of the trade unions by the end of the decade, led to another anti-Socialist reaction by the electorate. The uncertain attitude of the Liberals in regard to the government, demonstrated by the divisions over the so-called Lib-Lab pact in 1977–8, was hardly likely to help their electoral prospects given the fact that, with the odd exception like Liverpool, the party's support was concentrated in rural and non-Socialist areas. The sad end of Thorpe's parliamentary career further weakened the party's position. Forced to resign as leader in 1976 at a time of growing allegations of homosexuality and attempted murder, he made a brave decision to contest his North Devon seat in 1979. Although Thorpe's campaign no longer had the sparkle and vitality of former years, loyal supporters still regarded him as the 'uncrowned King of North Devon'. A factory foreman in the constituency summed up the feelings of many voters when he declared that the constituency owed a debt of gratitude to the disgraced Liberal leader:

> Before he came here it was a real Tory backwater, completely ignored, a depressed area with a lot of unemployment and low wages. Now the lowest-paid lift worker at this factory is getting £100 a week. That is the sort of thing Jeremy Thorpe has done for North Devon.[38]

In spite of such loyalty from many of his supporters, Thorpe was to lose the election by 8,473 votes. The negative atmosphere created by the scandal presumably had an influence on the result in adjacent constituencies since Pardoe was defeated in North Cornwall and Hicks increased his majority over Tyler from 665 to 10,029 votes. This reversal of fortunes in the Tamar zone, the main growth area for the British Liberals back in the 1950s, was not in line with national results since the party under the new leadership of David Steel actually did reasonably well in its strongholds. Locally, only Penhaligon, who enjoyed an increased majority in Truro, was able to beat the Conservatives. One could also argue that the personal style of Margaret Thatcher influenced the local outcome of the election results. The view that she was 'more of an old-fashioned Liberal than a Tory' seemed to apply to her stance on economic issues, with her defence of private enterprise, combined with calls for tax cuts, likely to go down well in a region that was dependent on small businesses.[39] Further research is necessary in order to see how far the strong moralistic image of Thatcher appealed to nonconformist voters, especially at a time when, according to Stevenson, the Liberals were in a vulnerable position over their 'carefully built-up reputation for probity and high principle'.[40] After all, Hearl suggests that, in contrast to Britain as a whole, religious belief continued to have 'political relevance' at least until the 1980s in the 'less developed and more traditional rural northern side' of Cornwall and Devon.[41]

The 1980s were to witness a new phase in the development of third-party politics. At the national level the formation of the Social Democratic Party in March 1981 and the subsequent Alliance between the Liberals and the SDP held out the prospect of a major realignment of British politics. In terms of electoral support the Alliance's share of the vote in 1983 and 1987, 25.4 and 22.6 per cent respectively, represented the best achievement for a third force since the 1920s. Yet while the number of Alliance MPs, twenty-three in 1983 and twenty-two in 1987, was an improvement on the 1960s and 1970s, it was still only a relatively small number even in comparison with the fifty-nine seats won back in 1929. This was clearly the case in the South-West where the Alliance was only able to win three seats (Truro, Yeovil and Devonport), which was actually the same number returned from the region as in 1966 and the two 1974 elections. Significantly, the Alliance failed to win a single seat in the Cornwall–Devon border area, and this limited its success to the isolated victories of Paddy Ashdown in Yeovil and Dr David Owen in Devonport, seats that had not really featured in the first post-war revival. Following a distinguished military and diplomatic career, Ashdown had cultivated Yeovil assiduously for eight years before achieving his eventual victory.[42] Owen, in contrast, had been a Labour MP in Plymouth since 1966, representing Sutton before moving to Devonport in February 1974, and a rising star in the Callaghan administration as Britain's youngest Foreign Secretary. His strong views on defence, out of place in a Labour party committed to nuclear disarmament, were naturally reinforced by the fact that he enjoyed the support of the workers at the naval docks in Devonport.[43] In that sense Owen's defection to the SDP in 1981 was reminiscent of Leslie Hore-Belisha's move to the Liberal Nationals fifty years before, which had also been influenced by concerns over the threat that Labour posed to the local defence interest.

As the decade went by the prospect of further parliamentary gains remained elusive. Nationally, the by-election record of the Alliance seemed encouraging, with sensational wins at places like Brecon & Radnor and Ryedale, but local activists did not have the good fortune to see a by-election for a Conservative seat in the South-West. Towards the end of 1986, however, came the tragic death of Penhaligon in a car accident, a sad event that robbed his party of a leading personality and potential leader. His seat was retained with an increased majority in the following March by Matthew Taylor, Penhaligon's research assistant, who now became at 24 the youngest member of the House of Commons.[44] This victory, following the triumph of Rosie Barnes for the SDP at Greenwich a month earlier, appeared to pave the way for success at the next election. In the event, however, there was no breakthrough.[45] Although there were some signs of progress in the 1987 election, particularly in the old Tamar zone where Liberal candidates were able to reduce the size of the Conservative majorities, a general recovery in the Labour vote blunted the challenge of the Alliance. This left the centre parties restricted once again to three scattered constituencies. Even this base did not seem totally secure since Taylor's majority was

Figure 8.2: David Penhaligon, MP for Truro (1974–86), meets a group of young people, early 1980s.

sharply reduced in comparison to his by-election landslide just three months earlier.

Yet in the area of local government the Alliance was achieving a breakthrough. During the early years of the Thatcher era the third force was steadily building up its strength at the grassroots, winning a strong bloc of seats as early as 1979 on Yeovil district council, later renamed as South Somerset, and scoring a series of wins in the mid-Cornwall councils of Restormel and Carrick in 1983. The first significant result occurred in the 1985 county council elections when, in a swing reminiscent of the Liberal landslide of 1923, the third party staged a major advance from Cornwall to Wiltshire. Much to their surprise the Alliance emerged as the single-largest group on the county councils of Devon, Somerset and Cornwall, which led to the first experience of real power with minority administrations formed in all three councils with the support of Labour and sympathetic Independents. This result marked a turning point in the public perception of the third force, when Penhaligon pointed out that only eight years before the Liberals had 'only two councillors in Devon and Cornwall, now we have 67'.[46] Two years later on the eve of the 1987 general election the Alliance parties strengthened their grip on the district councils with a net gain of seventy-three seats across the four counties. Apart from winning outright control of South Somerset, the Alliance was the single-largest group on a further five councils (Bath, Mendip, Carrick, Kerrier and Restormel). Despite the fact that much of the region had a strong Liberal tradition, the SDP was playing a quite important role in some areas at this time. Owen's personal bastion at Plymouth was the obvious case, with the SDP spearheading the breakthrough in the county council elections and winning eight of the ten Alliance seats on the city council in 1987. The new party also won more seats than its Liberal allies at Taunton Deane and Bath, while even in Liberal Cornwall the Social Democrats led the Alliance challenge on Kerrier and Penwith in the far west.[47] Significantly, these were all areas, with the possible exception of Bath, where the Liberals had failed to sustain a breakthrough in the 1960s and 1970s.

In total the Alliance held 293 district council seats in the South-West by 1987, which compared favourably with the Conservatives and Independents on 453 and 342 respectively. This figure was also significantly higher than the Labour party, reduced to just ninety-five seats and effectively pushed back to the urban enclaves of Plymouth and

Exeter.[48] Although even greater results were to be achieved in the following decade, it was clear already that the nature of party politics was changing at the local level. A quiet revolution was effectively taking place, removing the old image of the Liberals as just the local protest party for parts of Cornwall and Devon in Westminster elections and creating a new role as a more broadly based party that could channel discontent into the creation of a series of municipal powerbases throughout the region. Indeed, Richard West in the *Spectator,* commenting on the efficiency of the Liberal by-election campaign at Truro in March 1987, claimed that a 'great many people' now had a vested interest in the election of Alliance MPs like Matthew Taylor. Whereas just twenty years before the party only appealed to idealists and traditional voters, it was now, according to West, attracting the 'purely ambitious professionals, scenting the possibility of lucrative and powerful office; even at last, government office'. This process was creating a 'Liberal Tammany Hall', particularly in Cornwall, with the party now having the potential to control the patronage system in local government, the regional NHS and the police.[49] Whatever the truth of West's claims, it was undoubtedly the case that the Alliance was now consolidating its position as a powerful and influential force at the county and district council level. What the Liberals and their SDP allies now needed to do, however, was to translate this success in local government into seats at Westminster.

Ashdown's Liberal Democrats

In the immediate aftermath of the 1987 election the prospect of large-scale parliamentary gains seemed even more remote. Steel's call for a merger of the centre parties soon led to complete disarray, with Owen's continuing SDP, and later an independent Liberal Party led by David Morrish, competing with the new Social and Liberal Democrats for the old Alliance vote. Presiding over this difficult period in the history of third-party politics was Ashdown. Following Steel's decision not to contest the leadership of the SLD, Ashdown emerged as the obvious choice to replace him and he was duly elected to the post in August 1988. His fresh and dynamic image as an ex-marine commando concerned some Liberal activists, who were concerned that he was the 'new man with new ideas who might turn the SLD into something they don't recognise', but it placed him in a strong position to remould the new

Democrats into a more effective force.[50] In the short term, however, the party was soon fighting for its very existence. The 1989 county council elections saw a sharp reversal of the gains of 1985, with the Conservatives winning outright control of both Devon and Somerset. Only Cornwall went against the trend with the Democrats marginally increasing their number of councillors. An even greater setback occurred in the European elections a month later when the Democrats found themselves forced into fourth place, with the Greens on 22.4 per cent briefly taking over their role as the second party in Devon, Dorset and Somerset. The average vote for the Democrats in these three counties was just 11.7 per cent. Once again the far west broke this pattern with Paul Tyler, the former Liberal MP for Bodmin, retaining second place in the Cornwall & Plymouth seat with 31.5 per cent of the vote. Notwithstanding the Cornish result, the European elections were a low point in the South-West that was only comparable to 1951.[51]

As the party, now renamed as the Liberal Democrats, moved into the nineties, the political landscape began to change in its favour. A succession of impressive by-election results as the Thatcher era gave way to the Major years, along with solid progress in local government, once again provided a sense of momentum. Perhaps surprisingly, then, the Liberal Democrats were able to make quite significant progress through-out the four counties in 1992. Apart from victories in North Cornwall and North Devon, Bath was captured from the Conservatives for the first time since 1923. In total five constituencies were won throughout the region, though paradoxically at the national level the party's share of the vote, 18.3 per cent, had declined in comparison with the previous decade. Political observers pointed to the growing concern of voters over a variety of issues, such as the government's agricultural policy, defence cuts and water charges, which had particular significance for voters in the peninsula. In the late 1950s the impact of the centre–periphery cleavage had been restricted to Cornwall and North Devon, but by the early nineties there was a feeling that the interests of the wider South-West were affected by its 'remoteness from Westminster'.[52] Regional discontent continued to grow after the general election. By 1994 a Gallup poll for the *Daily Telegraph* placed the Conservatives in third place throughout the South-West, with the Major government now being blamed for a whole series of regional problems, ranging from unemployment to fears over a reduction in local services following rail

219

privatization. It was predicted that the Liberal Democrats, nicknamed as the 'Yellow Peril', would sweep to victory in virtually all of the county divisions, with Labour taking Plymouth and Exeter and the Conservatives forced back to the solitary seat of East Devon. By 1996 the party controlled thirteen major councils in the area, held six seats at Westminster following the defection of Emma Nicholson from the Conservatives and two of the four seats in the European parliament.[53]

Only Tony Blair's New Labour, riding high in the opinion polls and the national beneficiary of Conservative unpopularity, threatened to blunt this regional challenge. Although committed to fighting every seat in Britain, Ashdown believed that a more professional approach for the party, with a greater emphasis on target seats, would make the difference. This concern with targeting was increasingly shared with the other parties, but it became an essential ingredient in the Liberal Democrat campaign in 1997 given the fact that their vote was likely to be squeezed elsewhere. The most winnable fifty seats were provided with considerable resources from the centre, especially in terms of funding and computers, while thirty full-time agents, including nine in Cornwall and Devon alone by 1995, were appointed across the country.[54] Ashdown concluded in May 1996 that its local election success had 'given the Liberal Democrats the best launch pad we have ever had for a General Election campaign'. Determined to maintain this momentum the party launched a 'Big Push Campaign' at the grassroots level in the summer of that year, which aimed to ensure 'more newsletters are delivered, more doors knocked and more electors contacted'. When this professional approach was linked to the willingness of many voters to give tactical support to the opposition party that had the best chance of defeating a government candidate, the potential for realignment now seemed promising.[55]

In the event the Liberal Democrats with forty-six seats emerged as the strongest third force at Westminster in nearly seventy years. Locally, the most sweeping changes occurred in Cornwall where, with more echoes of 1929, not a single Conservative was returned. Only Falmouth & Camborne, a three-way marginal won by Labour, prevented the Liberal Democrats from monopolizing the area's parliamentary representation. This success was linked to a variety of local factors, ranging from the traditional strength of the party to the way in which the above-average vote given to the Referendum party presumably

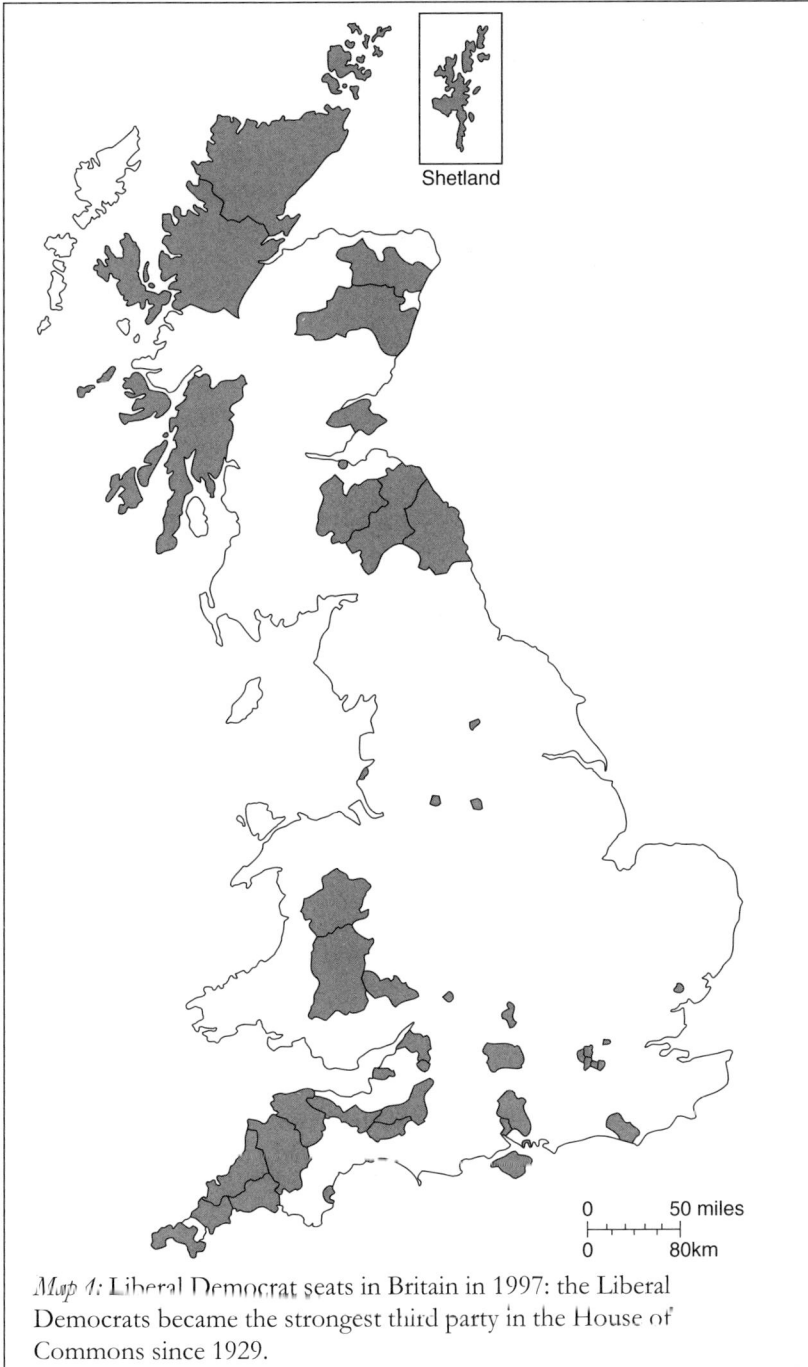

Shetland

0   50 miles

0   80km

Map 1: Liberal Democrat seats in Britain in 1997: the Liberal
Democrats became the strongest third party in the House of
Commons since 1929.

Figure 8.3: Emma Nicholson—with Liberal Democrat candidates Adrian Sanders (MP for Torbay since 1997) on the right and Colin Breed (MP for SE Cornwall since 1997) far left—campaigning against rises in prescription charges in 1996.

Figure 8.4: Paddy Ashdown on the campaign trail, with Colin Breed on his right and Owen May, chairman of the local police authority, on his left, during the run-up to the 1997 election.

helped to push Conservative support below 30 per cent in three of the five constituencies.[56] Furthermore, the local agenda of the Liberal Democrats reflected the specific concerns of Cornish voters. The *Daily Telegraph* in 1994 had suggested that regional discontent was greater in Cornwall, which had the highest concentration of unemployment on a county basis and a sense of remoteness from both national and regional centres of power. Under the slogan of a 'Fair Deal for Cornwall' the Liberal Democrats developed a specific plan for the county during the years running up to the election, with a pledge to create a separate Cornish Development Agency to back local businesses providing the centrepiece of their economic policy.[57]

Whilst the Cornish breakthrough was in line with long-term voting patterns, some of the other results seemed more surprising. Table 8.4 suggests that the greatest change since 1964 had actually occurred in Somerset. Ashdown's success at Yeovil and his enhanced prestige as party leader, combined with victory in the 1993 county council elections, created a domino effect leading to victory in the seats of Bath (won in 1992), Somerton & Frome, Taunton and Weston-super-Mare. Since these gains were obtained in three-cornered contests, it could be said that the Somerset results were even more spectacular than in the last Liberal landslide of 1923. On that occasion the Conservatives had only been narrowly defeated in straight fights. In contrast, the average vote per candidate in Devon had only increased fractionally since the mid-1960s. This reflected a low vote in Exeter and the Plymouth area, which had moved to Labour following Owen's withdrawal from the political scene in 1992, along with an inability to make real inroads into the Conservative bastion of East Devon. North Devon was retained, with exactly the same vote as in 1964, while West Devon & Torridge, part of Mark Bonham Carter's old seat of Torrington, was finally won in a general election. The main improvement in Devon came in Torbay and the surrounding area. Teignbridge and Totnes came out of the election as Conservative marginals, with Torbay narrowly falling to a local Liberal Democrat, Adrian Sanders, by a mere twelve votes. Dorset, as in 1923, remained with the Conservatives. Frank Byers' old seat of North Dorset had the third-highest Conservative majority in the region, even if this was only 5.2 per cent, but the real improvement in the long term came in the seats of West Dorset and Dorset Mid & Poole North which the Liberal Democrats failed to win by just a small margin. In spite of these

Table 8.4: A comparison of the average percentage vote for Liberal and Liberal Democrat candidates in 1964 and 1997.

Election	Tamar Zone	Cornwall	Devon	Dorset	Somerset
1964	43.4 %	33.5 %	30.8 %	24.1 %	20.3 %
1997	48.2 %	43.7 %	30.9 %	33.4 %	41.7 %
Change	+4.8 %	+10.2 %	+0.1 %	+9.3 %	+21.4 %

qualifications the Ashdown advance had transformed the political world of the South-West. The dozen Conservatives that survived in 1997 were fortunate since an extra swing of just 1.8 per cent to the Liberal Democrats would have given that party an extra seven seats.[58]

Conclusion

The regional breakthrough of the Liberal Democrats in 1997 marked the culmination of a gradual and difficult process of rebirth. Local activists in the mid-1950s would surely have been amazed to think that it would eventually take more than forty years before their party would again be on equal terms with the Conservatives. Although the lengthy nature of this process no doubt reflected a variety of short-term factors, the failure to consolidate the Liberal vote in the middle decades of this century was crucial. Only in the 1980s, with success in county and municipal elections, was there a new factor capable of transforming party politics at the grassroots. Surprisingly, however, there remains some continuity with the past. Even religious nonconformity, admittedly no longer the social force that it was in the past, is still represented in the House of Commons since three of the four Liberal Democrat MPs in Cornwall have connectionw with the Methodist Church. Above all, success in 1997 reflected long-term themes, such as local discontent with central government over issues like agriculture and unemployment, the personal appeal of individual candidates and the strong image of the Liberal Democrats as the principal centre-left party of the four counties.[59] It is this historical legacy from the days of Isaac Foot that will continue to provide the inspiration for regional Liberal Democracy in the years to come.

Appendix

Parliamentary representation for the four counties of the South-West, 1918–1997

Election	Liberals	Conservatives*	Labour	Other	Total
1906	28	6	—	—	34
1910 (Jan.)	17	17	—	—	34
1910 (Dec.)	12	22	—	—	34
1918	3	24	—	—	27
1922	5	22	—	—	27
1923	18	8	1	—	27
1924	1	26	—	—	27
1929	8	16	2	1	27
1931	2	25	—	—	27
1935	2	25	—	—	27
1945	2	18	6	1	27
1950	—	23	3	—	26
1951	—	24	2	—	26
1955	—	25	1	—	26
1959	1	24	1	—	26
1964	2	23	1	—	26
1966	3	20	3	—	26
1970	2	23	1	—	26
1974 (Feb.)	3	22	1	—	26
1974 (Oct.)	3	22	1	—	26
1979	1	24	1	—	26
1983	3	24	—	—	27
1987	3	24	—	—	27
1992	5	21	1	—	27
1997	12	12	4	—	28

* Includes the allies of the Conservative party. Liberal Unionists (until December 1910); Lloyd George Liberals (1918–22); an independent Conservative MP in 1922; a Constitutionalist MP (1924); and the Liberal Nationals (1931–66).

Notes

Introduction

1. K. Laybourn, *The Rise of Labour: The British Labour Party, 1890–1979* (London, 1988) and H. Pelling, *Popular Politics and Society in Late Victorian Britain* (London, 1968); other publications which essentially reflect this approach include K. Laybourn and J. Reynolds, *Liberalism and the rise of Labour, 1890–1979* (London, 1984); H.C.G. Matthew, R.I. Mckibbon and J. Kay, 'The franchise factor in the rise of the Labour party', *English Historical Review* (1976).
2. T. Wilson, *The Downfall of the Liberal Party, 1914–1935* (London, 1966); K. Morgan, *The Age of Lloyd George: The Liberal Party and British Politics, 1890–1929* (London, 1971); D. Tanner, 'The Parliamentary Electoral System: the 'Fourth' Reform Act and the Rise of Labour in England and Wales', *Bulletin of the Institute of Historical Research*, Vol. LVI (1983); for a discussion of this subject see G.R. Searle, *The Liberal Party: Triumph and Disintegration, 1886–1929* (London, 1992).
3. C. Cook, *The Age of Alignment: Electoral Politics in Britain, 1922–1929* (London, 1975), p. 343.
4. All statistics in this book, unless otherwise indicated, are based upon F.W.S. Craig, *British Parliamentary Election Results, 1918–1949* (Glasgow, 1969) and F.W.S. Craig, *British Parliamentary Election Results, 1950–1970* (Chichester, 1971).
5. Examples include D. Clark, *Colne Valley: Radicalism to Socialism* (London, 1981); I. McLean, *The Legend of Red Clydeside* (Edinburgh, 1983) and P. Wyncoll, *The Nottingham Labour Movement, 1880–1940* (London, 1985).

1 Politics in the Provinces

1. M. Kinnear, *The British Voter: An Atlas and Survey since 1885* (London, 1968).

2. S. Rokkan, *Citizens Elections Parties: Approaches to the Comparative Study of the Processes of Development* (Oslo, 1970), pp. 127, 141 and 282.

3. Ibid, p. 237.

4. Ibid, pp. 100–6.

5. R. Millward and A. Robinson, *The South West Peninsula* (London, 1971), pp. 5, 12, 52 and 54.

6. *Census of England and Wales. 1921—County of Devon* (London, 1923), p. ix; *The Times*, 23 October 1924 and 28 June 1945.

7. *The Times*, 1, 2 and 8 December 1923; *Western Morning News*, 1 November 1928; *Cornish Guardian*, 30 November and 7 December 1923; J. Ramsden (ed.), *Real Old Tory Politics: The Political Diaries of Sir Robert Sanders, Lord Bayford, 1910–35* (London, 1984), p. 211.

8. W. Gore Allen, *The Reluctant Politician: Derick Heathcoat Amory* (London, 1958), pp. 25 and 36; *Dorset County Chronicle*, 28 October 1931; *Western Gazette*, 7 August and 23 October 1931; *The Times*, 26 October 1931.

9. *Western Morning News*, 4 October 1930.

10. Ibid.

11. *Mid-Devon Advertiser*, 18 November 1944.

12. Rokkan, *Citizens Elections Parties*, p. 196.

13. E.W. Martin, *The Shearers and the Shorn: A Study of Life in a Devon Community* (London, 1965), pp. 1, 116, 136 and 152; F.E. Halliday, *A History of Cornwall* (London, 1959), p. 308; interview with Eric Higgs (20 November 1993).

14. A.L. Rowse, *St Austell Church: Town; Parish* (St Austell, 1960), p. 82.

15. J. Morris, 'Introduction: The European Petite Bourgeoisie 1914–1945: Encounters with the State' in *Contemporary European History* (Vol. 5, Part 3, Cambridge, 1996), pp. 279–85.

16. J. Morris, 'Retailers, Fascism and the Origins of the Social Protection of Shopkeepers in Italy', pp. 285–318 and T. Ericsson, 'Shopkeepers and the Swedish Model: The Petite Bourgeoisie and the State during the Inter-War Period, pp. 357–70 in *Contemporary European History* (Vol. 5, Part 3, Cambridge, 1996).

17. *Western Gazette*, 15 June 1945.

18. M.I. Baines, 'The Survival of the British Liberal Party, 1932–1959', PhD thesis (Oxford University, 1991), p. 60; *Wells Journal*, 7 July 1945.

19. Morris, 'Introduction: The European Petite Bourgeoisie' in *Contemporary European History*, p. 281.

20. Kinnear, *British Voter*, p. 121; see also W.M. Williams, *A West Country Village: Ashworthy—Family, Kinship and Land* (London, 1963), p. 10.

21. *Economist*, 21 November 1959.

22. *Western Gazette*, 23 October 1931.

23. P. Heyrman, 'Belgian Government Policy and the Petite Bourgeoisie (1918–1940)' in *Contemporary European History* (Vol. 5, Part 3, 1996); P.

Campbell, 'Le Mouvement Poujade', *Parliamentary Affairs*, Vol. X (1956–7), pp. 362–7.

24. *The Liberal Magazine*, Vol. 38 (1930), p. 33.

25. N. Orme (ed.), *Unity and Variety: A History of the Church in Devon and Cornwall* (Exeter, 1991) pp. 140–54.

26. Kinnear, *British Voter*, pp. 125–9.

27. See also J.C.C. Probert, *The Sociology of Cornish Methodism* (Truro, 1971), pp. 70 and 77; Martin, *Shearers and the Shorn*, p. 179; interview with David and Joan Morrish (16 September 1994); Cornish Methodist Records (Cornwall Record Office), MR/A/64, Schedule Book of the St Austell Wesleyan Circuit, 1923–33.

28. Martin, *Shearers and the Shorn*, p. 76.

29. Rowse, *St Austell*, p. 82; A.L. Rowse, *A Man of the Thirties* (London, 1979), p. 56; Martin, *Shearers and the Shorn*, p. 45; R. Currie, A. Gilbert and L. Horsley, *Churches and Churchgoers: Patterns of Church Growth in the British Isles since 1700* (Oxford, 1977), p. 56.

30. Martin, *Shearers and the Shorn*, p. 76.

31. A.M. Dawson, 'Politics in Devon and Cornwall, 1900–31', PhD thesis (London University, 1991), p. 133.

32. Rev. T. Shaw, *A History of Cornish Methodism* (Truro, 1967), p. 99; Kinnear, *British Voter*, p. 126.

33. Interview with F.L. Harris (10 June 1990); *Western Morning News*, 3 November 1924.

34. Interviews with David and Joan Morrish (16 September 1994); Chris and Bridget Trethewey (21 October 1994).

35. N. Smart, 'The Age of Consolidation: South-Western Constituency Politics and Electoral Change in the Age of Alignment', *Southern History*, Vol. 12 (1990).

36. H. Pelling, *Social Geography of British Elections, 1885–1910* (London, 1967), pp. 125, 141 and 158.

37. R. Manning-Sanders, *The West of England* (London, 1949); C. Hollis, *Along the Road to Frome* (London, 1958), p. 183.

38. P. Payton, *The Making of Modern Cornwall: Historical Experience and the Persistence of 'Difference'* (Redruth, 1992), pp. 7–20.

39. For a more detailed discussion of this subject see G. Tregidga, 'The Politics of the Celto-Cornish Revival 1886–1939' in P. Payton (ed.), *Cornish Studies: Five* (Exeter, 1997), pp. 125 50.

40. *Cornish Guardian*, 6 September 1912.

41. Penryn & Falmouth Conservative Association papers (Cornwall Record Office), DDX/551/11, electoral address of the Liberal candidate for Penryn & Falmouth in 1935.

42. *Cornish Guardian*, 16 February 1923.

43. See Payton, *The Making of Modern Cornwall*, p. 18.

44. These seats were centred on the historic counties of Devon (Devon West & Torridge, Devon North and Torbay) and Somerset (Taunton, Yeovil, Somerton & Frome, Weston-super-Mare and Bath). While the Liberal Democrats had some success in the Hampshire area (Winchester, Portsmouth South, Eastleigh and the Isle of Wight), they failed to win a single seat in Wiltshire which was a Liberal stronghold in 1923.

45. Pelling, *Social Geography*, pp. 172 and 174; interview with Chris and Bridget Trethewey (21 October 1994); *Western Morning News*, 1 June 1929; Kinnear, *British Voter*, p. 126; S.G. Putt, *Wings of a Man's Life* (London, 1990), pp. 6 and 24.

46. Quoted in P. Payton 'Cornwall in Context: The New Cornish Historiography' in P. Payton (ed.), *Cornish Studies: Five* (Exeter, 1997), p. 9.

47. See *Devon and Cornwall—A Preliminary Survey: A Report issued by the Survey Committee of the University College of the South West* (Exeter, 1947).

2 Keeping the Faith: 1918–1929

1. C. Cook, *The Age of Alignment: Electoral Politics in Britain, 1922–1929* (London, 1975).

2. For example, D. Clark, *Colne Valley: Radicalism to Socialism* (London, 1981); I. Mclean, *The Legend of Red Clydeside* (Edinburgh, 1983); P. Wyncoll, *The Nottingham Labour Movement, 1880–1940* (London, 1985); K. Laybourn, *The Rise of Labour: the British Labour Party, 1890–1979* (London, 1988).

3. The Labour percentage vote in Motherwell, Doncaster, Aberavon in 1918 was only 23.2, 25.0 and 35.7 per cent; by 1929 the party's share of the vote had risen to 58.0, 56.0 and 55.9 per cent respectively.

4. *Cornish Guardian*, 21 February 1918; see also A.L. Rowse, *St Austell: Church; Town; Parish* (St Austell, 1960), p. 82.

5. B. Deacon, 'Conybeare for Ever!' in T. Knight (ed.), *Old Redruth: Original Studies of the Town's History* (Redruth, 1992), pp. 37–43.

6. Acland papers (Devon Record Office), 1148 M 14/667, Francis Acland to Eleanor Acland, late 1917.

7. *Western Morning News*, 12, 30 and 31 December 1918.

8. J. Ramsden (ed.), *Real Old Tory Politics: The Political Diaries of Sir Robert Sanders, Lord Bayford, 1910–35* (London, 1984), pp. 193 and 210; A.F. Cooper, *British Agricultural Policy, 1912–36: A Study in Conservative politics* (Manchester, 1989), p. 66; *The Times*, 28 and 30 October 1922; 22 November 1923; 2 and 8 December 1923; *Western Morning News*, 17 November 1922.

9. *Western Morning News*, 20 October 1924; M. Kinnear, *The British Voter: An Atlas and Survey since 1885* (London, 1968).

10. *Western Morning News*, 1 December 1923.
11. *Royal Cornwall Gazette*, 22 November 1922; *West Briton*, 2 November 1922.
12. J. Rowe, 'The Declining Years of Cornish Tin Mining' in J. Porter (ed.) *Education and Labour in the South West* (Exeter, 1975), pp. 66 and 73; *West Briton*, 24 October 1935; *Cornish Guardian*, 23 March 1939.
13. P. Payton, *The Making of Modern Cornwall: Historical Experience and the Persistence of 'Difference'* (Redruth, 1992), pp. 139–60; see also R. Perry, 'A Remission in the Great Paralysis?' in *Cornish History Network Newsletter*, Issue 3, December 1998, pp. 2 and 3; R. Perry, 'Celtic Revival and Economic Development in Edwardian Cornwall' in P. Payton (ed.), *Cornish Studies: Five* (Exeter, 1997), pp. 112–24.
14. *Cornish Guardian*, 3 March 1922 and 15 December 1960; interview with F.L. Harris (10 June 1990).
15. *The Times*, 5 December 1918, 17 November 1922 and 14 May 1929; *Western Morning News*, 3 and 16 November 1922.
16. *The Liberal Agent*, Vol. 30 (1929), p. 43; *Western Morning News*, 3 November 1928, 6 June 1929 and 14 March 1930.
17. *The Times*, 28 October 1922; Kinnear, *British Voter*, p. 128.
18. *The Times*, 2 December 1923 and 22 October 1924; H. Pelling, *Social Geography of British Elections, 1885–1910* (London, 1967), pp.149–51.
19. *The Times*, 25 October 1924.
20. *Western Morning News*, 1, 5, 7 and 8 December 1923.
21. *Western Morning News*, 8 December 1923.
22. *Cornish Guardian*, ? January 1924.
23. *The Times*, 23 January 1924.
24. *Cornish Guardian*, ? January 1924; *West Briton*, ? January 1924.
25. *The Times*, 23 January 1924.
26. *Cornish Guardian*, ? October 1924; *Western Morning News*, 28 October 1924.
27. East Dorset Women's Liberal Association papers (University of Bristol), DM 1193, Alec Glassey's 1924 election address; executive committee minutes, 5 May 1924, 2 February 1927 and 27 March 1929; *Dorset County Chronicle*, 6 June 1929; *Liberal Agent*, Vol. 29 (1928).
28. *Western Morning News*, 28 October 1924; *The Times*, 18 and 25 October 1924.
29. *The Times*, 18 October 1924.
30. *Western Morning News*, 31 October and 1 November 1924; *The Times*, 21 October 1924; Pelling, *Social Geography*, p. 171.
31. *Western Morning News*, 31 October 1924.
32. *Cornish Guardian*, 7 November 1924; *Western Morning News*, 1 November 1924.
33. *Royal Cornwall Gazette*, 22 October 1924; *Cornish Guardian*, 8, 15 and 22 January 1926 and 5 March 1926; A.M. Dawson, 'Politics in Devon and Cornwall, 1900–31', PhD thesis (London University, 1991), pp. 255–61.

34. *Wells Journal*, 24 May 1929; *Somerset County Gazette*, 18 May 1929; *The Times*, 6 March 1928; C. Cook and J. Ramsden (eds), *By-elections in British Politics* (London, 1973), p. 108; Western Counties Liberal Federation papers (University of Bristol), DM 1172, executive committee minutes, 16 July 1929.

35. *Liberal Agent*, Vol. 29 (1928), pp. 46 and 47; Western Counties Liberal Federation, DM 1172, executive committee minutes, 21 January 1928.

36. *Cornish Guardian*, 11 January 1929.

37. *Western Morning News*, 1 May 1929; *The Times*, 6 May 1929.

38. Penryn & Falmouth Conservative Association papers (Cornwall Record Office), DDX/551/10/1, committee minutes, 9 October 1929; *The Times*, 13 May 1929; *Western Morning News*, 1 and 11 May 1929.

39. For a detailed study of the subject of ideology see W.H. Greenleaf, *The British Political Tradition: The Ideological Heritage*, Vol. 2 (London, 1983); T. Wilson, *The Downfall of the Liberal Party, 1914–1935* (London, 1966), p. 341.

40. *Western Morning News*, 1 November 1924.

41. Ibid., 21 May 1929.

42. A.M. Dawson, 'Politics in Devon and Cornwall, 1900–31', PhD thesis, London University, 1991, p. 343; *Liberal Magazine*, Vol. 37 (1929), p. 1.

43. Runciman papers (Newcastle-upon-Tyne University), WR 219, Runciman to Ilford Liberal association, n.d. (*c.*1928); *Liberal Magazine*, Vol. 35 (1927), p. 219.

44. Runciman papers, WR 331, newspaper article, 9 May 1929; WR 332, newspaper article, 17 May 1929.

45. *Liberal Magazine*, Vol. 35 (1927), p. 219.

46. National Liberal Club Collection (Bristol University), DM 668, 1929 election addresses of Liberal candidates in the South-West; *Western Morning News*, 10 May 1929.

47. *Dorset County Chronicle*, 9 and 30 May 1929; *Dorset Daily Express*, 25 and 30 May 1929; East Dorset Women's Liberal Association, DM 1193, committee minutes, 26 July 1928; *Western Morning News*, 1, 14, 15 and 18 May 1929.

48. *Dorset Daily Express*, 25 May 1929.

49. *Western Morning News*, 17 and 18 May 1929; see also Ramsden, *Real Old Tory Politics*, p. 238.

50. *Dorset County Chronicle*, 16 May 1929.

51. Camborne Conservative Association papers (Cornwall Record Office), DDX/387/3, executive committee minutes, 21 October 1929; see also *Royal Cornwall Gazette*, 24 April, 15 May and 5 June 1929.

52. Runciman papers, WR 219, Runciman to Ilford Liberals, n.d. (*c.*1928).

53. S. Ball, *Baldwin and the Conservative Party: The Crisis of 1929–1931* (London, 1988), p. 4; *Dorset County Chronicle*, 2 and 16 May 1929; *Bath Chronicle*, 25

May 1929; *Western Morning News*, 1 May 1929; *The Times*, 17 May 1929; Western Counties Liberal Federation, DM 1172, committee minutes, 24 September 1928.

54. *Western Morning News*, 1 November 1928 and 1 May 1929; *The Times*, 20 May 1929: North Dorset Conservative Association papers (Dale House, Blandford Forum), executive committee minutes, 5 April 1929; Camborne Conservative Association, DDX/387/3, committee minutes, 21 October 1929.

55. *Wells Journal*, 24 May 1929; *Western Morning News*, 15 May 1929; *Bath Chronicle*, 25 May 1929.

56. *Dorset County Chronicle*, 23 May 1929.

57. *Dorset Daily Express*, 17, 23 and 25 May 1929; West Dorset Conservative Association papers (Dorset Record Office), D/399/5/1, 1928 Report; *Bath Chronicle*, 16 March and 25 May 1929.

58. *Western Morning News*, 14 May 1929.

59. Ball, *Baldwin and the Conservative Party*, p. 5; North Dorset Conservative Association, committee minutes, 25 August 1927; finance and advisory committee minutes, 25 February 1928.

60. Ball, *Baldwin and the Conservative Party*, p. 19; Kinnear, *British Voter*, pp. 84 and 120; *Dorset Daily Express*, 29 May 1929.

61. Dawson, 'Politics in Devon and Cornwall', p. 196.

62. *Cornish Guardian*, 6 June 1929; *Somerset County Gazette*, 1 June 1929; *Dorset County Chronicle*, 30 May 1929.

63. *The Times*, 13 May 1929.

64. *Devon and Cornwall—A Preliminary Survey: A Report issued by the Survey Committee of the University College of the South West* (Exeter, 1947), pp. 239, 242, 246 and 247.

65. Camborne Conservative Association, DDX/387/3, committee minutes, 21 October 1929.

66. Kinnear, *British Voter*, p. 48.

67. Cook, *Age of Alignment*, p. 339.

68. N. Smart, 'The Age of Consolidation: South-Western Constituency Politics and Electoral Change in the Age of Alignment', *Southern History*, Vol. 12 (1990), pp. 118 and 128.

69. *Western Morning News*, 3 June 1929.

70. *Cornish Guardian*, 6 June 1929.

71. *Bath Chronicle*, 1 June 1929; *Western Morning News*, 1 June 1929; *The Times*, 23 October 1924 and 14 May 1929; *Cornish Guardian*, 6 June 1929.

72. Smart, 'Age of Consolidation', p. 123.

73. *Cornish Guardian*, 8 January 1926.

74. *Western Morning News*, 2 November 1928 and 1 May 1929.

75. Ibid., 1 November 1928; *Bath Chronicle*, 25 May 1929.

76. *Dorset County Chronicle*, 30 May 1929.

77. *Western Morning News*, 14 May 1929; *The Times*, 14 May 1929.

3 Into the Wilderness: 1929–1935

1. T. Wilson, *The Downfall of the Liberal Party, 1914–1935* (London, 1966), p. 351.
2. Western Counties Liberal Federation (Bristol University), DM 1172, executive committee minutes, 18 January 1930 and 25 April 1931; A. Thorpe, *Britain in the 1930s: The Deceptive Decade* (Oxford, 1992), p. 35; *Western Gazette*, 9 October 1931; *Western Morning News*, 8 March 1930.
3. Wilson, *Downfall of the Liberal Party*, p. 354; Sir C. Mallet, *Mr. Lloyd George: A Study* (London, 1930), pp. 302–13.
4. *West Briton*, 26 March 1931.
5. *Wells Journal*, 24 April 1931; *Western Morning News*, 18 October 1930.
6. *Western Gazette*, 23 October 1931; Runciman papers (Newcastle-upon-Tyne University), WR 252, Velden to Runciman, 20 September 1931.
7. *Western Morning News*, 28 November 1930.
8. A. Thorpe, *The British General Election of 1931* (Oxford, 1991), p. 62.
9. *Cornish Guardian*, 10 September 1931.
10. *Western Gazette*, 3 July 1931.
11. *Western Morning News*, 25 January and 6 July 1930.
12. *Western Morning News*, 14 March and 11 July 1930; Wilson, *Downfall of the Liberal Party*, pp. 357–8.
13. Wilson, *Downfall of the Liberal Party*, pp. 356–60.
14. D. Foot, 'The Liberal Crisis', *Contemporary Review*, Vol. 139 (May 1931), p. 585.
15. *Western Morning News*, 12 December 1930.
16. See Wilson, *Downfall of the Liberal Party*, p. 360.
17. *Western Morning News*, 21 and 23 March 1930; *Liberal Magazine*, Vol. 39 (1931), p. 155.
18. *Express and Echo*, 6 October 1931; *Western Morning News*, 25 November and 3 December 1930; Western Counties Federation papers, DM 1172, executive committee minutes, 25 April 1931.
19. *Western Morning News*, 28 January, 15 March and 24 July 1930.
20. *Liberal Magazine*, Vol. 39 (1931), p. 268.
21. *Cornish Guardian*, 10 and 24 September 1931; C. Cook, *A Short History of the Liberal Party, 1900–84* (London, 1984), p. 115.
22. *Wells Journal*, 16 October 1931; *Cornish Guardian*, 17 September 1931.
23. *West Briton*, 16 September and 7 October 1931; *Western Gazette*, 25 September 1931.
24. *Liberal Gazette*, Vol. 39 (1931), p. 155; Hore-Belisha papers, HOBE/1/1, Hore-Belisha's manifesto to MacDonald, 18 September 1931; *Wells*

Journal, 9 October 1931; Western Counties Federation papers, DM 1172, executive committee minutes, 23 January 1932.

25. *Dorset County Chronicle,* 29 October 1931; *Wells Journal,* 23 October 1931; *Cornish Guardian,* 15 October 1931.

26. *Western Gazette,* 23 October 1931; *Wells Journal,* 16 October 1931; *Dorset County Chronicle,* 22 October and 5 November 1931; N. Smart, 'The Age of Consolidation: South-Western Constituency Politics and Electoral Change in the Age of Alignment', *Southern History,* Vol. 12 (1990), p. 129.

27. Sir Donald Maclean papers (Bodleian Library, Oxford), fol. 147, notes for a speech, n.d. [*c.*1932].

28. C.T. Stannage, *Baldwin Thwarts the Opposition: The British General Election of 1935* (London, 1980), p. 86; Cook, *Short History of the Liberal Party,* p. 118.

29. *Cornish Guardian,* 4 May and 9 November 1933; D.M. Rees, 'The disintegration of the Liberal Party, 1931–33', MA (University of Wales, Aberystwyth, 1980), p. 195.

30. *The Times,* 25 June 1934; calculations for by-election results based on F.W.S. Craig (ed.), *British Parliamentary Election Results, 1918–1949* (Glasgow, 1969).

31. Stannage, *Baldwin Thwarts the Opposition,* p. 103; *Wells Journal,* 25 January and 5 April 1935; *Cornish Guardian,* 25 October 1934.

32. *West Briton,* 31 October 1935.

33. Wilson, *Downfall of the Liberal Party,* p. 377.

34. *West Briton,* 24 and 31 October 1935; *Cornish Guardian,* 14 November 1935; *Wells Journal,* 5 April 1935.

35. *Cornish Guardian,* 22 November 1934.

36. Cook, *Short History of the Liberal Party,* pp. 120–5.

37. J. Stevenson; *Third Party Politics since 1945: Liberals, Alliance and Liberal Democrats* (Oxford, 1993), p. 20; *Cornish Guardian,* 25 October and 29 November 1934.

38. *Somerset County Gazette,* 7 November 1931 and 2 November 1935; *Western Morning News,* 2 November 1931, 2 November 1932 and 1 November 1934; *Bath Chronicle,* 3 November 1934.

39. *Dorset County Chronicle,* 9 November 1933; *Somerset County Gazette,* 2 November 1929 and 4 November 1933.

40. Based on local newspaper reports of borough council elections. Some caution should be attached to the accuracy of these figures since some party candidates were listed as Independents.

41. *Liberal Magazine,* Vol. XLII (1934), pp. 156 and 166.

42. M.I. Baines, 'The Survival of the British Liberal Party, 1932–59', PhD thesis (Oxford University, 1991), p. 16.

43. *Cornish Guardian,* 24 October 1935.

44. *Cornish Guardian,* 5 April 1934.

45. Thurso papers (Churchill College, Cambridge), THRS II 56/2, a meeting

for discussion of a women's programme, 24 January 1935; F.W.S. Craig (ed.), *British General Election Manifestos, 1918–1966* (Chichester, 1970), p. 85.

46. Wilson, *Downfall of the Liberal Party*, pp. 378–9.
47. Runciman papers (Newcastle-upon-Tyne University), WR 252, report of a visit to Penzance by Major Broadhurst, 6 April 1936.
48. Stannage, *Baldwin Thwarts the Opposition*, p. 233.
49. *Cornish Guardian*, 14 July 1932; *Western Morning News*, 27 November 1935; interview with David and Joan Morrish (16 September 1994).
50. *Western Morning News*, 2 December 1935.
51. *The Times*, 13 November 1935.
52. *Dorset Daily Echo*, 14 and 19 November 1935.
53. *Express and Echo*, 28 October and 2 November 1935; Thurso papers, THRS II 58/1, annual report of the Devon and Cornwall Liberal Federation, 1936.
54. J. Ramsden (ed.), *Real Old Tory Politics: The Political Diaries of Sir Robert Sanders, Lord Bayford, 1910–35* (London, 1984), p. 247.
55. Thorpe, *British General Election of 1931*, pp. 240, 241 and 282; *Cornish Guardian*, 22 October 1931.
56. *Wells Journal*, 9, 16 and 23 October 1931.
57. *Express and Echo*, 25 September 1931; *Western Morning News*, 5, 8 and 11 December 1930; see also A.M. Dawson, 'Politics in Devon and Cornwall, 1900–31', PhD thesis (London University, 1991), pp. 205 and 206.
58. *Western Gazette*, 23 October 1931; *Cornish Guardian*, 29 November 1931.
59. *Cornish Guardian*, 28 July 1932; Rees, 'Disintegration of the Liberal Party', p. 192; *Liberal Magazine*, Vol. XL (1932), p. 574.
60. *Cornish Guardian*, 30 November 1933 and 6 December 1934.
61. *Dorset Daily Echo*, 4 November 1934; Stannage, *Baldwin Thwarts the Opposition*, p. 163; *Cornish Guardian*, 21 November 1935.
62. *Dorset Daily Echo*, 31 October and 4 November 1935.
63. *Liberal Magazine*, Vol. 38 (1930), p. 2; Foot, 'Liberal Crisis', pp. 582–8.
64. *Cornish Guardian*, 4 July 1929 and 16 January 1930.
65. *Western Morning News*, 13 and 25 October 1930.
66. *Western Morning News*, 6 March 1930.
67. *Western Morning News*, 27 February 1930.
68. *Western Morning News*, 15 February, 15 March and 24 July 1930.
69. *Western Morning News*, 31 January 1930.
70. *Cornish Guardian*, 9 January 1930.
71. Wilson, *Downfall of the Liberal Party*, p. 377; Stannage, *Baldwin Thwarts the Opposition*, p. 95.
72. Ibid., p. 103.
73. Lothian papers (Scottish Record Office), GD40/17/283, Lothian to Johnstone, 13 November 1934; Johnstone to Lothian, 19 November

1934.

74. Cook, *Short History of the Liberal Party*, p. 122.
75. *West Briton*, 18 July 1935, Western Counties Federation papers, DM 1172, finance and general purposes committee, 1929 and 1934.
76. *Liberal Magazine*, Vol. XL (1932), p. 592.
77. Thurso papers, THRS II 57/2, Pall to Sinclair, 16 August 1935; THRS II 56/3, Mackenzie to Harris, 15 October 1935 and Harris to Mackenzie, 18 October 1935.
78. *Cornish Guardian*, 7 November 1935; Lothian papers, GD40/17/301, Isaac Foot to Lothian, 28 October 1935.
79. Interview with Chris and Bridget Trethewey (21 October 1994).
80. Stannage, *Baldwin Thwarts the Opposition*, p. 99.
81. *West Briton*, 24 October and 14 November 1935.
82. Stannage, *Baldwin Thwarts the Opposition*, p. 85.
83. *Cornish Guardian*, 30 June, 21 July and 28 July 1932.
84. *Wells Journal*, 25 January 1935; Thurso papers, THRS II 58/1, annual report of the Devon and Cornwall Liberal Federation, February 1936.
85. *Express and Echo*, 28 October 1935; *Cornish Guardian*, 25 October 1934.
86. *Cornish Guardian*, 9 August 1934 and 29 October 1935.
87. *Cornish Guardian*, 5 November 1931, 16 November 1933 and 1 August 1935.
88. *Wells Journal*, 21 June 1935; *Cornish Guardian*, 29 November 1934.

4 Advance and Retreat: 1936–1945

1. C. Cook and J. Ramsden (eds), *By-elections in British Politics* (London, 1973), p. 116.
2. B. Pimlott, *Labour and the Left in the 1930s* (Cambridge, 1977), pp. 143–52.
3. C. Cook, *A Short History of the Liberal Party, 1900–84*, (London, 1984) pp. 123–5; G.J. De Groot, *Liberal Crusader: The Life of Sir Archibald Sinclair* (London, 1993), p. 130.
4. Cowling, *Impact of Hitler*, p. 210.
5. *Report of the Labour Annual Conference, 1939*, pp. 236, 295 and 299.
6. Thurso papers (Churchill College, Cambridge), THRS II/39/3, Sinclair to Wood, 4 May 1938.
7. De Groot, *Liberal Crusader*, pp. 130–45.
8. Thurso papers, THRS II/67/3, Sinclair to Enid Lakeman, 9 December 1938; THRS II/65/5, Mackenzie to Raymond Jones, 10 December 1938; THRS II/65/5, Mackenzie to James, 21 February 1939.
9. Ibid., THRS II/63/3, Davies to Sinclair, 25 February 1939; THRS II/63/3, Davies to Taylor, 17 February 1939.
10. B. Pimlott, *Hugh Dalton* (London, 1985), pp. 261 and 262; *Report of the*

Labour Annual Conference, 1939, pp. 231 and 301.

11. Pimlott, *Labour and the Left in the 1930s*, p. 176.

12. Thurso papers, THRS II/58/1, Annual report of the Devon and Cornwall Liberal Federation, February 1936; Frome Labour Party papers (Somerset Record Office), A/AAW/26, executive committee minutes, 12 March and 14 May 1938; *Cornish Guardian*, 6 July 1939.

13. Thurso papers, THRS II/62/4, memorandum entitled 'Political Inferences from the Miniature General Election' (1937).

14. Runciman papers (Newcastle-upon-Tyne University), WR 252, Broadhurst to Runciman, 19 March 1937; *Cornish Guardian*, 24 June 1937.

15. *Dorset Daily Echo*, 14 and 16 July 1937; Thurso papers, THRS II/62/4, 'Political Inferences from the Miniature General Election' (1937).

16. *Bridgwater Mercury*, 27 April, 29 June and 12 October 1938; *Somerset County Gazette*, 8 and 22 October 1938; Cook and Ramsden (eds), *By-elections in British Politics*, p. 151.

17. *Cornish Guardian*, 16 March 1939; *Western Morning News*, 22 November 1938; Lloyd George papers, H/33, *News Chronicle* article on the Bridgwater by-election.

18. *Cornish Guardian*, 8 December 1938 and 18 May 1939.

19. *Western Morning News*, 19 and 23 November 1938.

20. *Somerset County Gazette*, 31 December 1938; *Western Gazette*, 31 March 1939.

21. *Western Morning News*, 30 December 1938; *West Briton*, 2 January 1939; M.I. Baines, 'The Survival of the British Liberal Party, 1932–1959', PhD thesis (Oxford University, 1991), p. 34.

22. *Western Morning News*, 23 and 28 June 1939.

23. *Cornish Guardian*, 20 July 1939.

24. *Western Morning News*, 28 November 1938; *Dorset Daily Echo*, 5 April 1939.

25. *Cornish Guardian*, 15 March 1945; *North Devon Journal-Herald*, 12 July 1945.

26. *Western Morning News*, 25 April 1945; *Herald and Express*, 18 June 1945.

27. *Cornish Guardian*, 21 and 28 June 1945; Baines, 'Survival of the British Liberal Party', p. 34; T.L. Horabin, *Politics Made Plain: What the Next General Election will Really be About* (London, 1944), pp. 96–128.

28. *Cornish Guardian*, 1, 8 and 15 March 1945.

29. *Western Morning News*, 17 April 1945.

30. *Western Morning News*, 25 July and 3 October 1942.

31. W.L. Arnstein, 'The Liberals and the General Election of 1945: A Sceptical Note', *Journal of British Studies*, Vol. XIV (May 1975), p. 121.

32. *Western Morning News*, 30 May 1945; S. Gorley Putt, *Wings of a Man's Life* (London, 1990), p. 173.

33. *New Statesman*, 4 August 1945.

34. Cook, *Short History of the Liberal Party*, pp. 123–5; Baines, 'Survival of the British Liberal Party', p. 42.

35. *Cornish Guardian*, 18 February 1937.
36. *Western Morning News*, 23 November 1938 and 29 July 1939.
37. Western Counties Liberal Federation papers (Bristol University), DM 1172, finance and general purposes committee minutes, 18 February 1939; executive committee minutes, 5 June 1939.
38. *Dorset Daily Echo*, 5 July and 31 August 1939; *Bridgwater Mercury*, 16 February 1938.
39. *Dorset Daily Echo*, 22 February 1939; West Dorset Conservative Association papers (Dorset Record Office), D399/3/1, executive committee minutes, 1937–9.
40. Thurso papers, THRS II/58/1, Annual Report of the Devon and Cornwall Liberal Federation, February 1936.
41. *Western Morning News*, 4 January 1939; *Cornish Guardian*, 16 March 1939.
42. Thurso papers, THRS II/64/1, a meeting at the National Liberal Club, 21 June 1938.
43. Ibid., THRS II/63/3, Davies to Sinclair, 25 February 1939.
44. Cowling, *Impact of Hitler*, p. 111.
45. Thurso papers, THRS II/62/2, A. Campbell Johnson to Sinclair, 11 June 1937; *Dorset Daily Echo*, 22 July 1939.
46. Thurso papers, THRS II/62/4, 'Political Inferences from the Miniature General Election', *Cornish Guardian*, 24 June 1937 and 6 July 1939; A.J. Sylvester (edited by C. Cross), *Life with Lloyd George: The Diary of A.J. Sylvester* (London, 1975), p. 232.
47. *Cornish Guardian*, 10 August 1939; *Wells Journal*, 11 August 1939.
48. P. Addison, *The Road to 1945: British Politics and the Second World War* (London, 1975), p. 258; K. Jefferys, *The Churchill Coalition and Wartime Politics, 1940–1945* (Manchester, 1991), pp. 141 and 201.
49. Western Counties Federation papers, DM 1172, executive committee minutes, 8 December 1939 and 17 February 1940.
50. Ibid., DM 1172, finance and general purposes committee minutes, 17 February 1941.
51. Bodmin Liberal Association papers (Liskeard Liberal Democrat Office), executive committee minutes, February 1941 and May 1945.
52. Groot, *Liberal Crusader*, pp. 216–17.
53. Putt, *Wings of a Man's Life*, p. 178.
54. Ibid., p. 169.
55. *Western Morning News*, 15 February 1950.
56. *Mid-Devon Advertiser*, 24 March 1945; *Western Morning News*, 17 February 1950.
57. *Cornish Guardian*, 5 July 1945; interview with David and Joan Morrish (16 September 1994); Western Counties Federation papers, DM 1172, finance and general purposes committee minutes, 9 August 1945.
58. *Wells Journal*, 13 April 1945; Putt, *Wings of a Man's Life*, p. 168.

59. *Western Evening Herald*, 4 and 6 July 1945; *Herald and Express*, 14 June 1945; *Cornish Guardian*, 21 and 28 June 1945.

60. Thurso papers, THRS II/60/1, correspondence between Sinclair and Crinks, November 1935–January 1936; De Groot, *Liberal Crusader*, pp. 121 and 125; Cowling, *Impact of Hitler*, p. 112.

61. *Bridgwater Mercury*, 16 February 1938; *Wells Journal*, 6 January 1939.

62. Thurso papers, THRS II/66/3, leaflet entitled 'The Liberal Policy for Today's Needs'; THRS II/66/12, programme of the 1939 Annual Conference of the National League of Young Liberals; *Liberal Magazine*, Vol. XLIV (1936), p. 193.

63. *Bridgwater Mercury*, 16 February 1938; Thurso papers, THRS II/65/5, Mackenzie to Jones, 5 December 1938.

64. Thurso papers, THRS II/66/13, copy of the monthly report of the Devon and Cornwall Federation, undated (*c.*March 1939); A.L. Rowse, 'Present and Immediate Future of the Labour Party', *Political Quarterly*, p. 29.

65. Thurso papers, THRS II/62/4, minutes of a meeting of federation secretaries, 7 December 1939.

66. Ibid., THRS II/65/5, Crinks to Sinclair, 8 February 1939; THRS II/66/10, Pearce to Sinclair, 1 July 1939.

67. *Western Gazette*, 6 January 1939; C. Smith, 'The Government and the Farmers', *Fabian Quarterly*, No. 22 (Summer, 1939), pp. 13–18.

68. R. Eatwell, 'Munich, Public Opinion and the Popular Front', *Journal of Contemporary History*, Vol. 14 (1971), p. 134; Cook and Ramsden, *By-elections in British Politics*, p. 157.

69. *Bridgwater Mercury*, 26 October, 9 November and 19 November 1938; *Western Morning News*, 5 January 1939; Lloyd George papers, H/33, *News Chronicle* article on the Bridgwater by-election; Smith, 'Government and the Farmers', p. 17.

70. *Wells Journal*, 6 January 1939.

71. W. Roberts, 'The Programme We Want: A Popular Front Programme', *NFRB Quarterly*, No. 13 (Spring, 1937), p. 18.

72. *Wells Journal*, 6 January 1939; *Dorset Daily Echo*, 22 February 1939; *Cornish Guardian*, 26 January 1939; THRS II/66/10, Pearce to Sinclair, 1 July 1939.

73. De Groot, *Liberal Crusader*, p. 59; Thurso papers, THRS II/67/7, Pearce to Mackenzie, 7 May 1938.

74. Thurso papers, THRS II/62/4, 'Political Inferences from the Miniature General Election'; National Liberal Club collection of by-election addresses (Bristol University), DM 688, Liberal election address (St Ives, 1937).

75. *Wells Journal*, 6 January 1939.

76. De Groot, *Liberal Crusader*, p. 206.

77. Ibid., p. 220; Horabin, *Politics Made Plain*, pp. 124–6; *Western Morning News*, 25 August and 7 September 1942.

78. *Western Evening Herald*, 29 May 1945.

79. *Cornish Guardian*, 28 June 1945.

80. *Western Morning News*, 21 March 1942; *Western Gazette*, 3 August 1945.

81. *Dorset County Chronicle*, 7 and 21 June 1945.

82. *News Chronicle*, 11 July 1935.

83. *Express and Echo*, 16 June 1945; *Mid-Devon Advertiser*, 5 July 1945; *Wells Journal*, 3 August 1945; *Herald and Express*, 5 July 1945; *North Devon Journal-Herald*, 5 July 1945.

84. *Cornish Guardian*, 3 July 1945.

85. *Wells Journal*, 22 June 1945.

86. *Cornish Guardian*, 8 October 1936; Thurso papers, THRS II/62/4, 'Political Inferences from the Miniature General Election'.

87. *Mid-Devon Advertiser*, 9 December 1944 and 12 May 1945; see also *Western Morning News*, 12 and 15 September 1939.

88. *Western Morning News*, 4 July 1945; *North Devon Journal-Herald*, 2 August 1945; interview with David and Joan Morrish (16 September 1994).

89. *Cornish Guardian*, 28 June 1945.

90. *Western Evening Herald*, 26 July 1945; Penryn and Falmouth Conservative Association papers (Cornwall Record Office), DDX/551/16, committee minutes, [n.d., 1945].

91. *The Times*, 9 February 1950; statistical calculations for this section based on F.W.S. Craig, *British Parliamentary Election Results 1918–1949* (Glasgow, 1969).

92. *North Devon Journal-Herald*, 5 July 1945; *Western Gazette*, 12 January 1945.

93. *Western Gazette*, 12 January 1945.

94. *Royal Cornwall Gazette*, 30 August 1944; see also *Western Morning News*, 23 January 1950.

95. *Mid-Devon Advertiser*, 17 February and 24 March 1945; *Wells Journal*, 30 June 1944, 23 March and 12 May 1945; *Herald and Express*, 5 July 1945; *Western Gazette*, 22 June and 3 August 1945.

5 Crusade for Survival: 1945–1950

1. *Western Morning News*, 18 March 1946.

2. *Western Morning News*, 31 March 1947 and 15 February 1950.

3. *Bath Chronicle*, 24 September 1947 and 18 February 1949.

4. *Western Morning News*, 15 February 1950.

5. *Cornish Guardian*, 24 October 1946; *Western Morning News*, 21 March 1947.

6. *Western Morning News*, 26 January 1950; *The Times: House of Commons* (London, 1950), pp. 136 and 210.

7. *Western Morning News*, 25 January 1950; A. Watkins, *The Liberal Dilemma* (London, 1966), p. 45.

8. *The Times*, 18 March 1946; *Cornish Guardian*, 24 October 1946.

9. *Western Morning News*, 10 and 17 February 1950.

10. *Western Morning News*, 25 February 1950.

11. *West Briton*, 23 February 1950; *Somerset County Herald*, 11 February 1950; Samuel papers (House of Lords Record Office), A/129, Frank Byers to Samuel, 30 December 1949.

12. R. Eatwell, *The 1945–1951 Labour Governments* (London, 1979), p. 130.

13. *Somerset County Herald*, 14 January 1950; R.S. Milne and H.C. Mackenzie, *Straight Fight: A Study of Voting Behaviour in the Constituency of Bristol North-East at the General Election of 1951* (London, 1954), p. 126.

14. *Somerset County Herald*, 15 March 1950; *Poole & Dorset Herald*, 1 March 1950; Thurso papers (Churchill College, Cambridge), THRS IV/7/7, Sinclair to Foot, 9 November 1949.

15. *Western Morning News*, 13 February 1950.

16. *Dorset Daily Echo*, 19 January 1950.

17. *Dorset Daily Echo*, 20 January 1950; Dingle Foot papers (Churchill College, Cambridge), DGFT/1/5, a speech by Foot, 19 May 1950; *Somerset County Herald*, 14 January 1950; *Western Morning News*, 21 January 1950.

18. *Dorset Daily Echo*, 19 January 1950; *Western Morning News*, 22 February 1950.

19. Conservative Central Office, *Campaign Guide*, pp. 576–7.

20. *Poole & Dorset Herald*, 15 February 1950; *Somerset County Herald*, 18 February 1950.

21. *Western Morning News*, 13 February 1950.

22. *Western Morning News*, 21 and 25 February 1950.

23. J.S. Rasmussen, *The Liberal Party: A Study of Retrenchment and Revival* (London, 1964), p. 95; C. Cook, *A Short History of the Liberal Party, 1900–84* (London, 1984), p. 132.

24. Women's Liberal Federation papers (Bristol University), DM 193, Mrs Brinsley to Miss Harvey (Exmouth), 19 November 1948; see also Bodmin Liberal Association papers (Liskeard Liberal Democrat Office), executive committee minutes, 4 September 1948 and 1 October 1949.

25. *West Briton*, 19 January, 27 February and 2 March 1950; interview with Jack and Lillian Prowse (12 September 1994).

26. *Western Morning News*, 13 and 22 February 1950; West Dorset Conservative Association papers (Dorset Record Office), D399/3/2, executive committee minutes, 25 July 1949.

27. *Cornish Guardian*, 21 February 1946; Western Counties Liberal Federation papers (Bristol University), DM 1172, executive committee minutes, 12 July 1947.

28. *Western Morning News*, 2 November 1945, 2 November 1946, 31 October

1947 and 3 November 1947.

29. *Bath Chronicle*, 8 November 1947, 14 May 1949 and 13 May 1950,

30. *Express and Echo*, 2 November 1946 and 3 November 1947.

31. *Poole & Dorset Echo*, 18 May 1949.

32. *Bath Chronicle*, 8 November 1947, 14 May 1949 and 13 May 1950; *Express & Echo*, 13 May 1949 and 12 May 1950.

33. *Western Morning News*, 22 February 1950.

34. *Western Morning News*, 18 , 19 and 25 January and 22 February 1950.

35. *Dorset County Chronicle*, 23 May and 27 June 1946, 10 December 1946, 6 March 1947, 11 November and 9 December 1948.

36. *Western Morning News*, 8 February 1950.

37. *Dorset County Chronicle*, 6 January and 23 June 1949.

38. *Dorset County Chronicle*, 23 February 1950.

39. *The Times: House of Commons* (London, 1950), based on pages 169–209; *Western Morning News*, 27 January 1950.

40. *Western Morning News*, 13 and 21 February 1950.

41. *Western Morning News*, 13 and 25 February; E.W. Martin, *The Shearers and the Shorn: A Study of Life in a Devon Community* (London, 1965), pp. 9, 118 and 122.

42. *Western Morning News*, 6 February 1950.

43. Martin, *Shearers and the Shorn*, p. 136.

44. Interviews with William Hosking (31 March 1994), Jack and Lillian Prowse (12 September 1994), David and Joan Morrish (16 September 1994) and Baroness Seear (9 November 1994); *The Times*, 31 March 1950; *Western Morning News*, 6 May 1955; *Devon and Cornwall—A Preliminary Survey: A Report Issued by the Survey Committee of the University College of the South West* (Exeter, 1947), p. 15.

45. W. Gore Allen, *The Reluctant Politician: Derick Heathcoat Amory* (London, 1958), p. 78.

46. R. Perry, 'Cornwall Circa 1950' in P. Payton (ed.), *Cornwall Since the War: The Contemporary History of a European Region* (Redruth, 1993), p. 37.

47. *Western Morning News*, 8 February 1950; interview with David and Joan Morrish (16 September 1994).

48. S. Rokkan, *Citizens Elections Parties: Approaches to the Comparative Study of the Processes of Development* (Oslo, 1970), p. 106.

49. *Western Morning News*, 8 and 9 February 1950.

50. *Western Morning News*, 27 January, 31 January and 4 February 1950.

51. *Western Morning News*, 31 January and 22 February 1950.

52. *Western Morning News*, 19 and 23 February 1950.

53. *Western Morning News*, 8 February 1950.

54. *Devon & Cornwall—A Preliminary Survey,* pp. 13–34.

55. *Western Morning News*, 26 March 1947.

56. *Western Morning News*, 9 February 1950.

57. *Cornish Guardian*, 16 May 1946; *Western Morning News*, 20 February 1950.

58. J.D. Hoffman, *The Conservative Party in Opposition, 1945–51* (London, 1964), pp. 45–165.

59. *Western Morning News*, 17 February 1947.

60. *Western Morning News*, 26 March 1947; Foot papers, DGFT/1/3, Sir Archibald Sinclair to Dingle Foot, 6 February 1947.

61. *Western Morning News*, 17 February and 22 March 1947.

62. *Western Morning News*, 22 and 25 March 1947; Foot papers, DGFT/1/3, Sinclair to Foot, 6 February 1947; R. Douglas, *History of the Liberal Party, 1895–1970*, (London, 1971), p. 253.

63. Foot papers, DGFT/1/3, meeting between Foot and Peter Thorneycroft, 20 January 1947.

64. Interviews with Lord Foot (27 January 1991) and Baroness Seear (9 November 1994); Foot papers, DGFT/1/3, Sinclair to Foot, 6 February 1947.

65. Ibid., DGFT/1/3, meeting between Foot and Thorneycroft, 20 January 1947.

66. *Cornish Guardian*, 27 September 1945 and 4 October 1946; *Western Morning News*, 13 February 1947.

67. M.D. Kandiah, 'Lord Woolton's Chairmanship of the Conservative Party, 1946–1951', PhD thesis (Exeter University, 1992), pp. 68, 71 and 72.

68. Hoffman, *Conservative Party in Opposition*, pp. 46, 146 and 280; *Western Morning News*, 8 October 1951.

69. *Western Morning News*, 30 January 1950.

70. *Somerset County Herald*, 21 and 28 January 1950; Western Counties Liberal Federation papers, DM 1172, executive committee minutes, 2 April 1949.

71. *Western Morning News*, 8 and 10 February 1950; Bodmin Conservative Association papers (Cornwall Record Office), DDX/385/1, executive committee minutes, 13 November 1948; Foot papers, DGFT/1/5, president of St Ives and Penzance groups to Foot, 28 March 1949.

72. Rasmussen, *Liberal Party*, pp. 17 and 18.

73. Foot papers, DGFT/1/4, copy of *Liberal Magazine* (February 1946), pp. 55–7.

74. Western Counties papers, DM 1172, executive committee minutes, 2 April 1949; interview with Jack and Lillian Prowse (12 September 1994); calculations based on Craig's *British Parliamentary Election Results*.

75. House of Commons Sessional papers (1950), Paper No. 146, Vol. XVIII, p. 311.

76. Watkins, *Liberal Dilemma*, p. 42.

77. Foot papers, DGFT/1/3, Sinclair to Foot, 6 February 1947; see also Thurso papers, THRS IV/7/3, Sinclair to Clement Davies, 23 and 30 September 1947; Davies to Sinclair, 29 August and 19 September 1947.

78. Samuel papers, A/129, Earl of Reading to Samuel, 29 December 1949; Lord Rennell to Samuel, 4 January 1950.
79. Rasmussen, *Liberal Party*, p. 95.
80. Samuel papers, A/129, Samuel to Reading, 6 January 1950; see also Byers to Samuel, 30 December 1949.

6 Towards the Promised Land: 1950–1955

1. J.S. Rasmussen, *The Liberal Party: A Study of Retrenchment and Revival* (London, 1965), p. 19.
2. Western Counties Liberal Federation papers (Bristol University), DM 1172, executive committee minutes, 20 May and 22 July 1950; 29 September 1951.
3. *Cornish Guardian*, 26 April, 1, 8 and 22 March and 20 September 1951; interview with Jack and Lillian Prowse (12 September 1994) and Eric Higgs (20 November 1993).
4. Western Counties Federation papers, DM 1172, executive committee minutes, 24 September 1949 and 21 June 1952.
5. *The Times: House of Commons* (London, 1951), p. 171; Elizabeth Rashleigh to David Morrish, 5 April 1951 (letter in the possession of David Morrish); *Dorset Daily Express*, 12 November 1951.
6. D.M. Roberts, 'Clement Davies and the British Liberal Party, 1929–1956', MA thesis (University of Wales, Aberystwyth, 1977), pp. 147–59; M.D. Kandiah, 'Lord Woolton's Chairmanship of the Conservative Party, 1946–1951', PhD thesis (University of Exeter, 1992), pp. 198–213; Samuel papers (House of Lords Record Office), A/130, Violet Bonham Carter to Samuel, 5 May 1950; A/130, memorandum presented to a meeting of the Liberal Party Committee by Megan Lloyd George and Dingle Foot, 23 May 1950.
7. *Dorset Daily Express*, 3, 5 and 16 October 1951; interview with Baroness Seear (9 November 1994).
8. Roberts, 'Clement Davies and the Liberal Party', pp. 161 and 162.
9. *Dorset Daily Express*, 15, 18, 23 and 24 October 1951.
10. Interviews with Jack and Lillian Prowse (12 September 1994), David and Joan Morrish 16 September 1994) and Lord Foot (27 January 1991).
11. A.J. Allen, *The English Voter* (London, 1964), p. 5.
12. C. Cook, *A Short History of the Liberal Party, 1900–84* (London, 1984), p. 135.
13. A. Watkins, *The Liberal Dilemma* (London, 1966), p. 79.
14. Rasmussen, *Liberal Party*, p. 20; F.W.S. Craig (ed.), *British Electoral Facts, 1832–1980* (Chichester, 1981), p. 110.
15. *Economist*, 14 May 1955; Watkins, *Liberal Dilemma*, pp. 20–73; interview

with Lord Banks (12 November 1994).

16. *Economist*, 14 May 1955; Watkins, *Liberal Dilemma*, pp. 70 and 80.

17. Ibid. and p. 68; Conservative and Unionist Central Office, *The Campaign Guide, 1955: The New Political Encyclopaedia* (London, 1955), p. 548.

18. Liberal Party Organization papers (Bristol University), DM 668, memorandum on party strategy, November 1951.

19. *Western Morning News*, 10 April 1953 and 1 April 1954; Conservative Central Office, *Campaign Guide, 1955*, p. 548.

20. *Annual Report of the Liberal Party Organization, 1953* (No. 14), p. 21 and *Annual Report of the LPO, 1954* (No. 15), p. 23; A. Cyr, *Liberal Party Politics in Britain* (London, 1977), p. 104; *The Times*, 13 May 1949, 10 May 1952, 14 May 1954 and 13 May 1955.

21. *Annual Report of the LPO, 1953* (No. 14), p. 32; *Annual Report of the LPO, 1955* (No. 16), p. 30 and *Annual Report of the LPO, 1956* (No. 17), p. 40; *Economist*, 1 May 1954.

22. *The Times*, 20 and 24 December 1954; Conservative Central Office, *Campaign Guide, 1955*, p. 544.

23. Watkins, *Liberal Dilemma*, p. 73; *Western Morning News*, 24 December 1954; *Economist*, 1 January 1955.

24. *West Briton*, 27 January 1955; *Cornish Guardian*, 10 February 1955; *Western Morning News*, 6 May 1955.

25. *Western Morning News*, 2 May 1955.

26. Western Counties Federation papers, DM 1172, executive committee minutes, 11 July 1953.

27. Women's Liberal Federation papers (Bristol University), DM 1193, Mrs O'Sullivan to Miss F. Davey (secretary of Exmouth WLA), 13 June 1952.

28. *Western Morning News*, 10 April 1953; Western Counties Federation papers, DM 1172, finance and general purposes committee minutes, 28 November 1953 and 17 December 1955.

29. *Express and Echo*, 13 May 1949, 12 May 1950 and 11 May 1951; *Bath Chronicle*, 13 May 1950 and 12 May 1951; *Poole & Dorset Herald*, 17 May 1950, 28 March and 14 May 1951.

30. *Western Morning News*, 1 April 1953 and 27 April 1955; *Somerset County Gazette*, 15 May 1954.

31. Based on newspaper reports, particularly in *The Times*, of borough election results from 1949 to 1956.

32. North Devon Liberal Association papers (Barnstaple Liberal Democrat Office), report of Thorpe's adoption meeting, 6 May 1955; secretary's report (1955/6); Barnstaple Women's Liberal Association papers, report of AGM (5 March 1953).

33. *Western Morning News*, 3, 7 and 14 December 1951.

34. *Western Morning News*, 10 April 1953 and 21 April 1954.

35. *West Briton*, 21 April 1955.

36. *Annual Report of the LPO, 1956* (No. 17), p. 29.

37. *Economist*, 19 September 1953; *Cornish Guardian*, 2 June 1955; interview with William Hosking (31 March 1994).

38. *The Times: House of Commons* (London, 1955), pp. 57, 138, 142 and 144; Watkins, *Liberal Dilemma*, pp. 70 and 80; interview with Lord Banks (12 November 1994).

39. *Western Morning News*, 5 May 1955.

40. *The Times: House of Commons*, p. 142; *Western Morning News*, 6 May 1955; interview with William Hosking (31 March 1994).

41. National Liberal Club collection of election addresses (Bristol University), DM 668, 1955 election addresses of James Holland (Poole) and Peter Mayne (Devonport); Truro Conservative Association papers (Cornwall Record Office), DDX/551/16, executive committee minutes, 8 September and 10 November 1954; *Western Morning News*, 17 May 1955.

42. *Cornish Guardian*, 11 February, 15 April, 27 May and 22 July 1954; *Western Morning News*, 12 April 1954.

43. *Cornish Guardian*, 24 June 1954; interview with Lord Foot (27 January 1991).

44. *Cornish Guardian*, 4 September 1952

45. Bodmin Conservative Association papers, DDX/385/4, 1955 election address of Stuart Roseveare; *Cornish Guardian*, 8 May 1952, 15 April and 22 July 1954.

46. *Cornish Guardian*, 31 July 1952.

47. Rasmussen, *Liberal Party*, p. 123.

48. *Somerset County Gazette*, 9 May 1953 and 2 April 1955; *Cornish Guardian*, 4 February and 11 April 1954; *Western Morning News*, 7 May 1952, 20 April 1954 and 5 May 1955.

49. *Dorset Daily Echo*, 13 May 1955; *West Briton*, 3 May 1955; *Cornish Guardian*, 15 April and 22 July 1954; Bodmin Conservative papers, DDX/385/4, 1955 election address of Stuart Roseveare.

50. Conservative Central Office, *Campaign Guide, 1955*, pp. 449–69; *West Briton*, 5 May 1955; *Poole and Dorset Herald*, 23 March 1955; *Western Morning News*, 28 May 1955.

51. R.S. Milne and H.C. Mackenzie, *Marginal Seat, 1955: A Study of Voting Behaviour in the Constituency of Bristol North-East at the General Election of 1955* (London, 1958), pp. 47–56, 133 and 174–84.

52. *Cornish Guardian*, 28 February 1952.

53. *North Devon Journal-Herald*, 12 May 1955; see also *Poole and Dorset Herald*, 11 May 1955.

54. *West Briton*, 3 May 1955; Truro Conservative papers, DDX/551/16, executive committee minutes, 14 September 1955; Milne and Mackenzie, *Marginal Seat*, pp. 111 and 160.

55. *North Devon Journal-Herald*, 8 September 1955; *Western Morning News*, 9 and

16 May 1955.

56. *Western Morning News*, 7 May 1955.

57. Rasmussen, *Liberal Party*, p. 278.

58. *Cornish Guardian*, 4 September 1952; see also W. Wallace, 'The Liberal Revival—The Liberal Party in Britain, 1955–1966', PhD thesis (Cornell University, 1968), p. 97; *Economist*, 1 January and 24 September 1955.

59. *Cornish Guardian*, 4 September, 23 October and 27 November 1952; *Western Morning News*, 17 May 1955.

60. *Western Morning News*, 11 April 1953; interview with Baroness Seear (9 November 1994).

61. *Western Morning News*, 6, 17 and 28 May 1955; *Cornish Guardian,* 24 January 1952; Bodmin Conservative papers, DDX/385/2, executive committee minutes, 28 March 1953 and 25 June 1955.

62. *Western Morning News*, 11 April 1953; J. Stevenson, *Third Party Politics since 1945: Liberals, Alliance and Liberal Democrats* (Oxford, 1993), p. 35; interviews with David and Joan Morrish (16 September 1994) and Lord Banks (12 November 1994).

63. *Western Morning News*, 11 April 1953; Rasmussen, *Liberal Party*, p. 136; interview with David and Joan Morrish (16 September 1994); National Liberal Club collection, DM 668, 1955 election address of Jeremy Thorpe (North Devon).

64. *Poole and Dorset Herald*, 23 June and 28 July 1954; *Western Morning News*, 9 March and 2 May 1955.

65. *Western Morning News*, 13 April 1953 and 6 May 1955; *Devon and Cornwall— A preliminary Survey: A Report issued by the Survey Committee of the University College of the South-West* (Exeter, 1947), pp. 13, 15 and 17.

66. NLC collection, DM 668, 1955 election address of Edwin Malindine (North Cornwall).

67. *Western Morning News*, 10 May 1955.

68. NLC collection, DM 668, election address of Malindine.

69. V. Bogdanor (ed.), *Liberal Party Politics* (Oxford, 1983), p. 245; P. Payton, *The Making of Modern Cornwall: Historical Experience and the Persistence of 'Difference'* (Redruth, 1992), p. 194.

70. *Cornish Guardian*, 27 May, 22 July and 19 August 1954; *West Briton*, 27 January and 15 May 1955; Bodmin Conservative papers, DDX/385/4, the 1955 election address of Stuart Roseveare.

71. *Cornish Guardian*, 8 May 1952.

7 The Dawn of Victory: 1955–1959

1. *Western Morning News*, 10 and 15 December 1955; V. Bogdanor (ed.), *Liberal Party Politics* (Oxford, 1983), p. 80.

2. West Dorset Conservative Association papers (Dorset Record Office), D399/3/2, executive committee minutes, 9 July 1957; Conservative Central Office papers (Bodleian Library, Oxford), General Director's Office, CO/20/2/64, Oliver Poole to J.H. Randolph, 5 June 1957.

3. *Western Morning News*, 23 September 1959; C. Cook and J. Ramsden (eds), *By-elections in British Politics* (London, 1973), pp. 366–80; *The Times*, 29 March 1958.

4. Watkins, *Liberal Dilemma*, p. 90.

5. *The Times*, 13 and 14 June 1959; Conservative Central Office papers, General Director's Office, CO/20/2/74, report on the Weston-Super-Mare by-election, 30 May 1958; Cook and Ramsden, *By-elections in British Politics*, p. 196.

6. Bodmin Liberal Association papers (Liskeard Liberal Democrat Office), newspaper article *(Cornish Times,* 9 May 1958).

7. Bodmin Liberal papers, *Cornish Times*, 4 April 1958.

8. *Western Morning News*, 21 September 1959.

9. A. Cyr, *Liberal Party Politics in Britain* (London, 1977), pp. 104–5; statistics based on the report of local election results in *The Times*, 9 May 1959.

10. *Dorset Daily Echo*, 14 January 1958, 9 May 1958 and 8 May 1959; Western Counties Liberal Federation papers (Bristol University), DM 1172, executive committee minutes, 17 December 1955.

11. *Bath Chronicle*, 14 May 1955, 12 May 1956, 10 May 1958 and 9 May 1959.

12. *Express and Echo*, 11 May 1956, 9 May 1958, 8 May 1959, 12 May 1961, 11 May 1962 and 10 May 1963; interview with David and Joan Morrish (16 September 1994).

13. *The Times*, 9 May 1958 and 9 May 1959.

14. *Somerset County Gazette*, 19 September 1959; *The Times*, 9 May 1959.

15. *Poole & Dorset Herald*, 20 March 1957, 15 May 1957, 3 July 1957 and 13 May 1959; *The Times*, 9 May 1958 and 11 May 1962.

16. *Western Gazette*, 16 October 1959.

17. *Western Morning News*, 22 and 25 September and 2 October 1959; Bodmin Liberal papers, newspaper article *(Cornish Times*, 12 April 1957).

18. C. Driver, *A Future for the Free Churches* (London, 1962).

19. Bogdanor, *Liberal Party Politics*, p. 202; J.S. Rasmussen, *The Liberal Party: A Study of Retrenchment and Revival* (London, 1965), p. 288; Cyr, *Liberal Party Politics in Britain*, p. 119; Liberal Party Organisation papers (Bristol University), DM 668, report of the Political Research Unit, 1960.

20. Cyr, *Liberal Party Politics*, pp. 115–21.

21. Cook and Ramsden, *By-elections in British Politics*, p. 211; W. Wallace, 'The Liberal Revival—the Liberal Party in Britain, 1955–1966', PhD thesis (Cornell University, 1968), p. 350.

22. LPO papers, DM 668, report of the Political Research Unit, 1960.

23. N. Tiratsoo, *Reconstruction, Affluence and Labour Politics: Coventry, 1945–60*

(London, 1992), p. 3; D.E. Butler and R. Rose, *The British General Election of 1959* (London, 1960), pp. 14 and 200.

24. J.H. Goldthorpe et al., *The Affluent Worker: Political Attitudes and Behaviour* (Cambridge, 1968), pp. 31, 72 and 73.

25. Tiratsoo, *Reconstruction, Affluence and Labour Politics*, p. 115.

26. Butler and Rose, *British General Election of 1959*, p. 33; Bogdanor, *Liberal Party Politics*, pp. 102–10.

27. *Somerset County Gazette*, 26 September 1959; Butler and Rose, *British General Election of 1959*, pp. 51 and 71.

28. *The Times: House of Commons, 1959* (London, 1959), contains a copy of the Liberal manifesto *People Count*, p. 256.

29. North Devon Liberal Association papers (Barnstaple Liberal Democrat Office), booklet containing a series of statements from a 'cross-section of North Devon's electorate' in 1959; *Somerset County Gazette*, 29 August 1959.

30. *The Times: House of Commons, 1959*, p. 256.

31. *North Devon Journal Herald*, 17 April 1958; Watkins, *Liberal Dilemma*, p. 90; interview with Jack and Lillian Prowse (12 September 1994); North Devon Liberal papers, executive committee minutes, 28 November 1958 and 10 January 1959.

32. Watkins, *Liberal Dilemma*, p. 80.

33. *Western Morning News*, 28 January and 2, 5, 13 and 17 April 1956; Butler and Rose, *British General Election of 1959*, p. 36.

34. *The Times*, 15 and 16 February 1956.

35. J. Stevenson, *Third Party Politics since 1945: Liberals, Alliance and Liberal Democrats* (Oxford, 1993), p. 128.

36. P. Campbell, 'Le Mouvement Poujade', *Parliamentary Affairs*, Vol. X (1956–7), pp.362–7; A.J. Allen, *The English Voter* (London, 1964), p. 203; G. Allen, 'National Farmers' Union as a Pressure Group: II', *Contemporary Review*, Vol. 195 (1959), p. 323.

37. *The Times*, 16 February 1956.

38. Dingle Foot papers (Churchill College, Cambridge University), DGFT/1/7, memorandum on the Liberal vote, 1957.

39. W.M. Williams, *A West Country Village: Ashworthy—Family, Kinship and Land* (London, 1963), p. 10.

40. Wallace, 'Liberal Revival', p. 337; Conservative and Unionist Central Office, *The Campaign Guide 1959; The Unique Political Reference Book* (London, 1959), pp. 156 and 614; Rasmussen, *Liberal Party*, p. 137; Watkins, *Liberal Dilemma*, p. 92.

41. Conservative Central Office, *Campaign Guide 1959*, p. 614.

42. Rasmussen, *Liberal Party*, p. 140; *Western Morning News*, 11 April 1954 and 9 September 1959.

43. Interview with David and Joan Morrish (16 September 1994); *Western*

Morning News, 9, 11, 14 and 16 September 1959; National Liberal Club collection of election addresses (Bristol University), DM 668, the 1959 election address of Peter Bessell (Bodmin).

44. *Western Morning News*, 10 October 1959; *Annual Report of the Labour Party Conference, 1959*, p. 94.

45. *Western Morning News*, 3 October 1959; North Somerset Divisional Labour Party (Somerset Record Office), A/AAW/21, press statement of the Somerset Federation of Labour Parties for the Somerset County Council Elections, 1958.

46. Bodmin Liberal papers, newspaper article, 25 September 1958.

47. *Cornish Guardian*, 8 and 15 October 1959; *Western Morning News*, 25 September and 5, 8 and 10 October 1959; *North Devon Journal-Herald*, 15 October 1959.

48. *Poole and Dorset Herald*, 28 July, 23 September and 3 November 1954.

49. *Poole and Dorset Herald*, 13 May 1959 and 13 May 1960.

50. *Poole and Dorset Herald*, 15 May 1957, 13 May 1959 and 18 May 1960.

51. Bogdanor, *Liberal Party Politics*, p. 47 and 51.

52. *Western Morning News*, 9, 13 and 15 December 1955.

53. *The Times*, 16 February 1956.

54. *Western Morning News*, 5 and 6 April 1956.

55. *The Times*, 24 and 29 March 1958; *North Devon Journal-Herald*, 20 March and 2 April 1958.

56. *The Times: House of Commons*, p. 19; *Western Morning News*, 17, 21, 22, 23 and 28 September 1959; Butler and Rose, *British General Election of 1959*, pp. 37 and 41; *Cornish Guardian*, 17 September 1959.

57. NLC collection of election addresses, DM 668, 1955 election address of Jo Grimond (Orkney & Shetland); Bodmin Liberal papers, newspaper article, 25 September 1958; North Devon Liberal papers, 1959 election address of Jeremy Thorpe; *Western Morning News*, 28 September 1959; *The Times: House of Commons, 1959*, p. 257.

58. *North Devon Journal-Herald*, 8 October 1959; *Western Morning News*, 1 October 1959.

59. *West Briton*, 11 May and 8 October 1959; *Western Morning News*, 30 September and 2 October 1959; *New Cornwall*, Vol. 7, No. 6 (Oct–Nov, 1959), pp. 8–9.

60. *The Times*, 24 March 1958; *Western Morning News*, 5 October 1959.

61. *Dorset Evening Echo*, 28 October 1959; *Cornish Guardian*, 1 October 1959.

62. *Western Morning News*, 9 and 10 October 1959; Butler and Rose, *British General Election of 1959*, pp. 194 and 198.

63. *Western Morning News*, 5 October 1959.

64. *Western Morning News*, 10 October 1959.

65. *North Devon Journal-Herald*, 15 October 1959.

66. Butler and Rose, *British General Election of 1959*, p. 155; *Western Morning*

News, 5 October 1959.

67. Williams, *West Country Village*, pp. 7, 191 and 192.

68. N. Orme (ed.), *Unity and Variety: A History of the Church in Devon and Cornwall* (Exeter, 1991), p. 161; Martin, *Shearers and the Shorn*, p. 179.

69. *Cornish Guardian*, 24 September 1959; *West Briton*, 17 September 1959.

70. Bodmin Liberal papers, newspaper article, 29 March 1957.

71. *Poole and Dorset Herald*, 13 February 1957; see also L.D. Epstein, *British Politics in the Suez Crisis* (London, 1964), pp. 103 and 113.

72. *Somerset County Gazette*, 17 October 1959; Bodmin Liberal papers, newspaper article, 6 October 1959; *Western Morning News*, 3 October 1959; *West Briton*, 1 October 1959.

73. *Western Morning News*, 10, 12 and 15 December 1955; Wallace, 'Liberal Revival', p. 116.

74. Bodmin Liberal papers, newspaper article (*Cornish Guardian*, 3 April 1958).

75. *The Times*, 13 June 1958.

76. Conservative Central Office, *Campaign Guide, 1959*, p. 611.

77. Bogdanor, *Liberal Party Politics*, p. 81; *The Times,* 10 September 1959.

78. *Western Morning News*, 1 October 1959; *The Times*, 10 September 1959.

79. M.I. Baines, 'The Survival of the British Liberal Party, 1932–1959', PhD thesis (Oxford University, 1991), p. 101.

80. North Devon Liberal papers, executive and organization committee minutes, 25 February 1957, 14 February 1958 and 10 January 1959; AGM minutes, 2 March 1956 and 19 April 1958; *Western Morning News*, 6 October 1959.

81. *Western Morning News*, 6 October 1959; Butler and Rose, *British General Election of 1959*, pp. 50 and 65.

82. Watkins, *Liberal Dilemma*, p. 97.

83. *Western Morning News*, 1 October 1959.

84. North Devon Liberal papers, executive committee minutes, 3 September 1956, 26 November 1956, 28 November 1958 and 30 June 1960; AGM minutes, 2 March 1956 and 9 May 1959; interview with Jack and Lillian Prowse (12 September 1994).

85. Bodmin Liberal papers, finance and general purposes committee minutes, 15 August 1958 and newspaper article (*Cornish Times*, 4 April 1958); *Cornish Guardian*, 1 October 1959.

86. Bodmin Conservative Association papers (Cornwall Record Office), DDX/385/2, executive committee minutes, 28 November 1959.

87. *Western Morning News*, 21 September 1959; Butler and Rose, *British General Election of 1959*, p. 150.

88. Western Counties federation papers, DM 1172, executive committee minutes, 5 October 1957 and 5 December 1959.

89. *Western Morning News*, 15 December 1955.

90. Ibid., 21 September 1959.

91. Bodmin Conservative papers, DDX/385/2, executive committee minutes, 28 November 1959; interview with Eric Higgs (20 November 1993); communication received from a Liberal activist.

92. *The Times*, 7 October 1959; *Western Morning News*, 23 September 1959.

93. *Economist*, 3 October 1959.

94. *Cornish Guardian*, 17 and 24 September 1959; Bodmin Liberal papers, newspaper articles (*Western Morning News*, 28 February 1958; *Cornish Times*, 7 March 1958.

8 Past to Present: 1997 in Context

1. S. Rokkan, *Citizens Elections Parties: Approaches to the Comparative Study of the Processes of Development* (Oslo, 1970), p. 128.

2. Ibid., p. 100, 125 and 237.

3. S. Henig and J. Pinder (eds), *European Political Parties* (London, 1969), pp. 94, 163, 340–3; A.S. Banks (ed) *Political Handbook of the World: 1976* (New York, 1976), pp. 337, 341 and 343.

4. Scandinavian results calculated from a list of election results in Henig and Pinder, *European Political Parties*, pp. 336–43. The term 'Old Left' is used in its Scandinavian sense. It therefore includes the Agrarian and religious 'allies' of the Liberals.

5. Statistical Office of the United Nations, *Demographic Yearbook, 1959* (New York, 1959), p. 122. The population of the United Kingdom (1951 census), 50,225,224; Denmark (1955) 4,448,401; Finland (1950) 4,029,803; Iceland (1950) 143,973; Norway (1950) 3,278,546; Sweden (1950) 7,041,829; Rokkan, *Citizens Elections Parties*, pp. 77–91.

6. Ibid., pp. 5, 108–34; Henig and Pinder, *European Political Parties*, p. 324; Banks, *Political Handbook of the World*, pp. 94, 95, 115, 163, 275 and 347.

7. Henig and Pinder, *European Political Parties*, p. 518.

8. Banks, *Political Handbook of the World*, pp. 94 and 347; Henig and Pinder, *European Political Parties*, pp. 327, 330, 344 and 350.

9. M. Kinnear, *The British Voter: An Atlas and Survey since 1885* (London, 1968), p. 120.

10. Ibid., pp. 119–21.

11. A.J. Allen, *The English Voter* (London, 1964), p. 203; Rokkan, *Citizens Elections Parties*, p. 227; G.R. Searle, *The Liberal Party: Triumph and Disintegration, 1886–1929* (London, 1992).

12. A.M. Dawson, 'Politics in Devon and Cornwall, 1900–31', PhD thesis (London University, 1991).

13. The area in question essentially covered the county constituencies of Devon, Dorset, Somerset, Gloucestershire, Hampshire, Isle of Wight,

Berkshire and Wiltshire.

14. See Dawson, 'Politics in Devon and Cornwall'.

15. Kinnear, *British Voter*, p. 48.

16. Searle, *Liberal Party*, p. 159.

17. Kinnear, *British Voter*, pp. 122–4.

18. Ibid., p. 58.

19. Interviews with David and Joan Morrish (16 September 1994), Jack and Lillian Prowse (12 September 1994) and William Hosking (31 March 1994); information obtained from questionnaire survey of Liberal party activists in the South-West; A.L. Rowse Collection (University of Exeter Library), notes for a political speech, *c.* 1930.

20. Interview with Eric Higgs (20 November 1993).

21. Interviews with Lord Foot (27 January 1991) and David and Joan Morrish (16 September 1994).

22. Searle, *Liberal Party*, p. 20.

23. Interview with David and Joan Morrish (16 September 1994).

24. Henig and Pinder, *European Political Parties*, p. 330.

25. *The Times*, 11 May 1962; *Express and Echo*, 11 May 1962 and 10 May 1963; *Poole and Dorset Herald,* 18 May 1960.

26. Interview with William Hosking (31 March 1994); 1964 Liberal election address for Truro which was formerly in the possession of the late William Hosking.

27. J. Vincent, 'What Kind of Third Party?' in *New Society*, 26 January 1967.

28. K. Young, 'Orpington and the Liberal Revival' in C. Cook and J. Ramsden (eds), *By-elections in British Politics* (London, 1997), pp. 157–80; J. Stevenson, *Third Party Politics since 1945: Liberals, Alliance and Liberal Democrats* (Oxford, 1993), p. 51.

29. *Economist*, 21 January and 2 December 1967.

30. *New Society*, 26 January 1967.

31. Interview with Chris and Bridget Trethewey (21 October 1994); for a national study of this period see D. McKie, 'By-elections of the Wilson Government' in Cook and Ramsden, *By-elections in British Politics*, pp. 180–94.

32. *Economist*, 9 March 1974.

33. *The Times*, October 1974.

34. J. Vincent, 'Tomorrow's Liberals' in *New Society*, 6 May 1976; West Dorset Liberal Association papers (Dorset Record Office), D/1446/3/2/1, constituency newsletter: by-election number, n.d., *c.*1973; R. Jay, 'Lincoln and the Liberal surge, 1972–73' in Cook and Ramsden, *By-elections in British Politics*, pp. 194–215.

35. Quoted in P. Payton, *The Making of Modern Cornwall* (Redruth, 1992), p. 228.

36. Ibid., p. 229.

37. Statistics calculated on the basis of F.W.S. Craig (ed.), *British Parliamentary Election Results, 1974–1983* (Chichester, 1984); West Dorset Liberal papers, D/1446/3/12, press release regarding the selection of Trevor Jones of Dorchester as Liberal parliamentary candidate for West Dorset, 22 January 1977.

38. *The Times*, April 1979; D. Brack (ed.), *Dictionary of Liberal Biography* (London, 1998), pp. 356–60; interviews with Lord Foot (27 January 1991) and David Morrish (16 September 1994).

39. *Spectator*, 20 June 1987; *Economist* 7 April, 28 April and 12 May 1979.

40. Stevenson, *Third Party Politics since 1945*, p. 60.

41. G. Davie and D. Hearl, 'Religion and Politics in Cornwall & Devon' in M. Havinden, J. Queniart and J. Stanyer (eds), *Centre and Periphery: Brittany and Cornwall & Devon Compared* (Exeter, 1991), pp. 220–2.

42. *The Times*, 12 May 1988; I. Crewe and A. Fox, *British Parliamentary Constituencies: A Statistical Compendium* (London, 1984), p. 354.

43. *Spectator*, 7 March 1987; Crewe and Fox, *British Parliamentary Constituencies*, p. 260.

44. *News from the Liberals: Truro by-election special*, March 1987; *Western Morning News*, 16 February 1987.

45. For a wider discussion of the Alliance period and the early years of the Liberal Democrats see Stevenson, *Third Party Politics since 1945*, pp. 74–142.

46. *Liberal News*, 15 and 22 May 1979; *Western Morning News*, 4 May 1985.

47. *Daily Telegraph*, 9 May 1987.

48. Based on results in *Daily Telegraph*, 9 May 1987.

49. *Spectator*, 7 March 1987.

50. *The Times*, 12 May 1988.

51. R. Morgan (ed.) *The Times Guide to the European Parliament 1994* (London, 1994), pp. 47–58; for a discussion of the Cornish situation at this time see Payton, *Making of Modern Cornwall*, pp. 226 and 233.

52. *Sunday Express*, 16 May 1993; *Western Morning News*, 11 May 1993; interviews with Eric Higgs (20 November 1993) and William Hosking (31 March 1994); *Cornish Voice: Special Election Edition* (St Austell and District 1992).

53. *Daily Telegraph*, 25 April 1994; *Devon & Cornwall Focus: News from the Liberal Democrats*, Summer 1995, Winter 1995 and Summer 1996.

54. D.E. Butler (ed.), *The British General Election of 1997* (London, 1997), pp. 68–70; *Devon & Cornwall Focus: News from the Liberal Democrats*, Winter 1995.

55. Butler, *British General Election of 1997*, p. 310; *Devon & Cornwall Focus: News from the Liberal Democrats*, Winter 1995 and Summer 1996; *Cornish Voice* (Restormel edition), Spring 1995.

56. The Referendum party's average vote per candidate at the state level in

1997 was 3.1 per cent. This compared with 4.1, 4.4 and 4.7 per cent in Devon, Somerset and Dorset respectively, but in Cornwall the figure was even higher at 6.6 per cent.

57. *Daily Telegraph*, 25 April 1994; *Cornish Guardian*, 23 February 1995; *Western Morning News*, 27 March 1995; *Cornish Voice: Special Election Edition*, 1992; *Cornish Voice* (Restormel), Spring 1995.

58. *The Times*, 3 May 1997; results calculated on the basis of national statistics in Butler, *British General Election of 1997*.

59. Brack, *Dictionary of Liberal Biography*, p. 54; information on Liberal Democrat MPs supplied by Rev. Stephen Dawes (12 July 2000); interview with Trevor Jones, 29 June 1998; small businesses were also discontented with the Major government in the 1990s, *Cornish Voice: Special Election Edition* (1992) and *Western Morning News*, 27 March 1995.

Bibliography

Private Papers

Acland family papers (Devon Record Office).
Lord Beaverbrook papers (House of Lords Record Office).
Dingle Foot papers (Churchill College, Cambridge University).
Lord Hore-Belisha papers (Churchill College, Cambridge University).
Earl Lloyd George papers (House of Lords Record Office).
Lord Lothian papers (Scottish Record Office, Edinburgh).
Sir Donald Maclean papers (Bodleian Library, Oxford).
Dr A.L. Rowse papers (University of Exeter).
Runciman papers (Newcastle-upon-Tyne University).
Viscount Samuel papers (House of Lords Record Office).
Viscount Thurso papers (Churchill College, Cambridge University).
Sir Charles Trevelyan papers (University of Newcastle-Upon-Tyne).

Records of Political Parties

(1) Conservative Party
Conservative Central Office papers (Bodleian Library, Oxford).
Conservative and Unionist Central Office, *General Election 1950: The Campaign Guide* (Westminster, 1949).
Conservative and Unionist Central Office, *The Campaign Guide, 1955: The New Political Encyclopaedia* (London, 1955).
Conservative and Unionist Central Office, *The Campaign Guide 1959: The Unique Political Reference Book* (London, 1959).
Bath Conservative Association papers (Archives and Record Office, Bath).
Bodmin Conservative Association (Cornwall Record Office).
Falmouth & Camborne Conservative Association (Cornwall Record Office).
North Cornwall Conservative Association (Cornwall Record Office).
North Dorset Conservative Association.

Penryn & Falmouth/Truro Conservative Association (Cornwall Record Office).
West Dorset Conservative Association (Dorset Record Office).

(2) Labour Party
Reports of the Annual Conference, 1928–1940.
Frome/North Somerset Divisional Labour Party (Somerset Record Office).
Yeovil Divisional Labour Party (Somerset Record Office).

(3) Liberal Party
Bodmin Liberal Association (Liskeard Liberal Democrat Office).
Divisional correspondence of the Women's Liberal Federation (Bristol University).
Liberal Agent, Vol. 28–30 (1927–9).
Liberal Magazine, 1929–36/*Liberal News,* 1979.
National Liberal Club Collection (Bristol University).
North Devon/Barnstaple Liberal Association (Barnstaple Liberal Democrat Office).
Reports of the Annual Assembly, 1941–59.
West Dorset Liberal Association (Dorset Record Office).
Western Counties Liberal Federation papers (Bristol University).

Personal collection of regional Liberal Democrat leaflets from the 1990s.

Other Records

Census of England and Wales since 1921.
Cornish Methodist Records (Cornwall Record Office).
House of Commons Sessional papers: election expenses.

Interviews

Fred L. Harris, Redruth, 10 June 1990.
Dr A.L. Rowse, St Austell, 15 June 1990.
John Tonkin, Bugle, 14 October 1990.
Lord Foot, Tavistock, 27 January 1991.
Eric Higgs, Lanlivery, 20 November 1993.
Mildred Curtice, St Austell, 29 March 1994.
William Hosking, Newquay, 31 March 1994.
Jack and Lillian Prowse, Barnstaple, 12 September 1994.
David and Joan Morrish, Exeter, 16 September 1994.
Chris and Bridget Trethewey, Torquay, 21 October 1994.

Baroness Seear, London, 9 November 1994.
Lord Banks, Chesham, 12 November 1994.
Trevor Jones, Dorchester, 29 June 1998.

Newspapers and Journals

Bath Chronicle, Bridgwater Mercury, Cornish Guardian, Daily Telegraph, Dorset County Chronicle, Dorset Daily Echo, Dorset Evening Echo, Economist, Express and Echo, Herald and Express, Mid-Devon Advertiser, New Cornwall, New Society, New Statesman, North Devon Journal-Herald, Poole and Dorset Herald, Royal Cornwall Gazette, Somerset County Gazette, Somerset County Herald, Spectator, The Times, Wells Journal, West Briton, Western Evening Herald, Western Gazette, Western Morning News.

Reference Works

Cook, C., *Sources in British Political History, 1900–1951* (London, 1977).

Craig, F.W.S. (editor), *British General Election Manifestos, 1918–1966*, Chichester, 1970.

———— (compiler and editor), *British Parliamentary Election Results 1885–1918* (London, 1974); *1918–1949* (Glasgow, 1969); *1950–1970* (Chichester, 1971); *1974–83* (Chichester, 1984).

———— *British Electoral Facts, 1832–1980* (Chichester, 1981).

Crewe, I. and A. Fox, *British Parliamentary Constituencies: A Statistical Compendium* (London, 1984).

Gallup, G.H., *The Gallup International Public Opinion Polls: Great Britain, 1937–1975, Volume One, 1937–1964* (New York, 1976).

Morgan, R., (editor), *The Times Guide to the European Parliament* (London, 1994).

Statistical Office of the United Nations, *Demographic Yearbook, 1959* (New York, 1959).

The Times: House of Commons, (London): elections of 1950, 1951, 1955 and 1959.

Memoirs and Biographies

Allen, W.G., *The Reluctant Politician: Derick Heathcoat Amory,* London, 1958.

Bartlett, V., *I Know What I Liked,* London, 1975.

Brack, D., *Dictionary of Liberal Biography,* London, 1998.

Dalton, H., *The Fateful Years: Memoirs, 1931–1945,* London, 1957.

De Groot, G.J., *Liberal Crusader: The Life of Sir Archibald Sinclair,* London, 1993.

Hocking, S.K., *My Book of Memory: A String of Reminiscences and Reflections by Silas K. Hocking,* London, 1923.

Hollis, C., *Along the Road to Frome,* London, 1958.

Macmillan, H., *Riding the Storm, 1956–9,* London, 1971.

Mallet, C., *Mr. Lloyd George: A Study,* London, 1930.

Pimlott, B., *Hugh Dalton,* London, 1985.

Putt, S.G., *Wings of a Man's Life,* London, 1990.

Ramsden, J. (editor), *Real Old Tory Politics: The Political Diaries of Sir Robert Sanders, Lord Bayford, 1910–35,* London, 1984.

Rowse., A.L., *A Man of the Thirties,* London, 1979.

Sylvester, A.J. (edited by C. Cross), *Life with Lloyd George: The Diary of A.J. Sylvester,* London, 1975.

Trevail, C.T.T., *The Life and Reminiscences of C.T.T. Trevail,* Bristol, 1926.

Other Published Works

Addison, P., *The Road to 1945: British Politics and the Second World War,* London, 1975.

Allen, A.J., *The English Voter,* London, 1964.

Allen, R.W., *Methodism and Modern World Problems,* London, 1926.

Ball, S., *Baldwin and the Conservative Party: The Crisis of 1929–1931,* London, 1988.

Banks, A.S. (editor), *Political Handbook of the World: 1976,* New York, 1976.

Bentley, M., *The Liberal Mind, 1914–1929,* Cambridge, 1977.

Bogdanor, V. (editor), *Liberal Party Politics,* Oxford, 1983.

Butler, D.E., *The British General Election of 1951,* London, 1952.

———— (editor), *The British General Election of 1997,* London, 1997.

Butler, D.E and Rose, R., *The British General Election of 1959,* London, 1960.

Clark, D., *Colne Valley: Radicalism to Socialism,* London, 1981.

Cook, C., *The Age of Alignment: Electoral Politics in Britain, 1922–1929,* London, 1975.

———— *A Short History of the Liberal Party, 1900–84,* London, 1984.

Cook, C. and Ramsden, J. (editors), *By-elections in British Politics,* London, 1993.

Cooper, A.F., *British Agricultural Policy, 1912–36: A Study in Conservative Politics,* Manchester, 1989.

Cowling, M., *The Impact of Hitler: British Politics and British Policy, 1933–1940,* Cambridge, 1975.

Currie. R., Gilbert, A. and Horsley, L, *Churches and Churchgoers: Patterns of Church Growth in the British Isles since 1700,* Oxford, 1977.

Cyr, A., *Liberal Party Politics in Britain,* London, 1977.

Devon and Cornwall—A Preliminary Survey: A Report issued by the Survey Committee of the University College of the South West, Exeter, 1947.

Douglas, R., *The History of the Liberal Party, 1895–1970,* London, 1971.

Driver, C., *A Future for the Free Churches,* London, 1962.

Eatwell, R., *The 1945–1951 Labour Governments,* London, 1979.

Epstein, L.D., *British Politics in the Suez Crisis,* London, 1964.

Freeden, M., *Liberalism Divided: A Study in British Political Thought, 1914–1939,* Oxford, 1986.

Goldthorpe, J.H. et al., *The Affluent Worker: Political Attitudes and Behaviour,* Cambridge, 1968.

Greenleaf, W.H., *The British Political Tradition: The Ideological Heritage,* Vol. 2, London, 1983.

Halliday, F.E., *A History of Cornwall,* London, 1959.

Havinden, M., Queniart, J. and Stanyer, J. (editors), *Centre and Periphery: Brittany and Cornwall & Devon Compared,* Exeter, 1991.

Henig, S. and Pinder, J. (editors), *European Political Parties,* London, 1969.

Hoffman, J.D., *The Conservative Party in Opposition, 1945–51,* London, 1964.

Hollis, C., *Along the Road to Frome,* London, 1958.

Horabin, T.L., *Politics Made Plain: What the Next General Election will Really be About,* London, 1944.

Jefferys. K., *The Churchill Coalition and Wartime Politics, 1940–1945,* Manchester, 1991.

Kinnear, M., *The British Voter: An Atlas and Survey since 1885,* London, 1968.

Koss, S., *Nonconformity in Modern British Politics,* London, 1975.

Laybourn, K., *The Rise of Labour: The British Labour Party, 1890–1979,* London, 1988.

Laybourn, K. and Reynolds, J., *Liberalism and the rise of Labour, 1890–1979,* London, 1984.

McLean, I., *The Legend of Red Clydeside,* Edinburgh, 1983.

Manning-Sanders, R., *The West of England,* London, 1949.

Martin, D., *A Sociology of English Religion,* London, 1967.

Martin, E.W., *The Shearers and the Shorn: A Study of Life in a Devon Community,* London, 1965.

Milne, R.S. and Mackenzie, H.C., *Straight Fight: A Study of Voting Behaviour in the Constituency of Bristol North-East at the General Election of 1951,* London, 1954.

———— *Marginal Seat, 1955: A Study of Voting Behaviour in the Constituency of Bristol North-East at the General Election of 1955,* London, 1958.

Milward, R. and Robinson, A., *The South West Peninsular,* London, 1971.

Morgan, K., *The Age of Lloyd George: The Liberal Party and British Politics 1890–1929,* London, 1971.

Nicholas, H.G., *The British General Election of 1950,* London, 1951.

Orme, N. (editor), *Unity and Variety: A History of the Church in Devon and Cornwall,* Exeter, 1991.

Payton, P., *The Making of Modern Cornwall: Historical Experience and the Persistence of 'Difference',* Redruth, 1992.

———— (editor), *Cornwall Since the War: The Contemporary History of a European Region* (Redruth, 1992).

———— *Cornwall* (Fowey, 1996).

Pelling, H., *Popular Politics and Society in Late Victorian Britain*, London, 1968.
——— *Social Geography of British Elections, 1885–1910,* London, 1967.
Pimlott, B., *Labour and the Left in the 1930s,* Cambridge, 1977.
Pinto-Duschinsky, M., *British Political Finance, 1830–1980,* Washington, 1981.
Probert, J.C.C., *The Sociology of Cornish Methodism,* Truro, 1971.
Pugh, M., *Women and the Women's Movement in Britain, 1914–1959,* London, 1992.
Rasmussen, J.S., *The Liberal Party: A Study of Retrenchment and Revival,* London, 1964.
Rokkan, S., *Citizens Elections Parties: Approaches to the Comparative Study of the Processes of Development,* Oslo, 1970.
Rowse, A.L., *St Austell: Church; Town; Parish,* St Austell, 1960.
Searle, G.R., *The Liberal Party: Triumph and Disintegration, 1886–1929*, London, 1992.
Shaw, T., *A History of Cornish Methodism,* Truro, 1967.
Stannage, C.T., *Baldwin Thwarts the Opposition: The British General Election of 1935,* London, 1980.
Stevenson, J., *Third Party Politics since 1945: Liberals, Alliance and Liberal Democrats,* Oxford, 1993.
Stevenson, J. and Cook, C., *The Slump: Society and Politics During the Depression,* London, 1977.
Thorpe, A., *The British General Election of 1931,* Oxford, 1991.
——— *Britain in the 1930s: The Deceptive Decade,* Oxford, 1992.
Tiratsoo, N., *Reconstruction, Affluence and Labour Politics: Coventry, 1945–60,* London, 1992.
Watkins, A., *The Liberal Dilemma,* London, 1966.
Weinbren, D., *Generating Socialism: Recollections of Life in the Labour Party,* Stroud, 1997.
Williams, W.M., *A West Country Village: Ashworthy—Family, Kinship and Land,* London, 1963.
Wilson, T., *The Downfall of the Liberal Party, 1914–1935,* London, 1966.
Wyncoll, P., *The Nottingham Labour Movement, 1880–1940,* London, 1985.

Articles

Allen, G., 'National Farmers' Union as a Pressure Group: II', *Contemporary Review,* Vol. 195, 1959.
Arnstein, W.L., 'The Liberals and the General Election of 1945: A Sceptical Note', *Journal of British Studies,* Vol. XIV, May 1975.
Bonham, J., 'The Middle Class Revolt', *Political Quarterly,* Vol. 33, 1962.
Campbell, P., 'Le Mouvement Poujade', *Parliamentary Affairs,* Vol. X, 1956–7.
Cleary, E.J., 'Liberal Voting at the General Election of 1951', *Sociological Review,* Vol. 6, 1971.

Deacon, B., 'Conybeare for Ever!' in Knight, T. (editor), *Old Redruth: Original Studies of the Town's History*, Redruth, 1992.

Eatwell, R., 'Munich, Public Opinion and Popular Front', *Journal of Contemporary History*, Vol. 14, 1971.

Ericsson, T., 'Shopkeepers and the Swedish Model: The Petite Bourgeoisie and the State during the Inter-War Period', *Contemporary European History* (Vol. 5, Part 3), Cambridge, 1996.

Foot, D., 'The Liberal Crisis', *Contemporary Review*, Vol. 139, 1931.

———— 'The Liberal Summer School', *Contemporary Review*, Vol. 140, 1931.

Fothergill, P., 'The Liberal Predicament', *Political Quarterly*, Vol. 24, 1953.

Grimond, J., 'The Principles of Liberalism', *Political Quarterly*, Vol. 24, 1953.

Heyrman, 'Belgian Government Policy and the Petite Bourgeoisie (1918–1940), *Contemporary European History* (Vol. 5, Part 3), Cambridge, 1996.

Koss, S., 'Lloyd George and Nonconformity: the last rally', *English Historical Review*, Vol. 89, 1974.

McCallum, R.B., 'Thoughts on the General Election', *Contemporary Review*, Vol. 196, 1959.

Matthew, H.C.G., Mckibbon, R.I. and Kay, J., 'The franchise factor in the rise of the Labour party', *English Historical Review*, 1976.

Morris, J., 'Introduction: The European Petite Bourgeoisie' in *Contemporary European History* (Vol. 5, Part 3), Cambridge, 1996.

———— 'Retailers, Fascism and the Origins of the Social Protection of Shopkeepers in Italy', *Contemporary European History* (Vol. 5, Part 3), Cambridge, 1996,

Perry, R., 'Celtic Revival and Economic Development in Edwardian Cornwall' in Payton, P. (editor), *Cornish Studies: Five*, Exeter, 1997.

———— 'Cornwall Circa 1950' in Payton, P. (editor), *Cornwall Since the War: The Contemporary History of a European Region*, Redruth, 1993.

———— 'A Remission in the Great Paralysis?', *Cornish History Network Newsletter*, Issue 3, December 1998.

Roberts, W., 'The Programme We Want: A Popular Front Programme', *NFRB Quarterly*, No. 13, 1937.

Rowe, J., 'The Declining Years of Cornish Tin Mining' in Porter, J. (editor), *Education and Labour in the South West*, Exeter, 1975.

Rowse, A.L., 'The Present and Immediate Future of the Labour Party', *Political Quarterly*, Vol. IX, 1938.

Smart, N., 'The Age of Consolidation: South-Western Constituency Politics and Electoral Change in the Age of Alignment', *Southern History*, Vol. 12, 1990.

Smith, C., 'The Government and the Farmers', *Fabian Quarterly*, No. 22, 1939.

Tanner, D., 'The Parliamentary Electoral System: the 'Fourth' Reform Act and the Rise of Labour in England and Wales', *Bulletin of the Institute of Historical*

Research, Vol. LVI, 1983.

Thorpe, A., 'J.H. Thomas and the Rise of Labour in Derby, 1880–1945', *Midland History,* Vol. 15, 1990.

Vincent, J., 'What Kind of Third Party?', *New Society*, 26 January 1967.

———— 'Tomorrow's Liberals', *New Society*, 6 May 1976.

Theses

Baines, M.I., 'The Survival of the British Liberal Party, 1932–1959', PhD, Oxford University, 1991.

Brier, A.P., 'A Study of Liberal Party constituency activity in the mid-190s', PhD, Exeter University, 1967.

Dawson, A.M., 'Politics in Devon and Cornwall, 1900–31', PhD, London University, 1991.

Kandiah, M.D., 'Lord Woolton's Chairmanship of the Conservative Party, 1946–1951', PhD, Exeter University, 1992.

Rees, D.M., 'The disintegration of the Liberal Party, 1931–1933', MA, University of Wales, Aberystwyth, 1980.

Roberts, D.M., 'Clement Davies and the Liberal Party, 1929–56', MA, University of Wales, Aberystwyth, 1977.

Wallace, W., 'The Liberal Revival—The Liberal Party in Britain, 1955–1966', PhD, Cornell University, 1968.

Index

265